A NATION
OF VICTIMS

Other books by Charles J. Sykes

ProfScam
The Hollow Men

A NATION OF VICTIMS

THE DECAY OF THE AMERICAN CHARACTER

Charles J. Sykes

ST. MARTIN'S PRESS
NEW YORK

Editor: George Witte

Design by Dorothy Isenberg

Library of Congress Cataloging-in-Publication Data

Sykes, Charles J.
    A nation of victims : the decay of the American character /
Charles J. Sykes.
      p.   cm.
    Includes index.
    ISBN 0-312-08297-5/HC   0-312-09882-0/PBK
    1. Victims of crimes—United States.   2. United States—
Social conditions—1980-   3. United States—Moral
conditions.   I. Title.
HV6250.3.U5S94   1992   92-21704
362.88'0973—dc20   CIP

For Diane

Important pp.: 40, 53, 59, 60, 61, 80, 88, 125, 127, 151, 164, 165, 168

CONTENTS

PREFACE

This book has its origins in my previous explorations into higher education, especially my encounters with those odd permutations of political correctness that can be found on so many American university campuses.* As anyone who has spent much time on campus these days knows, it is almost impossible to debate any issue of weight without running up against the politics of victimization; its legacy is the tone of shrill intolerance and ethnic division described, among others, by Dinesh D'Souza in *Illiberal Education*.

But this tone of debate is not limited to the universities. Increasingly, it seems to pervade American society. Portraying oneself as a victim has become an attractive pastime. Shelby Steele described eloquently the grim price that minorities have paid for embracing their victim status. But perhaps the most extraordinary phenomenon of our time has been the eagerness with which more and more groups and individuals—members of the white middle class, auto company executives and pampered academics included—have defined themselves as victims of one sort or another. This rush to declare oneself a victim cannot be accounted for solely in political terms. Rather it suggests a more fundamental transformation of American cultural values and notions of character and personal responsibility.

When I first broached the idea of exploring the implications of this

---

* I touch upon these developments in two previous books, *ProfScam: Professors and the Demise of Higher Education* (New York: St. Martin's Press, 1990) and *The Hollow Men: Politics and Corruption in High Education* (Washington, D.C.: Regnery Gateway, 1990).

embrace of victimhood, I received invaluable encouragement and advice from several friends and colleagues, who deserve special recognition. My old editor, Harry W. Crocker, former *National Review* literary editor Brad Miner, and my editor at St. Martin's Press, George Witte, were especially enthusiastic, and this book largely owes its existence to their belief in the importance of this topic.

I am also deeply grateful for the generous support I have received from the John M. Olin Foundation and the Wisconsin Policy Research Institute for this project. James Piereson of the Olin Foundation and James Miller of the Wisconsin Policy Research Institute have proven to be invaluable friends in this undertaking. Thanks also go to my agent, Glen Hartley, for his energetic exertions on my behalf, and to the Intercollegiate Studies Institute, which graciously sent me on a speaking tour of leading university campuses, where I had a chance to refine my understanding of the new politics of "sensitivity."

Special acknowledgment is due to my friend attorney Julie M. Buchanan, who unselfishly opened her files to me, providing me with many of the anecdotes and outrages that fill these pages. Much of this book would have been impossible if Ms. Buchanan—an expert in civil rights and employment law—had not so generously shared her insights with me.

To my family—Diane, Sandy, Jay, and Alexander—who have continued to tolerate me through all of this, my love and (continuing) gratitude.

Milwaukee, Wisconsin
February 1992

SECTION ONE

A Society of
Victims

Scenes from the Zeitgeist

An FBI agent embezzles two thousand dollars from the government and then loses all of it in an afternoon of gambling in
Atlantic City. He is fired but wins reinstatement after a court rules
that his affinity for gambling with other people's money is a "handicap" and thus protected under federal law.[1] (The court, of course,
should have described him as "differently abled.")

Fired for consistently showing up late at work, a former school
district employee sues his former employers, arguing that he is a
victim of what his lawyer calls "chronic lateness syndrome."[2] In
Framingham, Massachusetts, a young man steals a car from a parking
lot and is killed while driving it. His family then sues the proprietor
of the parking lot for failing to take steps to prevent such thefts.[3]

A man who by his own admission has exposed himself between
ten thousand and twenty thousand times (and been convicted of
flashing on more than thirty occasions) is turned down for a job as a
park attendant in Dane County, Wisconsin, because of his arrest
record but sues—on the grounds that he had never exposed himself
in a park, only in libraries and laundromats. Wisconsin employment
officials, ever accommodating to the expansion of human rights,
agree and make "an initial determination of probable cause" that the
flasher was the victim of illegal job discrimination.[4]

Surely it was some similar wrinkle in the Zeitgeist that induced a
professor of political science from a Midwestern college to write:

"I'm not female and I'm not black. I'm not even poor. Nevertheless, in the past few years, I've had the chance to taste powerlessness, to experience minority status, to be treated as a pariah by a society that embraces different values, to be subjected to ridicule, abuse and violence."

How?

"I've been riding a bicycle."

Like bigotry of gender (sexism) and race (racism), he insists, the bigotry of the highway also needs an "ism."

"The essence of 'motorism,' " he explains, "is the belief that having control over a vehicle equipped with an internal combustion engine creates an elite status. . . . In contrast with drivers generally, 'motorists' have a lot in common with racists and sexists. Bigotry in all its forms is about unequal power and lack of respect. It is about treating people as members of a class rather than as individuals. When I'm on a bicycle, who I am becomes irrelevant. Every personal trait is subsumed by my status as member of a despised group. The absence of motor brands me as 'other' and unworthy of respect."

Warming to his theme, he compares disrespect to bicyclists to "cross burning, swastika painting, gay bashing," and other "hate crimes motivated by the status of the victim." Emulating victims of racism and sexism, he writes, victimized bicyclers "adopt behaviors" that merely perpetuate their victimization. They "hunt for underused roads where traffic is light." Although there is simple prudence at work here, the professor declares that "there is also an element of self-hatred. . . . You begin to victimize yourself." All of this ends with a passionate peroration of liberation:

> Banding together, members of the underclass can abandon
> apprehension, experience the euphoria of empowerment, and for
> a moment free themselves of their victimization. This summer I
> joined about 10,000 other bicyclists in a ride across Iowa. . . .[5]

Indeed, the bicycle appears to be the locus of the fight against oppression these days. After *The New York Times* published a seemingly benign piece about bicycles built for two, attributing the renewed popularity of the tandem cycles to "family-oriented fitness enthusiasts, graying baby boomers," and new technology, one letter writer denounced the paper's failure to expose the repressive underside of the phenomenon. Because men often ride in the front, and women in the back, the indignant writer declared, "nowhere is male chauvinism more arrogant, or female subservience more pitiful, than on a tandem bike."[6]

The patriarchal bicycle, however, is nothing compared to lipstick. In one widely discussed book, author Naomi Wolf argues that conventional ideas of female beauty are actually part of a cultural conspiracy that has "reimposed onto liberated women's faces and bodies all the limitations, taboos, and punishments of the repressive laws, religious injunctions and reproductive enslavement that no longer carried sufficient force."[7] She denounces the emphasis on attractiveness, which she calls "the beauty backlash," as "totalitarian," a "replacement shackle," and a new "tactic of obstruction" designed by nervous men to keep women in their place.[8]

The same principle obviously could be—and has been—applied to education, especially to the books students have to read. Generations of reluctant scholars have grumbled over a forced march through Melville, but now annoyance can become grievance. Students who do not recognize themselves in Milton, fail to see their attitudes reproduced in Swift, or whose prejudices go unconfirmed in Dante can now denounce reading lists filled with "dead white males" as acts of cultural imperialism.

This is a charge led not by the students but by their professors, who are themselves fascinating artifacts of the modern age. They have tenure, sabbaticals, and summers off. They drive Volvos, invest in mutual funds, live in attractive Tudors, drink California wines, and insist they feel oppressed whenever anyone uses words like *classic* to describe a work of literature. They have transformed the intellectual landscape of academia.

A quarter century after its triumph, the Free Speech Movement has been replaced by attempts to impose official gag rules at major universities. The passions of the Sixties have been succeeded by "political correctness." Would-be Jacobins who stormed the barricades in 1968 today hold earnest seminars in "Empowering Women with Eating Disorders Through Fairy Tales and Dance Movement Therapy" and "Feminism and Animal Liberation: Making the Connection."[9]

In political correctness, as in the politics of victimization, the stakes are constantly being raised.

A Boston feminist organization's manifesto—"The Time for Access Is Now!"—demands the elimination of "ableist language and images from our poems, prose, doings, dances, artwork, and hearts."

Ableism, of course, describes the systematic oppression of and lack of sensitivity for the needs of the "physically challenged," or even more correctly, the "differently abled." (Use of the term *handicapped* is a sure sign of both political incorrectness and ableism.) To be absolutely free of ableism, the nonhandicapped should be referred to as the "temporarily abled." For the Boston group, the liberation of the differently abled requires, *inter alia*, that all announcements be read aloud twice for the benefit of the illiterate and dyslexic. Instruments of ableist oppression—which include perfumes, furniture, and various brands of soda—must also be confronted, the manifesto insists. "Commitments must be made to develop access for women with environmental illnesses," including creating "scent free" events at which official "sniffers" would be posted at the entrances to detect would-be violators. Other demands include wide chairs so that "large-sized women" would not be victimized by narrow seats, and readily available sugar-free drinks "as a form of accessibility" for women who are diabetic or "otherwise sugar-intolerant."[10]

Given the danger of transgressing these increasingly elaborate regulations of correctness, it is fortunate that there are now guidebooks for the perplexed. The University of Missouri School of Journalism has helpfully issued a handbook of phrases and words that should be shunned "in order to avoid offending and perpetuating stereotypes." Banned terms include *burly* ("too often associated with large black men, implying ignorance"); *glamorous* (sexist); gratuitous references to fried chicken (stereotypical of black cuisine); the exclamation *"Ugh!"* ("highly offensive" as a stereotype of Native Americans); and the word *white* (a product of the "racist power structure.") Other proscribed terms include *banana* (offensive to Asian Americans); *qualified minority* (because it implies some are not); *white bread* (offensive to whites and to bland people); any descriptions that imply a standard of beauty; *gyp* (offensive to Gypsies); *mafia* (offensive to Italians); *Dutch treat* (offensive to the Dutch); and *community* ("implies a monolithic culture in which people act, think, and vote in the same way.")[11]

A "Fact Sheet on Bias-Free Communication" distributed at Michigan State University goes even further, warning against the use of terms such as *culturally deprived, black mood, yellow coward,* and the pronoun *he,* and also cautioning staff members and students, "Be aware of seating patterns, eye contact, interruptions, and domination of the class by certain groups or individuals."[12]

Seating patterns? Eye contact? Interruptions? Well, who can say that poor eye contact might not hurt someone's feelings and thereby constitute an act of victimization? Especially when so many people seem so eager to feel annoyed.

In Chicago, a man complains to the Minority Rights Division of the U.S. Attorney's Office that McDonald's is violating federal equal-protection laws because their restaurants' seats are not large enough for his unusually capacious backside. Seething with indignation, the aggrieved party announces: "I represent a minority group that is just as visible as blacks, Mexicans, Latins, Asians, or women. Your company has taken it upon itself to grossly and improperly discriminate against large people—both tall and heavyset—and we are prepared, if necessary, to bring federal litigation against your company to comply with the Equal Rights in Public Accommodations Provision. . . . I have a 60-inch waist and am 6 feet 5 inches tall. It is absolutely impossible for me to get service in that restaurant because of the type of seating that you have installed. Furthermore, many of the single seats have such small platforms on the seats that it is impossible for the posterior of an overweight individual to sit on that seat.

"We are very serious in our demands that McDonald's recognize the existence of the large and heavy minority that make up nearly 20 percent of the American population, and take severe steps to provide at least 20 percent of the seating in your restaurants to be suitable . . . for large and heavy people.

"We will await bringing litigation for 30 days pending the possibility of a suitable plan being developed by McDonald's. . . ."

Commenting on the letter, *Chicago Tribune* columnist Mike Royko noted that despite the author's attempt to equate his status with that of blacks, Mexicans, Latins, Asians, and women, the writer "was not born with a 60-inch waist and an enormous butt. After a certain age, he created himself and his butt. They are his responsibility. And even the most liberal of liberals would have to agree that [the writer's] 60-inch waist and awesome butt should not be the responsibility of the United States of America."[13]

But Royko did not figure on the magnitude of the rights revolution: In some instances, discrimination against the self-inflicted obese is covered by federal law.

Attempting to cash in on rules guaranteeing that a certain percentage of work be set aside for members of minority groups, a 640-pound contractor demands that he be classified as a minority-group bidder on City of Baltimore contracts because of his weight—even though he is unable to visit job sites (he falls through wooden stairs).[14] A federal lawsuit by an obese nursing student goes all the way to the U.S. Supreme Court after she is denied her nursing degree in part because she fell on a dummy during CPR training and required assistance to be lifted off. "Had this been a real emergency," a spokesman for the school says, "it could have been a very dangerous situation."[15]

One woman who is so obese that she allegedly cannot sit behind the steering wheel of her car (apparently, she sits in the middle of the seat and drives with her left hand) appears on "The Oprah Winfrey Show" to charge that she is a victim of "size discrimination" after state officials require her to retake her driver's license test. She is joined by a representative of the national fat rights movement, who declares, "We don't get angry and that's our problem. We need to get angry like the people in the Civil Rights movement."[16]

Indeed, modeling itself on the NAACP, the National Association to Advance Fat Acceptance (NAAFA) bills itself as a "human rights" organization. It has already issued broadsides against the discriminatory portrayal of the large on television. "You rarely see fat women as love interests," the group's executive director has declared. "It's a shame we don't have more shows that show fat people in a positive light, where they're leading happy, healthy lives."[17]

That attitude is the soul of moderation compared with the stance of Susie Orbach, the author of the cult classic *Fat Is a Feminist Issue*. "Fat," declares Orbach, "is not about food." To attribute compulsive eating to a simple inability to control one's appetite is to engage in the "ineffective blame-the-victim approach," she insists. Instead, it is imperative to recognize that "Fat is a social disease, and fat is a feminist issue. Fat is *not* about lack of self-control or lack of will-power. . . . It is a response to the inequality of the sexes."

Being fat, Orbach declares, "represents an attempt to break free of society's sex stereotypes. Getting fat can thus be understood as a definite and purposeful act; it is a directed, conscious or unconscious, challenge to sex-role stereotyping and culturally defined experience of womanhood."[18]

It is not only the horizontally challenged who are having a rough time: Consider the couple with a combined annual income of $350,000 who keep running out of money by the end of every month. One month things got so bad, *The New York Times* reports, that "they found themselves penniless, their credit cards at their limit, their account overdrawn. They did not know how they would find the money to eat for the last few days of the month." Although the *Times* goes on to describe their "desperation," the term is somewhat relative. Apparently faced with starvation, "they cashed in their last liquid asset: travel and hotel awards they had earned from airline travel. The couple flew to Hawaii and stayed there in a hotel with a prepaid hotel plan.

"And so," the *Times* relates with an absolutely straight face, "they survived another month."

But it was a close call. The tale of the Hawaiian trip emerged during a meeting of a self-help group for compulsive spenders. In the support group, the compulsive couple learned they were not alone. "Those in the self-help group are part of a growing number of compulsive spenders for whom shopping has little or nothing to do with the specific objects purchased," the *Times* explains.

Experts quoted in the article estimate that as many as 6 percent of Americans "suffer" from this compulsion—which, we are told, has nothing to do with greed, acquisitiveness, or irresponsibility. Reports the *Times*: "Instead, new studies are finding, the trip to the store has become a ritual assurance of love and self-worth, offering an escape from loneliness, despair and anxiety."[19]

There seems to be a lot of that going around.

As it becomes increasingly clear that misbehavior can be redefined as disease, growing numbers of the newly diseased have flocked to groups like Gamblers Anonymous, Pill Addicts Anonymous, S-Anon ("relatives and friends of sex addicts"), Nicotine Anonymous, Youth Emotions Anonymous, Unwed Parents Anonymous, Emotional Health Anonymous, Debtors Anonymous, Workaholics Anonymous, Dual Disorders Anonymous, Batterers Anonymous, Victims Anonymous, and Families of Sex Offenders Anonymous.[20]

The young, however, seem to be able to find their own support groups. Affluent, suburban-bred teens apparently imagine themselves striking a blow against repression by attending, for example, a concert later described as "one long howl of fury and defiance"—featuring a white rapper "vowing to avenge police brutality, Trent Reznor of Nine-Inch Nails moaning, 'I'm gonna smash myself to pieces' or Perry Farrell of Jane's Addiction wailing: 'Ain't no wrong now; ain't no right. Only pleasure and pain.' "

Reports *The New York Times*: "The well-groomed, largely suburban audience shouted approval for every imprecation." The *Times*'s critic cannot resist resorting to the language of psychotherapy to describe the musicians of this "anthology of alienated rage." "In

Jane's Addiction," writes Jon Pareles, "the fury is connected to primal traumas; Mr. Farrell (as a pop psychologist might put it) held on to his inner child. That child is a bawling, squalling creature who wants everything right now, from sexual gratification to consumer goods."[21]

Mr. Farrell's inner child is hardly alone.

From the self-styled compulsive gamblers and spenders to the "chronically late," from victims of "lookism" and "ableism" to those oppressed by narrow restaurant seats, Herman Melville, lipstick, and bad eye contact, this squalling howl of grievance has become a national chorus.

ONE

A Society of Victims

S omething extraordinary is happening in American society. Criss-crossed by invisible trip wires of emotional, racial, sexual, and psychological grievance, American life is increasingly characterized by the plaintive insistence, *I am a victim.*

The victim-ization of America is remarkably egalitarian. From the addicts of the South Bronx to the self-styled emotional road-kills of Manhattan's Upper East Side, the mantra of the victims is the same: *I am not responsible; it's not my fault.*

Paradoxically, this don't-blame-me permissiveness is applied only to the self, not to others; it is compatible with an ideological puri-tanism that is notable for its shrill demands of psychological, political, and linguistic correctness. The ethos of victimization has an endless capacity not only for exculpating one's self from blame, washing away responsibility in a torrent of explanation—racism, sexism, rot-ten parents, addiction, and illness—but also for projecting guilt onto others.

If previous movements of liberation may have been characterized as Revolutions of Rising Expectations, this society is in the grips of a Revolution of Rising Sensitivities, in which grievance begets grievance. In the society of victims, individuals compete not only for rights or economic advantage but also for points on the "sensitivity" index, where "feelings" rather than reason are what count. This ethos is fueled by a hypersensitivity so delicately calibrated that it can detect racism in the inflection of a voice, discover sexism in a classroom's seating pattern, and uncover patriarchal oppression in a mascara stick or a Shakespeare sonnet.

The new culture reflects a readiness not merely to feel sorry for oneself but to wield one's resentments as weapons of social advantage and to regard deficiencies as entitlements to society's deference. Even the privileged have found that being oppressed has its advantages. On the campuses of elite universities, students quickly learn the grammar and protocols of power—that the route to moral superiority and premier griping rights can be gained most efficiently through being a victim—which perhaps explains academia's search for what one critic calls the "unified field theory of oppression."[1]

Americans, of course, have a long tradition of sympathy for the downtrodden; compassion for the less fortunate has always been a mark of the nation's underlying decency and morality. But our concern for the genuine victims of misfortune or injustice is sorely tested as the list of certifiable victims continues to grow; victim status is now claimed not only by members of minority groups but increasingly by the middle class, millionaire artists, students at Ivy League colleges, "adult children," the obese, codependents, victims of "lookism" (bias against the unattractive), "ageism," "toxic parents," and the otherwise psychically scarred—all of whom are now engaged in an elaborate game of victim one-upmanship. Celebrities vie with one another in confessing graphic stories of abuse they suffered as children, while television talk shows feature a parade of victims ranging from overweight incest victims to handicapped sex addicts.[2] "A Martian would be forgiven for thinking," columnist Barbara Amiel wrote in *McLean's*, "that the primary problem of North Americans is a population of females totally absorbed with their personal misery— addictions, abuse experiences and pain. . . . We are suffocating in our own pain."[3]

Describing the new "politics of dependency" of the poor in the 1990s, Lawrence Mead notes that its practitioners "claim a right to support based on the injuries of the past, not on anything that they contribute now. Wounds are an asset today, much as a paycheck was in progressive-era politics. One claims to be a victim, not a worker."[4]

Everybody wants in on this.

But the competition is stiff: If you add up all the groups—women, blacks, youths, Native Americans, the unemployed, the poor, etc.—

that consider themselves to be oppressed minorities, Aaron Wildavsky calculates, their number adds up to 374 percent of the population.[5] The media continue to create new categories of victimization. A recent CBS report, for example, breathlessly revealed the existence of "the hidden homeless"—people living with their relatives. As a reporter for *The Washington Post* pointed out, "Once we called these situations *'families'* . . ."[6]

Despite its complicity in spreading the epidemic of disability, the popular press seems to sense that something is amiss. In 1991 alone, *New York* magazine featured a cover story on "The New Culture of Victimization" with the headline: "Don't Blame Me!" *Time* followed with its own cover story on "Crybabies: Eternal Victims"; *Esquire* probed what it called "A Confederacy of Complainers"; while *Harper's* asked, "Victims All?"[7] Indeed, the new culture seems to grow by feeding on itself.

Armed with ever-more ingenious diagnoses of the therapeutic culture, we have multiplied the number of diseases exponentially. In place of evil, therapeutic society has substituted "illness"; in place of consequence, it urges therapy and understanding; in place of responsibility, it argues for a personality driven by impulses. The illness excuse has become almost routine in cases of public misconduct. When Richard Berendzen, the president of American University, was caught making obscene phone calls, he attributed his conduct to his having been an abused child and checked himself into a hospital for "treatment." Robert Alton Harris, a convicted murderer later executed for killing two sixteen-year-old boys, argued in court that he was the victim of fetal alcohol syndrome. San Francisco Supervisor Dan White invented the "Twinkie" defense during his trial for the murder of that city's mayor and a fellow supervisor. (White claimed that his addiction to and steady diet of junk food had clouded his brain and induced his violent outburst.)

By one estimate, 20 percent of Americans now claim to suffer from some form of diagnosable psychiatric disorder. The economic cost to society of such disorders comes to an estimated $20 billion a year. If addictive disorders and alcoholism are thrown in, the tab soars to more than $185 billion a year.[8] Dysfunction is, in every respect, a growth industry. In the 1990s, young people are ten times as likely to be depressed as their parents and grandparents were at their age.[9] Depending on the criteria used, as many as half of all Americans can be described as either obese or suffering from an "eating disorder."* Experts peg the number of alcoholics at 20 million or more. If family members are added—as "codependents"—the number affected rises to 80 million.[10] The National Association on Sexual Addiction Problems estimates that between 10 and 15 percent of all Americans—or about 25 million people—are "addicted" to sex. The National Council on Compulsive Gamblers claims that 20 million Americans are addicted to games of chance, while as many as 50 million Americans are considered "depressed and anxious." Premenstrual syndrome (PMS), once considered *the* disease of the Eighties, can theoretically be attributed to almost all women of a certain age.[11] Estimates for addicted shoppers and addicted debtors are less easily obtained, although both groups are busily forming support networks.

The movement to medicalize everything has meant literally *everything*. According to researchers Stan Katz and Aimee Liu, a national clearinghouse for self-help groups has even had inquiries about the possibility of a group for people who "drink a little too much but not too much Coca-Cola."[12]

In assigning responsibility for this explosion of victimization, there is a strong temptation to round up the usual suspects—simple demographics, for example. Baby boomers—who were assured they could have everything they wanted and came to believe they *should* have everything they wanted—now face a far less reassuring reality. Economically, the era of sustained growth that fueled postwar optimism is no longer guaranteed. Then, of course, there are the lawyers. In 1991, the United States had 281 lawyers per 100,000 population—compared with 82 per 100,000 in England and a meager 11 per 100,000 in Japan. In sheer volume, the United States had 70 percent of the world's total supply of lawyers. The evidence suggests that they were being kept busy. In 1960, fewer than 100,000 lawsuits were filed in federal courts; in 1990, 250,000 suits were filed there.[13] But although the most seductive words in the English language may be Shakespeare's injunction to "kill all the lawyers," blame for the national glut of litigation cannot be laid solely at the feet of the barristers, the boomers, or even the economy. The impulse to flee

---

*"Considering Americans who are 50 percent or more overweight, there are 15 million potential obesity patients (about 5 percent of the population). About a third of all Americans—approximately 70 million—consider *themselves* fat enough to diet or potentially to require treatment. On the other hand, by the standard of being 10 to 15 percent overweight, half of all Americans or more qualify as obese." Stanton Peele, *The Diseasing of America* (Lexington, Mass: Lexington Books, 1989), 134.

from personal responsibility and blame others seems far more deeply embedded within the American culture.

Whatever the future of the American mind—and the omens are not propitious—the destiny of the American character is perhaps even more alarming. In the evolution of the modern American, Economic Man has been succeeded by Anxious Man; Other-Directed Man by Narcissistic Man; but all have seemingly evolved into Annoyed Man, or rather . . . Annoyed Person.

The National Anthem has become The Whine.

Increasingly, Americans act as if they had received a lifelong indemnification from misfortune and a contractual release from personal responsibility. The British *Economist* noted with bemusement that in the United States, "If you lose your job you can sue for the mental distress of being fired. If your bank goes broke, the government has insured your deposits. . . . If you drive drunk and crash you can sue somebody for failing to warn you to stop drinking. *There is always somebody else to blame.*"[14] [Emphasis added.]

Unfortunately, that is a formula for social gridlock: the irresistible search for someone or something to blame colliding with the unmovable unwillingness to accept responsibility. Now enshrined in law and jurisprudence, victimism is reshaping the fabric of society, including employment policies, criminal justice, education, urban politics, and, in an increasingly Orwellian emphasis on "sensitivity" in language. A community of interdependent citizens has been displaced by a society of resentful, competing, and self-interested individuals who have dressed their private annoyances in the garb of victimism.

VICTIMSPEAK

The claim that we are all victims accounts not only for what one critic calls an outbreak of "emotional influenza" in the United States but also for the increasingly shrill and carping tone of social debate—and for the distrust and unease in our day-to-day relations. At times it seems that we can no longer talk to one another. Or rather, we can talk—and shout, demand, and vilify—but we cannot reason. We lack agreed-upon standards to which we can refer our disputes. In the absence of shared notions of justice or equity, many of the issues we confront appear increasingly to be unresolvable.

For many Americans, the politics of victimization has taken the place of more traditional expressions of morality and equity. "The simple act of naming and identifying victims becomes a substitute for conscience and public discourse," writes Joseph Amato. "Identifying oneself with the 'real suffering' of a chosen class, people, group, race, sex, or historical victim is the communion call of the twentieth-century secular individual. It is his sincerity, his holiness, his martyrdom."[15]

Political discourse and academic research alike have become dominated by what University of Chicago sociologist James Coleman calls the politics of "conspicuous benevolence," which is designed to "display, ostentatiously even, egalitarian intentions." Among his academic colleagues, Coleman gibes, postures of conspicuous benevolence have replaced "the patterns of conspicuous consumption that Thorstein Veblen attributed to the rich. . . . They display, conspicuously, the benevolent intentions of their supporters."[16]

This attitude may account not only for the paucity of serious public debate but also for growing divisiveness along lines of race, class, and gender, and for the tribalization of American society as groups define themselves not by their individual worth or shared culture but solely by their status as victims. Americans have long prided themselves on their pluralism and their tolerance of the incredible diversity of viewpoints and ideologies represented by this country's various cultural groups. But insistence on the irreducible quality of one's victimhood threatens to turn pluralism into a series of prisons. Only genuine victims can claim "sensitivity" and "authenticity," and only victims can challenge other victims.

Increasingly, debates take place between antagonists who deny their opponents' ability to understand their plight. Inevitably, that turns such clashes into increasingly bitter ad hominem attacks in which victim status and the insistent demands for sensitivity are played as trump cards. In a culture of sound bites and slogans substituted for rational argument, the claim that one is a victim has become one of the few universally recognized currencies of intellectual exchange. Victimspeak is the trigger that permits the unleashing of an emotional and self-righteous response to any perceived slight. Charges of racism and sexism continue to be the nuclear weapons of debate, used to shout down nuanced approaches to complex issues. Victimspeak insists upon moral superiority and moral absolutism and thus tends to put an abrupt end to conversation; the threat of its deployment is usually enough to keep others from even considering raising a controversial subject. Ironically, this style of linguistic bullying often parades under the banner of "sensitivity."

Of course, sensitivity to the needs and concerns of others is the mark of a civil and civilized society. But the victimist demand for sensitivity is more problematic. To be sensitive (in victimspeak) is not to argue or to reason but to *feel*, to attune one's response to another's sense of aggrievement. This politicized sensitivity (as distinct from decency, civility, and honesty) demands the constant adjustment of one's responses to the shifting and unpredictable demands of the victim. The greater the wounds, the louder the cries of injustice, the greater the demand for sensitivity—no matter how unreasonable. Asking the wrong questions can be perceived as insensitivity, but so can failing to ask the right ones. One can be insensitive without intending to be; only the victim can judge. Inevitably, this changes both the terms and the climate of debate. It is no longer necessary to engage in lengthy and detailed debate over such issues as affirmative action; it is far easier and more effective to simply brand a critic as insensitive.

This tactic tends to work as long as there is a consensus about who is the real victim and who the real oppressor. The hierarchy becomes less clear as victim groups begin to vie *with one another* for the right to define the nature of sensitivity. The dominance of victimspeak in American society was dramatically highlighted during the battle over the confirmation of Clarence Thomas to the U.S. Supreme Court, when both sides—accuser and accused alike—portrayed themselves as victims: one of sexual harassment, the other of racism and a "high-tech lynching."

Increasingly, victim-vs.-victim politics seems to frame our social and political debates. There was a certain poignant inevitability about the headline in *The Wall Street Journal* that declared, "Tales From an Oppressed Class"—the oppressed class in question being white males.[17] But the politics of racial resentment is not really all that different from the politics of racial grievance. White racist David Duke is not the opposite of black racist Louis Farrakhan; he is the mirror image. The same can be said of the relationship between the embryonic "men's rights" movement and the feminist movement— the men's movement is far closer to being a clone than a challenge.

Tragically, a victim's rage that is redirected from the oppressor toward rival victim groups ultimately turns against the victim himself. For self-hatred is the final destination of any attempt to yoke one's sense of identity and power to one's weaknesses, deficiencies, and perceived victimization. Victimism debilitates its practitioners by trapping them in a world of oppressive demons that they cannot, by definition, control. It is found at the interstices of self-assertion and self-loathing, of moral absolutism and self-doubt.

But victimism's larger sin is its reduction of human experience and the complexity of social relationships to a single monotonic worldview. Blaming one's ills on oppression, on society, on psychological maladjustment, on racism, or on sexism is tempting because those complaints provide clarity and certitude—and perhaps even identity as part of a *faux* community of victims. Such self-diagnoses are perhaps inevitable for a society that has grown unwilling to judge itself in terms of moral order or personal responsibility. But they are also fatally misleading, especially for those members of society who can least afford to indulge in fashionable myths.

COMPASSION FATIGUE

There are, of course, *real* victims. Neither racism nor sexism are myths; too many men and women continue to experience the injustice of prejudice. The handicapped still face the daunting barriers of everyday life. But here is the rub. The attempt to appropriate the moral qualities of genuine victims for the aggrandizement of less deserving groups and individuals poses no moral or political dilemma for those who refuse to recognize the legitimacy of the real victims. The challenge of the politics of victimization is to those who *do* care about genuine victims and who recognize that victimism reaps its advantage at the direct expense of those most deserving of compassion and support. *If everyone is a victim, then no one is.*

But this purposeful muddling is often a painful thing to acknowledge, especially when the reality of genuine victimization has so powerfully haunted our own times. What child of the 1960s was unaffected by the scenes of beefy white Southern sheriffs beating and bludgeoning peaceful civil rights marchers who had the temerity to ask that they be treated with dignity?

For many of us, it has been easy to judge people simply by whether they have compassion for the underdog. Morality blends imperceptibly into empathy for the downtrodden. So when philosopher John Rawls suggested that no one should ever endorse a social order that he could not accept if he were in the shoes of its most disadvantaged member, he seemed merely to be restating a truism.

If only it were so easy. Chaney, Goodman, and Shwerner, the three civil rights workers murdered in Mississippi, were obvious martyrs to racism. But what about Washington, D.C., Mayor Marion Barry, who claimed he was a victim of racism after he was caught smoking crack cocaine? Or the student who insists that only racism would cause someone to prefer the novels of Saul Bellow to those of Toni Morrison? And should concern for the unfortunate really extend to indignant bicycle riders? Or men with sixty-inch waists and large butts who can't fit into seats at fast-food restaurants? It often seems that there is a victimist version of Gresham's Law: Bogus victims drive out genuine victims.*

The need to start making careful distinctions between the legitimate objects of compassion and the products of the victimist culture is urgent. Beginning with Rousseau, progressive thinkers have imagined that it is possible to bind a society together not by self-interest but by compassion born out of equality.[18] Victimism, however, has exacted a heavy tax on our compassion and on the sense of guilt that is so integral a part of the politics of victimization.

Americans remain an extraordinarily compassionate people, but it is difficult to escape the sense that we are suffering from compassion fatigue. The excesses of victim politics have generated new skepticism, not only about the more bizarre claims of putative victims but about the very idea that individuals bear moral obligations to the less fortunate. The gridlock of national politics, the refusal of interest groups to surrender their demands to the larger public good, the growing provincialism and parochialism of national politics—all indicate a "What's in it for me?" mentality with troubling consequences for the future.

But if the middle class is truly feeling less guilty, won't victim politics, deprived of that rich source of nutrients, simply wither away in time? No: Victimism's influence is too pervasive. Draining the lake of universal compassion would reveal only the accumulated wreckage of the flight from responsibility and the culture of infinite entitlement. As compassion itself has diminished, society has degenerated into a community of insistent sufferers. What was once con-

---

*Named (erroneously) after the Elizabethan financier Sir Thomas Gresham, Gresham's Law is that bad money drives out good money.

ferred compassionately is now demanded by self-proclaimed victims in tones that seem increasingly shrill and meanspirited.

How did this happen? This degeneration is especially puzzling if we regard victimism as a movement based on liberalism and compassion, deriving its roots from the Christian vision of the sanctified and suffering victim. But such a reading of the politics of victimization fundamentally misunderstands its nature. Although victimism can trace its lineage to liberalism, it is not itself liberalism. Nor is it updated Christianity. It militates against ideas of equity, fairness, and process; its natural tone is one of assertion of prerogatives, a demand for reparations.

THE NO-FAULT, NO-PAIN SOCIETY

The rise of the Annoyed Person is inseparable from our society's attitude toward adversity and pain—but also toward happiness itself. In the tragic vision of life, pain was a central reality, part of the shared and inevitable suffering of the human condition. It marked the bounds of human possibility but also served as a goad to human progress. "Fear, pain, and grief," notes Robert Grudin, "helped to provoke the medical advances that have exponentially increased the human presence on earth. . . . If pain is physiologically a defensive warning signal, it is historically a spur to the expansion, through technology, of human power." But Grudin sees the driving impetus of the modern world as an attack on pain itself.

> As though in emulation of technology, other modern institutions have waged their own offensives against pain. Religious observances, once so full of suffering and awe, have become accommodating and benign. Teachers go out of their way to avoid embarrassing, insulting, overworking, or otherwise vexing their students. Each year public language is further purged of impurities that might injure sensitive groups. Prime-time television series seem dedicated to the comforting message that things are really okay.[19]

But the world is *not* endlessly plastic; pain *cannot* always be anesthetized; the promise of happiness is often illusory. For a society that has substituted techniques for values, however, the response to personal setbacks is either to redouble the search for nostrums or to let out the plaintive cry "It's not fair!" That attitude may be preferable to despair, but perhaps it is merely a byway that has the same destination. In place of a recognition that human life is marked by disappointment and limitation, we have enshrined the infinite expectation—for psychological gratification, self-actualization, self-realization, and happiness—not as a goal to be won but as an entitlement.

Although it is unfashionable to speak without derision of the values of bourgeois society, the bygone middle-class ethos had held such acquisitive tendencies in check by emphasizing archaic notions like self-restraint, probity, and character. Modernity can, in large measure, be described as the cultural assault on that ethos.

In his novel *Mr. Sammler's Planet*, Saul Bellow speculates: "You wondered whether . . . the worst enemies of civilization might not prove to be its petted intellectuals who attack it at its weakest moments—attacked it in the name of reason and in the name of irrationality, in the name of visceral depth, in the name of sex, in the name of perfect and instant freedom. *For what it amounted to was limitless demand—insatiability, refusal of the doomed creature (death being sure and final) to go away from this world unsatisfied. A full bill of demand and complaint was therefore presented by each individual. Non-negotiable. Recognizing no scarcity in any human department. Enlightenment? Marvelous! But out of hand, wasn't it?*" [Emphasis added.][20]

"It's as if some idiot raised the ante on what it takes to be a normal human being," remarks Dr. Martin Seligman.[21] By raising our standards of felicity, we have radically changed the terms of the pursuit of happiness. "Expectations have always run high in America, but in the last 30 years or so they have absolutely skyrocketed," writes Dr. Bernie Zilbergeld in *The Shrinking of America*.

> We want and expect far more than ever before. Parents expect more of their children and of themselves as parents and spouses; children expect more from their parents. . . . When our desires are not fulfilled, as is frequently the case, we are ready to complain, get assistance, try something else, or file a lawsuit to right the wrongs we think are done to us. Almost everyone seems to feel entitled to all sorts of successes, adventures, and joys right now, without having to make any great sacrifices to get them.[22]

Ironically, our special genius as a people has been to refine the language and definition of human failure and inadequacy, becoming connoisseurs of deficiency and specialists in enumerating our entitlements and rights. But human *success* is more problematic. Although we devote so much effort to its pursuit, happiness seems increasingly elusive, not because we cannot imagine it, but because we have so many images of it—so many models jostling and crowding one another, vying for our attention and in the seductiveness of their promises. Each tends to devalue the others as illusions or impostures. Global skepticism, once supposed to liberate us from dogma and dry convention, has now left us entangled in a permanent web of uncertainty.

AN IDEOLOGY OF THE EGO

Despite its pretensions, victimism is not idealism. Ultimately, victimism is concerned not with others, but with the *self.* The feminist self, the ethnic self, the addicted self, are not without importance and are deserving of attention, but they also need to be seen ultimately as projections from the Imperial Self—self-cleansing, self-serving, self-demanding poses, cloaking themselves in the garb of idealism and the armor of victimism.

Stripped of its idealistic pretensions, victimism is an ideology of the ego. But perhaps ideology is too strong a term; victimism can be seen as a generalized cultural impulse to deny personal responsibility and to obsess on the grievances of the insatiable self. It might even be called a habit of mind, but one with substantial institutional support; a reflex so ingrained that its premises are no longer apparent, nor its radical view of human nature even subject to debate. One need only spend time debating "multiculturalism" on university campuses to realize the truth of Jonathan Swift's remark that it is impossible to reason someone out of something he did not reason himself into in the first place.

Perhaps the finest—and certainly the most eloquent—discussion of the dilemma of victimism is Shelby Steele's *The Content of Our Character,* in which he describes the central tragedy of relations between blacks and whites. While one's victim status confers a sense of moral innocence and entitlement, Steele writes, "it is a formula that binds the victim to his victimization by linking his power to his status as a victim." As potent as victim politics has proved to be, "It is primarily a victim's power, grounded too deeply in the entitlement derived from past injustice. . . ."[23]

Steele's description need not be limited merely to those who cling to their race as the symbol of their victim status. The impotence Steele describes is a familiar feature not merely of the politics of race but of modern man in general. The complexity, impersonality, and uncertainty of modern life have made helplessness into an attractive escape hatch for members of all races. And though the surrender of responsibility was neither discovered nor first championed by black Americans, it is easy to lose sight of this, since the debate over victim politics often focuses on the status of blacks and because the consequences of race discrimination are so palpable and undeniable. The infrastructure of the culture of dependency, however, was inspired by the values and impulses of the larger culture.

Indeed, many black communities hold more firmly to the norms and values of middle-class life than their white counterparts. Black Americans are now beginning to understand the price they have paid for adopting the values of a cultural and intellectual elite—an elite that has not always shared with them the tragic consequences of their ideas.

Far less clear, however, is the future of America's general romance with inadequacy. The impotence that results from clinging to one's status as a victim has its own obvious attraction: a surcease from the strains, choices, and tensions of a life that often seems to lack direction or meaning. The rejection of the cold demands of personal accountability can mean a return to the warmth and security of childhood. Who, after all, abandons that safety and surety without regret?

But a society that insists on stressing self-expression over self-control generally gets exactly what it deserves. The sulking teenager who insists, "It's not fair!" is not referring to a standard of equity and justice that any ethicist would recognize. He is, instead, giving voice to the vaguely conceived but firmly held conviction that the world in general and his family in particular serve no legitimate function except to supply his immediate needs and desires. In a culture that celebrates self-absorption and instant gratification, however, this selfishness quickly becomes a dominant and persistent theme. No wonder, then, that the rage of the eternal victim—both black and white, male and female, "abled" and "disabled"—is so often expressed in the plaintive cry of disappointed adolescence. When I refer to America's "youth culture," I do not mean merely one that worships the young. I mean a culture that refuses to grow up.

Although it is tempting to begin any discussion of victim politics with the struggle of minority groups and the poor, we would do better to first examine the peculiar paradoxes at the heart of the American character: its innocence and its nagging anxieties; its naïveté and its pragmatism; its conservatism and its embrace of restless novelty—tensions that were once held in delicate balance by a system of values and norms that fell under the rubric of character. How, in short, did we ever get here from there?

SECTION TWO

The Roots of
Victimism

TWO

The Pursuit of Happiness

On July 18, 1955—nearly 180 years after the nation committed itself, at least in theory, to the "pursuit of happiness"—Disneyland opened its doors for the first time. Thousands of parents and children began gathering at the theme park at 2:00 A.M.—eight hours before its official opening. Five million visitors were expected in the first year. Covering 160 acres in Anaheim, California, the $17 million fantasy park employed 2,500 workers who worked until the last minute to complete the Peter Pan Fly-Through, a galleon trip to Never Land. Visitors to the park could move from the "car of the future" directly to a medieval castle, passing through Main Street USA and sampling along the way Mr. Toad's Wild Ride, Monstro the Whale's Water Slide, Dumbo the Flying Elephant's Aerial Ride, and even "a genuine, child-size, medieval torture chamber."

Disney had chosen the perfect historical moment for his fantasy kingdom, which seemed to mirror the only somewhat less fantastic society around it. Two weeks before Disneyland's opening, *Life* magazine described America as "up to its ears in domestic tranquility." Surveying the state of the nation on that Fourth of July, the magazine found Americans "purring with contentment—when they were not roaring with exuberance.

"Embroiled in no war, impeded by no major strikes, blessed by almost full employment, the U.S. was delighted with itself and almost nobody was mad with nobody. . . ." The nation itself had reached "a peak the [Founding Fathers] could scarcely have imagined. Everywhere there were crazy and spirited sidelights which spelled out prosperity as clearly as statistics did." The stock market had broken through 1929 pre-Crash levels, the auto industry had just come off the best first half in its history, family income and wages had never been higher, and the dollar was rock solid.[1] "Anybody who can't find cause for at least selective optimism," said a Seattle banker in 1955, "is just congenitally morose."[2] There were stirrings on campus, but even the student upheavals seemed saturated with the high-spirited mood of the era. At Harvard, a riot broke out at a rally to nominate the cartoon character Pogo for the presidency; disorders at Yale erupted after a Good Humor man got into a dispute over a parking place with a rival ice cream entrepreneur doing business under the name "Humpty Dumpty."[3]

At Disneyland, visitors arrived in the new V-8–powered '55 Chevy, a car that embodied power and speed; women strolled the grounds attired in the miracle of wrinkle-free Dacron (men would have to wait another year), wheeling children who were to be raised not by happenstance but under reliable scientific auspices. Women who had helped run the nation's war machine while their husbands were in Europe or the Pacific now turned anxiously to Dr. Spock for the most up-to-date advice on avoiding trauma in potty training. "Adorable as babies, cute as grade school pupils and striking as they entered their teens," William Manchester wrote of this privileged generation, "they would attend the best colleges and universities in the country, where their parents would be very, very proud of them."[4] In 1955, all things were possible. The Brooklyn Dodgers would win the World Series and the Mickey Mouse Club would premiere on television, bringing entertainment, education, marketing, and a blossoming Annette Funicello directly into the nation's living rooms. All and all, it was an encouraging beginning for adolescence.

The most profound definition of youth was written by Alfred North Whitehead: "Life as yet untouched by tragedy." Literally, of course, this did not apply to Americans, who had certainly confronted their share of misfortunes over the previous three decades. Yet neither Depression nor war had wrested from them their youthful conviction or disabused them of their innocence. This tenacity, mingled with naïveté, seemed to define the national character and set it apart.

For Europeans, whose exposure to Americans through two world wars had never completely unraveled the intricacies of their national personality, Disneyland would come to symbolize America's Happiness Culture and its radical innocence. No society had ever pursued "fun" with such single-mindedness or precision, nor had any culture been so aggressively ahistorical, abolishing its past as it celebrated its limitless potential and protean qualities. "America is a happiness society even more than it is a freedom society or a power society," wrote Max Lerner. "The underlying strivings may be toward success, acquisitiveness or power, toward prestige or security. But what validates these strivings for the American is the idea that he has a natural right to happiness."[5]

There were, however, undercurrents hinting that Disneyland was not the final word in American culture. Mumbling and sulking, James Dean embodied a sense of alienation among the younger generation. And the intellectuals were in a similarly bad mood. W. H. Auden christened the postwar era "the age of anxiety," a characterization embraced by a wide range of social critics.

William H. Whyte described the bureaucratization of middle-class culture in *The Organization Man*, echoing themes developed by C. Wright Mills in *White Collar: The American Middle Classes* and in Sloan Wilson's novel *The Man in the Gray Flannel Suit*. Each questioned the basis of American felicity, taking note of the growing isolation of individuals and the standardization of social and economic life. In 1951, Mills described a deep-rooted "malaise" in the apparently complacent middle class. The absence of "any order of belief," he wrote, "has left them morally defenseless and politically impotent as a group."

> Newly created in a harsh time of creation, white collar man has no culture to lean upon except the contents of a mass society that has shaped him and seeks to manipulate him to its alien ends.[6]

In 1953, Robert Nisbet had also dissented from the mood of self-celebration, describing in his book *The Quest for Community* "the spectre of insecurity" and "moral estrangement and spiritual isolation" of modern society. "Impersonality, moral neutrality, individualism, and mechanism have become in recent decades terms to describe the pathological condition of society," Nisbet wrote.[7]

If Huck Finn embodied the nineteenth century's spirit of liberation, hope, and the celebration of a world without limits, Franz Kafka reflected the twentieth century's mood of alienation and doubt. Kafka's work, Nisbet wrote, was a "symbolization of man's effort to achieve status, to uncover meaning in the society around him, and to discover guilts and innocences in a world where the boundaries between guilt and innocence become more and more obscured."[8] A sense of loss and dislocation pervaded the literature of the era. Nisbet commented:

> The notion of an impersonal, even hostile society is common—a society in which all actions and motives seem to have equal value and to be perversely detached from human direction. Common too is the helplessness of the individual before alien forces—not the hero who does things, but as Wyndham Lewis has put it, the hero to whom things are done. The disenchanted, lonely figure, searching for ethical significance in the smallest of things, struggling for identification with race or class or group, incessantly striving to answer the question, "Who am I, What am I," has become, especially in Europe, almost the central literary type of the age.
>   Not the free individual, but the lost individual; not independence but isolation; not self-discovery but self-obsession; not to conquer but to be conquered; these are the major states of mind in contemporary literature.[9]

If the man who had emerged from the Renaissance, Nisbet wrote, was "the reasonable man," and the representative figure of the nineteenth century was the economic and political man, "it is by no means unlikely that for our own age it is the alienated or maladjusted individual who will appear to later historians as the key figure of twentieth-century thought. Inadequate man, insufficient man, disenchanted man. . . ."[10]

THE AMERICAN PARADOX

Published two years before the opening of Disneyland, Nisbet's jeremiad could easily be seen as a case study of intellectual crankiness. That was certainly how it was received by some of his contemporaries. Liberals had little patience for doubts about the efficacy of twenty years of social progress, while conservatives, basking in the warm glow of capitalism *revivus*, could hardly be expected to embrace such counsels of pessimism. And indeed, no society had ever had such success in distributing either wealth or the fruits of felicity. The great social experiments of the century—the totalitarian states of the right and left—had either collapsed or been proven to be morally bankrupt. Marxism's historical determinism and doctrine of inevitable class struggle had been discredited by the extraordinary expansion of the middle class and the prosperity and growing leisure of the working class itself. But this only served to make the American paradox more pointed: Why, amid so much prosperity and in a society devoted to happiness, was there so much anxiety? All in all, the 1950s chose to defer the issue.

The psychological dance of optimism and anxiety could be temporarily glossed over but could not be ignored forever—it was not only a fundamental paradox of American life but also the paradox of modernity itself. The tension had always been present, but until the last half century, optimism had seemed to be in the ascendancy.

Even so, more than a century before Mills and Nisbet, Alexis de Tocqueville had remarked upon the uneasiness of the citizens of the young republic, who "are apt to imagine that their whole destiny is in their hands," an attitude that "throws him back forever upon himself alone and threatens to confine him entirely within the solitude of his own heart."[11]

The result of this attitude was the peculiar paradox of the American character. While residents of the Old World, in far less advantageous circumstances, tended not to dwell on their misfortunes, Tocqueville found that Americans "are forever brooding over advantages they do not possess. . . . It is strange to see with what feverish ardor the Americans pursue their own welfare, and to watch the vague dread that constantly torments them lest they should not have chosen the shortest path which may lead to it."[12]

INADEQUATE MAN

Tocqueville's description of that "vague dread" made him one of the prophets of modernity, as well as the keenest critic of early American society. He recognized a basic fact of life: Human happiness has never been an absolute. Indeed, prosperity could easily produce what Robert Nisbet would call "inadequate, insufficient, disenchanted man." Zealous in his pursuit of happiness and cosseted by enviable comforts, he could still be a lost soul, desperately in search of identity and meaning.

As it turned out, happiness proved surprisingly elusive for modern man. Expectation proved to be inseparable from anxiety, while the reliance on the self often cut man off from his neighbors and left him a prisoner of his own sense of entitlement.

There has been no shortage of attempts to substitute new values for discarded faiths and new arrangements for abandoned communities. Ultimately, none proved to be a sufficient antidote for the "vague dread" of modern man. The search for explanation and justification had to go on, accompanied by a raucous symphony of competing ideologies, dialectics, nostrums, and therapies.

Neither Tocqueville nor Nisbet had directly described the culture of victimization; but they were prophetic nonetheless. What they *had* described was the fertile soil from which victimism would later emerge and in which it would come to full bloom.

THREE

The
Therapeutic
Culture

In the late 1980s, the troubled New York Mets took a step that was unusual even for that idiosyncratic franchise: The team hired a psychiatrist. While managers had long interpreted their players' performance in terms of baseball mechanics—hitting, fielding, throwing, running—the Mets' top management apparently decided it was time to probe the inner selves of players who had trouble throwing the ball back to the pitcher and managers who had trouble communicating with—and relating to—their high-priced charges. There were, of course, skeptics. "If we need a team psychiatrist, what's this world coming to?" asked Mets catcher Gary Carter. A coach for the L.A. Dodgers mused: "What's a psychiatrist going to say? 'It's O.K. if you throw it away. I'll still like you'?"[1]

But the presence of the team shrink was another small victory in the cultural transformation that Phillip Rieff has called "The Triumph of the Therapeutic."

Over the last half century, the triumph of therapeutic thinking has been so complete that it is frequently taken for granted; what began with Dr. Freud is now the staple of daytime television talk shows, routine in politics, almost reflexive in matters of criminal justice and ethics. "It is so ingrained in modern American attitudes as hardly to be challenged," noted social scientist James Deese. "I once tried to dissuade an intelligent young undergraduate student in a seminar on ethics and psychology from the belief that anyone who committed a murder was *ipso facto* 'sick.' I failed."[2]

THE PSYCHOLOGICAL SOCIETY

Although the process of psychologization affected all of the Western world, Americans embraced it with a special fervor. "Psychological man is, I suggest, more native to American culture than the Puritan sources of that culture would indicate," Phillip Rieff noted.[3]

Indeed, a century before today's outbreak of psychological influenza, Americans experienced a collective attack of nerves—chronicled by George Beard in his 1881 book *American Nervousness*. Its manifestation was an epidemic of "neurasthenia," literally a weakness in the nerves, which was reflected in insomnia, hysteria, hypochondria, dyspepsia, and other related complaints. Beard regarded neurasthenia as a product of American civilization, while other observers blamed it on the pressures of modernity itself.[4]

Americans of that era turned with considerable enthusiasm to the therapeutic techniques available to them, from vegetarianism to cold baths, open windows, and graham crackers. As the mainline churches fell into decline, there was an upsurge in spiritualism and fundamentalism, as well as a fascination with "mind cures" and "New Thought," which "dwelt on life and light pointing the way to the mastery of all sorrow and suffering." By the time Freudianism first arrived here, Americans were already well-disposed to listen; the groundwork had been thoroughly laid.

The triumph of the therapeutic mentality reflected the general temper of the American personality, which insisted upon seeing the immemorial questions of human life as *problems* that required *solutions*. The therapeutic culture provided both in abundance: The therapists transformed age-old human dilemmas into psychological problems and claimed that they (and they alone) had the treatment. Psychotherapy, critic Thomas Szasz has noted, "conquered what is in effect the human condition by annexing it in its entirety to the medical profession."[5] The result was an explosion of inadequacy—or what psychologists themselves would prefer to call "deficits"—among the nonprofessional populace.

By the 1970s, approximately six million Americans were receiving some form of psychotherapy in clinics and hospitals, a million more from so-called lay therapists. Americans had more professional therapists than librarians, fire fighters, or mail carriers—and twice as many therapists as dentists or pharmacists.[6] Modern America and the Western world in general, Martin Gross wrote in the 1970s, had taken on "the tone of a giant psychiatric clinic. . . . [Psychotherapy's] pervasiveness in the fabric of our culture has become near total as it absorbs new disciplines each year. Armed with what it claims are the hidden truths about man's behavior, it has impressed its philosophical stamp on virtually all of contemporary life: mental health and illness, the arts, education, religion, medicine, the family, child care, business, the social sciences, history, government, language, advertising, law, crime and punishment, even architecture and economics."[7] The triumph of the therapeutic, however, reflected a larger cultural transformation.

ANXIOUS MAN

In 1950, David Riesman's *The Lonely Crowd* described a radical change in the American character—a convulsion Riesman felt was as momentous as the revolutions of the Renaissance, the Reformation, the Counter-Reformation, the Industrial Revolution, and the political upheavals of the seventeenth, eighteenth, and nineteenth centuries. Those movements had cut Western man off from the traditional forms of medieval life and led to the triumph of the bourgeoisie. This new revolution, Riesman argued, was marked by the gradual displacement of bourgeois man—whom he described as "inner-directed"—by a new personality who was "other-directed."

The analogy he applied to inner-directed man was the gyroscope, an internal navigation system that in Riesman's view represented the internalization of social norms and mores. The inner-directed personality could be highly individualized and was distinguished by its "hard enduringness and enterprise." It was, in fact, a type ideally suited for a world of social, economic, and technical change, able to adapt to changing conditions while maintaining a clear and stable identity.

The bourgeois society of the inner-directed personality had been held in balance by two separate but related forces: the transcendent ethic provided by Protestantism, with its emphasis on salvation and self-restraint, and a distinctive family structure that emphasized the sort of character required by this emerging society. Brigitte and Peter Berger have argued persuasively that this family structure was not simply an artifact of early capitalism but was a *precondition* for the creation of that society, as well of the modern world as a whole. The bourgeois family was uniquely fitted to the needs of the time because it "made it possible to socialize individuals with singularly stable personalities ('strong characters'), who were also ready for innovation and risk-taking in a society undergoing historically unprecedented transformations."[8] The goal of such families was to produce autonomous individuals who were both free *and* responsible, exactly those individuals described by Riesman as inner-directed. The importance of the family for bourgeois society, as well as for the democratic polity, the Bergers have asserted, was in its emphasis on the balance "between individualism and social responsibility, between 'liberation' and strong communal ties, between acquisitiveness and altruism."[9]

The bourgeoisie had, in effect, created a society founded on "character."

With the emergence of affluence, however, Riesman wrote, the essential problem faced by modern man was no longer material; now the central difficulty was other people. "Gyroscopic control is no longer sufficiently flexible," he wrote, "and a new psychological mechanism is called for." The New Man needed the psychological equivalent not of a gyroscope but of *radar*.[10]

Other-directed personalities sought their guidance not from tradition or families or a static set of values but from other people, and were driven by an insatiable need for the "respect and, more than the respect, the affection, of an amorphous and shifting, though contemporary jury of peers. . . . Instead of referring himself to the great men of the past and matching himself against their stars, the other-directed person moves in the midst of a veritable Milky Way of almost but not quite indistinguishable contemporaries."[11] He does this by developing "an exceptional sensitivity to the actions and wishes of others."[12]

While traditional inner-directed types were often quite concerned with "keeping up with the Joneses," Riesman wrote, "these conformities were primarily external, and despite his concern with his reputation, he was often quite independent of the vagaries of public opinion and changing fashion." In contrast, the other-directed personality "aims to keep up with them not so much in external details as in the quality of his *inner experience*."[13]

This obsession with the conformity of the inner self was reflected in the defining characteristic of the new personality. In traditional, clan-oriented societies, Riesman wrote, individuals were kept in line through *shame*. The inner-directed man suffered from *guilt*. But the distinctive psychology of the new American personality was altogether different. It was, Riesman noted, "a diffuse *anxiety*."[14]

An age of anxiety creates its own ideologies and myths, although it hardly recognizes that it is doing so. The professionalization of life—turning over larger and larger spheres of human existence to a new class of credentialed experts—seemed a perfectly reasonable response to the increasing complexity of the modern world as well as a recognition of the growing power of the scientific professions to make life more comprehensible and manageable. In particular, the rise of the therapeutic professions seemed to promise access to and understanding of the central preoccupation of the age, the self.

Like the other ideologies of the century, the therapeutic culture provided a sort of *faux* community to replace those genuine communities that had disappeared from the modern world. But while the utopian ideologies withered away, the therapeutic ideology survived and flourished.

The therapeutic culture, which includes the vast empires of psychotherapy and its related counseling and "helping" professions, is only infrequently classified as an ideology. But it often shares with the utopian ideologies of the twentieth century a faith in the limitless plasticity of reality and in the changeability of human nature. It is, moreover, the perfect ideology for the age of anxiety. It both explains and embraces.

No longer focused on survival or prosperity, the new psychological man turned inward to a self that could be shaped, molded, and created anew, the ultimate aesthetic act and perhaps the only one worth performing. With the self as the measure of all values, psychological man could transform the standards of morality, consequence, responsibility, and free will that had once seemed the unshakable pillars of bourgeois society.

THE MARKETING OF
THE THERAPEUTIC

Perhaps the greatest irony of the decline of the bourgeois ethos was the enthusiasm with which the therapeutic culture embraced the principles of the marketplace. In order to sell their services, the new professional therapeutists needed first to create a market—in this case, a market in human psychological deficit. "It is a basic tenet of therapeutic ideology that people are not okay as they are; that's why they need therapy," explains Dr. Bernie Zilbergeld in his book *The Shrinking of America*. "In the therapeutic view, people are not regarded as vile or as having done anything they should feel guilty about, but there is certainly something wrong with them. Specifically, they are too guilty, too inhibited, not confident and assertive enough, not able to express and fulfill themselves properly, and without a doubt not as joyful and as free from stress as they ought to be." In other words, we are "not getting all we can from life."[15]

Zilbergeld succinctly describes the four-step process employed by the therapeutic culture:

1. Continue the psychologization of life.*
2. Make problems out of difficulties and spread the alarm.
3. Make it acceptable to have a problem and to be unable to resolve it on one's own.
4. Offer salvation.[16]

The special talent of the psychologizers was their ability to detect mental disorder in just about anybody. In this, they were following the lead of Freud, who blazed the trail toward universal pathology. "Now every normal person is only approximately normal," he declared in his later years. "His ego resembles that of the psychotic in one point or another, in a greater or lesser degree."[17] His successors seemed to take him literally. In the 1950s, a major study of fifteen hundred New Yorkers "discovered" that almost a quarter were "impaired," while only one in five could be considered "well." That

---

*"By calling attention to symptoms they might otherwise ignore and by labeling those symptoms as signs of neurosis, mental health education can create unwarranted anxieties, leading those to seek psychotherapy who do not need it. . . . Psychotherapy is the only form of treatment which, at least to some extent, appears to create the illness it treats." Bernie Zilbergeld, *The Shrinking of America* (Boston: Little, Brown and Company, 1983), 88.

meant that fully 80 percent of the New Yorkers studied suffered from some form of disorder, even if they appeared to be living relatively normal and competent lives.[18] In the 1970s, a psychologist at the National Institute of Mental Health declared that "almost no family in the nation is entirely free of mental disorders" and estimated that up to 60 million Americans "exhibit deviant mental behavior related to schizophrenia."[19] Zilbergeld comments: "The truth is that mental health researchers and clinicians see problems and not strengths because that is what they are trained to see and *because it is in their interest to do so. The more pathology, the greater the need for more studies, more therapists, and more therapy.*"[20] [Emphasis added.]

Several experiments seem to bear out Zilbergeld's suspicion. In one test, eight "eminently normal" people gained admission to psychiatric hospitals. They behaved normally, exhibiting no signs of what could even remotely be considered disordered behavior. But not one was discovered to be a fake. One of the "patients" took extensive notes on his experiences, which doctors entered on his chart as "patient engaged in writing behavior."[21]

In another study, therapists and students listened to what they were told was a recording of a first therapy session. Actually, the client was an actor who played the role of a "relaxed, confident and productive man who was enjoying life and was free from psychological problems but who was curious about therapy." Forty-three percent of the therapists rated him as psychotic or neurotic, 19 percent found "mild adjustment problems," and only 38 percent saw him as "healthy." Remarks Zilbergeld: "Therapists simply don't know much about health or normal living."[22]

They *do*, however, understand the nature of their business. Practitioners have been zealous in crafting new maladies from the raw material of daily life. Fears become phobias, concerns become complexes, anxieties become compulsions. Smoking can be transmuted into "Tobacco Use Disorder," shyness into "Social Phobia," and lousy grades into "Academic Achievement Disorder."

Consider the explosion in therapeutic terminology that catalogs the multiplication of psychic infirmity: posttraumatic stress disorder, antisocial personality, identity crisis, libido, repressed, obsessive-compulsive, sadomasochistic, castration complex, acting out, introversion, phallic symbol, Oedipus complex, psychopathic deviate, seasonal affective disorder, penis envy, defense mechanism, inferiority complex, midlife crisis, authoritarian personality, sublimation, transference, death wish, projection, accident-prone, social maladjustment, transient situational disturbances, sleep disorders, the immature personality.

Following the inspiration of Freud, therapeutists made sexuality a particularly lucrative market, albeit one that often called for ingenuity. As Zilbergeld notes, the orgasm proved especially problematic. Freud regarded sexual intercourse as the only genuinely healthy way for women to have sexual pleasure. But in the 1960s and 1970s, that orthodox view was challenged by a revolution against the hegemony of the vaginal orgasm launched on behalf of the clitoris, which contended for orgasmic supremacy. What then to make of women who achieved orgasm only through intercourse and who thought that this was perfectly OK? Masters and Johnson quickly created a new category of disorder, which they named "masturbatory orgasmic inadequacy."[23]

With as much entrepreneurial zeal as scientific basis, therapists developed therapies to deal with all of these disorders, fashioning jogging therapies, dance therapy, scream therapy, creative-art therapy, camping therapy, skydiving therapy, thumb therapy ("just gently rub your thumb for diversion from minor pressures and tension"), sailing therapy, guided imagery, Gestalt, and movement therapy.[24] Sometimes they merely made use of whatever came to hand. Masturbation, once considered a cause and symptom of insanity, was resurrected as a psychotherapeutic technique; so was nudism, once stigmatized as both exhibitionistic and voyeuristic, but which, according to Thomas Szasz, made a startling comeback when the IRS declared "nude therapy" a deductible medical expense if a patient was referred by a practicing physician.[25]

"I DESERVE . . ."

With the aid of this seemingly infinite array of therapeutic techniques, the self no longer had to be regarded as a given or as a fixed reality. The Imperial Self (or the protean self, the saturated self, etc.) was a work in progress—a work that was, almost by definition, never finished—*because anything at all was possible.* Marital satisfaction, sexual bliss, fulfillment at work, self-actualization, were all obtainable. Dr. Martin Seligman describes this shift by contrasting the traditional New England self—dour, responsible, hardworking—with what he calls the "California self"—"the self taken 'to the max,' a self that chooses, feels pleasure and pain, dictates action and even has things like esteem, efficacy and confidence."[26]

If such a personality type could have a single war cry, it might be "I DESERVE . . ." As a 1986 book by that title declared in a statement of expectation and entitlement, "I deserve love. I deserve to be trusted. I deserve freedom. I deserve friendship. I deserve respect. I deserve sexual pleasure. I deserve happiness."[27] Only forty years earlier those notions would have been dismissed as absurdities. All of these things could, of course, be earned, sometimes at great cost. But they were simply *given* to no one. Over time, the rules had changed; the notion of what constituted "normal" had been radically revised.

All sorts of disappointments were declared superfluous. "If you're plagued by guilt or worry, mired in a marriage or a job that yields little satisfaction, unable to say no to things you don't want or afraid to go after the things you do," admonished the dust jacket of the 1976 bestseller *Your Erroneous Zones*, you needed to buy that book so you could find the "whole areas of your psyche that block you from all kinds of freedoms and experiences." The author, therapist Wayne Dyer, the flap copy declared, "admits unabashedly that he has done—and continues to do—everything he has ever wanted to in life, achieved all his goals and set new ones. . . ." Dyer's thesis was "remarkable in its simplicity."

> You are in charge of yourself! You can be whatever you choose
> to be. And since the choice is yours, why not choose to be
> happy rather than depressed, successful rather than overlooked,
> adventurous rather than timid?

The underlying philosophy of Dyer's book was reinforced by his frontispiece quote from Walt Whitman: "The whole theory of the universe is directed unerringly to one single individual—namely to You."[28]

Such books are not, of course, works of philosophy, nor do they claim to redefine metaphysics. But they are notable for their inversion of the classical notion that men are, by nature, social creatures whose virtues and strengths cannot be known apart from their roles and responsibilities in the larger community. In the classical view, the good life is "a complete human life lived at its best, and the exercise of the virtues is a necessary and central part of such life, not a mere preparation to secure such a life."[29] What is notable about the new doctrines of fulfillment is their rejection of that tradition and, indeed, of any reference to the duties, obligations, and sacrifices that might inconvenience one from laying one's hands on "all kinds of freedoms and experiences."

Also absent is any sense that by expanding without limit the definitions of human possibility, the new culture guarantees not fulfillment but a nagging sense of falling short, of not living up to one's full potential. By declaring that all manner of joy is indeed attainable, the culture manufactures a perpetual sense of grievance as the new techniques fail to fully compensate for the loss of the discarded values.

The therapeutic expansion of the notion of happiness also permits extraordinary enlargements and refinement in the most ancient human trait: envy. The multiplication of choices for consumers, the breakdown of traditional hierarchies and limits, has expanded exponentially the potential for jealousy. If I am not happy, why not? And if my neighbor is leaping from success to success, what does he know that I don't? Moreover: How dare he?

The French, who understand such things instinctively, have a word for the phenomenon: *ressentiment*, a term that is only weakly translated by the English "resentment." Ressentiment is the passionate envy of the qualities and possessions of another, carried to the point of spite and hatred. As the German sociologist Max Scheler described it, *ressentiment* "whispers continually: 'I can forgive everyone anything, but not that you *are*—that you are *what* you are—that I am not want you are—indeed that I am not *you*.'"[30] But Scheler wrote in 1915; how much worse then are the pangs of jealousy when the standards of "fulfillment" are changed as they have been so radically in the subsequent decades?*

Joseph Epstein, one of the keenest students of American society and of victimism, describes a modern quality he calls "disinterested envy," which arises from "one's own unmistakable sense that one ought to get more out of oneself." The success of others generates "a pang, a slight stab, if one is to be honest about it, of hatred," because "they seem to be living their lives to their full potential." This is an envy that has nothing to do with coveting the possessions or even the specific achievements of someone else. It is an envy that

---

*In their book *Cinderella & Her Sisters: The Envied and the Envying* (Philadelphia: Westminister Press, 1983), Ann and Barry Ulanov write: "The self who refuses to live revenges itself, turns on us and makes us miserable. Then we envy people who are really living themselves." This, of course, becomes problematic, since the notion of what constitutes "really living" is so chimerical.

festers *within* the self, which measures itself against the new and constantly shifting standards of self-realization and actualization. "At bottom," Epstein writes, "envy is self-disappointment."[31]

Americans have embraced the self, only to find that it is a mess. Garth Wood describes the new therapeutic personalities: "Mildly anxious and mildly depressed, they stumble though life living ineffectually and dreaming of improbable and fantastical victories which will transform them magically, through no effort of their own, into the sorts of individual they feel they have a right to be. . . . They blame others for their failures. Or, encouraged by psychoanalytic-type philosophies, they blame their families, their friends, their circumstances. These individuals are characterized by the 'if only' syndrome ('if only things had been different . . . 'if only I had been born more intelligent, with more money, taller, more attractive,' etc., etc.)."[32]

THE THERAPEUTIC FAMILY

From the beginning, the marketing of parental incompetence set the tone for the larger marketing of therapeutic techniques. For centuries, parents had raised children and somehow managed to survive such traumas as infancy, teething, diapering, toilet training, and even adolescence (actually a relatively modern concept and problem). But with the explosion of "helping" professionals, parents found that they required credentialed advice and counsel for virtually every aspect of child rearing.* This despite the therapeutic community's often woeful ignorance of the realities of "normal" family life. "They learn about their faults and problems, the ways they harm, oppress and limit," notes Bernie Zilbergeld. "They do not learn what a healthy or typical family looks like, the ways in which a family provides security, comfort, love, and direction."[33]

---

*Brigitte and Peter Berger write: "If the schools arose in the nineteenth century as an institution ancillary to the bourgeois family, the middle-class family in America *now became increasingly perceived as ancillary to the professional child-rearing establishment.* [Emphasis mine.] Who, after all, was to decide whether parents were living up to their 'professionalized' function? Well, there was no shortage of candidates for this evaluative role: not only sociologists (most of whom operated in the antiseptic milieu of academia, at a safe distance, except for purposes of research, from the messy world of nursery and school), but regiments of new experts on child-rearing, education and therapy." Brigitte Berger and Peter Berger, *The War over the Family* (New York: Anchor Books, 1984), 14.

Even so, the notion that professional advice was not merely helpful, but *essential*, quickly became ingrained in the psyches of anxious parents. Increasingly, parents stood in the dock of scientific scrutiny, on trial for undermining, sabotaging, or distorting their children's tender and fragile personalities.

In bourgeois society, the family had been the anchor as well as the focus of the cultural ethos. It kept that role in the therapeutic society. But the modern family had adjusted itself to the new demands of the social contract of the self. As Brigitte and Peter Berger point out, the family was increasingly regarded "not as an entity that transcended the individual" but merely as "an arrangement between individuals" that was judged as a success or failure to the degree to which it contributed to the self-realization of its members.[34] What mattered was not inculcation of values—the focus of the bourgeois family— but "self-expression," "creativity," "being one's self," all of which translated, as often as not, into a rigid adherence to the shifting norms of peer groups. Where parents had once emphasized obedience, the modern parent chose to encourage independence.* That too often proved illusory.

Parents who lacked the self-assurance to make decisions independent of the new therapeutic class or of their peers could hardly be expected to fill the role they were formerly allotted in the bourgeois family. The result was a generation that questioned the legitimacy of parental authority and scoffed at the idea of superior parental wisdom.† In the late 1940s, David Riesman had already found that parents "no longer feel themselves superior to the children. . . . The

---

*In 1924, mothers from "Middletown" (an incognito study site that turned out to be Muncie, Indiana) were surveyed and asked to choose three traits they wished their children to develop. Forty-five percent chose "strict obedience," 50 percent chose "loyalty to church," 31 percent chose "good manners." In contrast, a group of mothers surveyed in 1988 overwhelmingly rejected those priorities. Only 17 percent chose "strict obedience," 22 percent "loyalty to church," and 23 percent "good manners." Far more popular were "independence," chosen by 76 percent of the mothers, and "tolerance," chosen by 47 percent. (Only 25 percent of the 1924 mothers had chosen "independence," and a scant 6 percent had chosen "tolerance.") "From Obedience to Independence," *Psychology Today*, October 1988.

†An example of the new relationship between parents and children can be detected in the comments of a mother who said in 1988: "I've treated Alexis as if she had a mind of her own ever since she was a baby. When she was 6 months old and sitting in her crib, I used to ask her what she wanted to do next, what she wanted to eat or to wear. But now that's she's 4, sometimes I really want her to mind me. The other day I told her, 'Alexis, you're going to do this right now because I say so!' She looked up at me astounded—as if to say, 'What's going on here? You're changing the rules on me.' " "From Obedience to Independence," *Psychology Today*.

other-directed child is often more knowing than his parents." This was a lesson that the other-directed child could internalize. "What the other-directed child does learn from his parents," Riesman remarked, "is anxiety—the emotional tuning appropriate to his adjustment."[35]

In their eagerness to accommodate the needs of the new age, parents often willingly transferred the values of the therapeutic culture from the larger society to the family itself. Not only were children now accorded a standing once reserved for adults alone, but the family was increasingly expected to adopt the therapeutic values of "openness" and "sharing" that had once been reserved for the controlled settings of psychotherapeutic counseling. As early as 1953, Robert Nisbet could already write about "the staggering number of clinics, conferences, lectures, pamphlets and books on the subject of relations between parents and child, between husband and wife."

By transforming itself into a therapeutic entity, the modern family had eased the transition between traditional norms and the shifting values of society; it had erased the boundaries of particularity and idiosyncracy that had so often made the transition from childhood to adulthood awkward and painful. But by breaking down the walls that had shielded it from the outside world, the family had also robbed itself of the ability to provide a safe haven against shocks from without.

THE USES OF ADVERSITY

Nothing, perhaps, separates modern man from his forebears more definitively than his attitude toward adversity. Immanuel Kant expressed both the classical and Christian tradition when he argued that man should seek not to be happy but to be *deserving* of happiness. Man held no deed that entitled him to happiness, Kant said; he was only granted a charter to be worthy of it. Happiness was a *consequence* of the life well lived, a life attuned to the fixed realities of man's world and to his own metaphysical nature. Adversity—rather than consolation—was the central reality of his world: His ambitions often were frustrated, his plans came to naught, his loved ones died prematurely. Even the longest life could be a disappointment. This was the human condition.

None of the vagaries of life, however, released individuals from the ineradicable personal responsibility to pursue the good life. Saint Paul did not exhort the faithful to be themselves; he urged them to be perfect. It was a standard that skewed the curve.

The notion of achieving perfection, or at least redemption through adversity, was one of the most common themes of Western literature. In any story of a quest or journey, the hero endures hardship, danger, and pain to win his goal. In the heroic ideal, adversity is not merely unavoidable but a means for the individual to test and purify himself—or as the bourgeois would put it, to build his character.

Adversity was also the centerpiece of the moral order. Both classical and Christian societies were cultures of consequence and responsibility. Given the weight they attached to those consequences, they could be inflexible and unforgiving, not merely toward the transgressor but also toward the idiosyncratic and the dissenter. But they were anchored on the conviction that an individual's choices were decisive because they formed what a person was, often irreversibly shaping his life and destiny. Ultimately (and they meant *ultimately* not merely as a figure of speech), choices *mattered* because of their moral content as well as the social and economic consequences they carried. The final sanction for wrong choices was failure (or damnation), and bourgeois society did not doubt that the consequences of immorality, spendthrift behavior, indolence, dishonesty, injustice, and hubris was disease, ruin, and disgrace.

In premodern society, adversity was understood only through the prism of faith. Two contradictory lines of criticism are often advanced nowadays, portraying the religious attitude toward misfortune as either demanding fatalistic resignation or sentimental optimism, à la *Candide*; neither is completely accurate. Much of the criticism seems to assume the presence of a rigid and dogmatic set of precepts that effectively abolish existential doubt, dis-ease, and despair. Such a faith, with its assurance of a benevolent deity, can be caricatured as providing an emotional and metaphysical security blanket for the faithful, who are pictured huddling beneath it in naïveté and ignorance.

But the insistence on seeing religion merely as a palliative ignores its powerful recognition of evil. The premodern world had no illusions about the possibility of ill chance and disaster: these were everywhere in the shape of disease and natural and man-made calamity. Far from providing a set of operating instructions to the universe, the Book of Job declared creation's incomprehensibility while expressing the confusion and rage of the faithful against a God who permits evil to exist and flourish. That tradition left no room for using religion as wish fulfillment; the universe was a given, a preexistent reality formed not by an individual's needs nor by his desires. Not only was the world characterized by the fundamental presence of evil, but the reality of the cosmos was grounded in the radical Other. The dark night of the soul was not discovered by Freud; it was at the heart of the experience of faith.

Far from assuring the individual that the world exists as a stage for his self-actualization, the religious tradition demanded a surrender of self. It repudiated the power of magic to manipulate and reshape reality and set sharp limits on the powers of humankind to remake itself or the natural order. But above all, the broad historical religious tradition rejected the idea that "happiness" was at the top of the cosmic agenda.

This attitude would come to seem incomprehensible to modern generations. "Unable to conceive of a God who does not regard human happiness as the be-all and end-all of creation," writes Christopher Lasch, "[modernists] cannot see the central paradox of religious faith: that the secret of happiness lies in renouncing the right to be happy."[41]

What faith demanded was not quiescence or fatalistic resignation but acceptance. ("Thy will be done . . .") Bad things would happen. They were to be seen not as final judgments but rather as challenges. At the heart of the Protestant ethic was the insistence that man labor incessantly to improve himself; only through such efforts could man realize the meaning of his life and his place in the order of things. He was given no guarantees, only the injunction to work and to hope. Failure bore disgrace only if it was accompanied by surrender, cynicism, and the betrayal of the moral injunctions of God and man. As one historian of Puritanism explains, "The grace of God was free, and so all men were born free as well as equal. . . . Thus there might be help for any man, but this help came only from God and worked only through a man's own self. He must become a new man . . . fight his own weakness, blame none but himself for his troubles and failures, endeavor to be strong, believe that providence was with him, persevere, and trust that all would be well in the end."[42]

In 1867, Matthew Arnold heard the "melancholy, long, withdrawing roar" of the Sea of Faith. Once, that sea "at the full, and round earth's shore / Lay like the fold of a bright girdle furled," but the age of faith had not survived the nineteenth century. Nor could the culture of the bourgeoisie survive the decline of faith. "Without this religious foundation," Brigitte and Peter Berger remarked, "[one can see in retrospect that] this morality was bound to lapse into implausibility."[43] Social Darwinism and the rise of an insatiable consumer society—a culture of expectations and entitlements—were the flotsam and jetsam of the triumph of science over faith and the decline of the transcendent values that had underlain the social order. As early as 1904, Max Weber, who had chronicled the role of faith in the creation of the spirit of capitalism, felt that he had entered an era in which capitalism had been sundered from its religious roots. With asceticism abandoned, Weber wrote, "material goods have gained an increasing and inexorable power over the lives of men as at no previous period in history." Even the idea of duty in one's calling—so central to bourgeois society—"prowls about in our lives like the ghost of dead religious beliefs."

Daniel Bell would later argue that the development of consumer credit had been the decisive blow to the bourgeois ethic, because it undermined a culture built upon the delay of gratification. In place of that society of restraint, there arose a new culture built on consumption, in which impulses were both encouraged and gratified. This was a new society, defined no longer by its needs but by its *wants*. "Wants are psychological, not biological," Bell noted, "and are by their nature unlimited."[44]

But the attack on bourgeois society was more fundamental. Modernism, wrote Irving Howe, "strips man of his systems of belief and his ideal claims; and then proposes the one uniquely modern style of salvation: a salvation by, of, and for the self."[45]

This inward turn was the culmination of strains that had been latent within modern society. From the sixteenth century on, the emphasis of Western thought had been an historical shift away from traditional social bonds and toward the person. In traditional, premodern society, the focus of the culture had not been on the individual at all but on the "small, primary, personal relationships of society."[46]

Describing this world, historian Peter Laslett cautions that it was "no paradise or golden age of equality, tolerance or loving kindness." But it was a world that was familiar, personal, permanent. "Time was," Laslett writes, "when the whole of life went forward in the family, in a circle of loved, familiar faces, known and fondled objects, all to human size. That time is gone forever. It makes us very different from our ancestors."[47]

The bourgeois equilibrium had held the individualizing tendencies of modernity in check. With the decline of society's primacy, that equilibrium was wrecked. The results were not what the prophets of liberation had envisioned. In practice, the individual—abstracted and atomized from his social context—proved far less stable and resilient than the theorists of human liberation had believed. Somehow, as man became more and more highly individualized, he became less human, less attached to a sense of place or purpose that had been, it seemed in retrospect, an essential part of the human condition. Instead of being freed from the oppressive bonds of the past, he often found himself alone in a world without mooring, norms, sense of direction, or purpose. Instead of being inspired by affection or shared values, human relations were suddenly contingent, artificial, and increasingly based on narrow legalisms. This was a world made for the litigator, a figure who was to become dominant in our own time.

American society became extraordinarily mobile, which contributed to a sense of rootlessness. Tens of millions of Americans moved away from their birth communities to places where they had no social or familial ties. Work, which once involved a lifelong commitment, became a way station. Personal relationships, like job functions, became more impersonalized, more interchangeable.

Marx had erroneously identified this rootless individual with the bourgeoisie; in fact, he was a social type who would arise in the wake of the bourgeois collapse.

THE GOD THAT FAILED

The triumph of the therapeutic can perhaps best be understood as the ascendancy of a substitute faith. Filling the vacuum created by the decline of institutional faith and the collapse of the moral order it has provoked, psychoanalysis has assumed many of the functions traditionally performed by religion, and has done so by translating many of the theological and existential issues of human life into therapeutic terms. What had once been the "cure of souls" by the church has now become the treatment of psychological illness by medical science.[36] The animus between the two worldviews was apparent from the beginning. Franz Kafka called the therapeutic claims of psychoanalysis "an impotent error," declaring:

All these so-called illnesses, however sad they may look, are facts of *belief*, the distressed human being's anchorages in some maternal ground or other; thus it is not surprising that psychoanalysis finds the primal ground of all religions to be precisely the same thing as what causes the individual's illnesses.[37]

The prophets of the therapeutic seemed to agree, at least to the extent of recognizing religion as the greatest barrier and rival to their nascent movement. The doctrines that were to evolve into a sort of universal tolerance for every sort of peculiarity, deviance, abnormality, and even crime began with a virulent intolerance for traditional forms of faith. The therapeutic, Philip Rieff asserts, "tolerates no revealed, eternal, and commanding truths" and represents "an assault, more and more successful, upon all sacred barriers."[38]

Rieff recognizes that it is part of the human condition to be buffeted by "the infinite variety of panics and emptiness." Traditionally, the role of culture—and of the faith that infused it—was to fill this emptiness by communicating ideals and internalizing transcendent moral values. "Culture," writes Rieff, "is another name for a design of motives directing the self outward, toward those communal purposes in which alone the self can be realized and satisfied. . . . Each culture is its own order of therapy—a system of moralizing demands, including remissions that ease the pressures of communal purposes."[39] The limits of traditional and bourgeois society had, ironically enough as viewed by modern lights, provided a sort of salvation by training individuals to express "fixed wants" that conformed to both reality and the values of the society itself. "The limitation of possibilities," Rieff writes, "was the very design of salvation."[40]

In place of the bourgeois culture of character and denial, the therapeutic culture proposed a culture of fulfillment whose horizons knew no limit but the appetite and ambition of the self. Fulfillment, however, demanded tearing out by force the mores and norms that stood in its way. "The systematic hunting down of all settled convictions represents the anti-cultural predicate upon which modern personality is being reorganized," Rieff says.* And the "unreligion of the age and its master science" was the therapeutic, "with nothing at stake beyond a manipulable sense of well-being."[48]

---

*Where the culture of the West had once imagined itself inside of a church, writes Rieff, modern man now "feels trapped in something like a zoo of separate cages."

Freud himself set the tone for the assault on faith. He regarded religion in all its forms as an illusion and therefore recast it as a form of neurosis.* There was no room in the new world for both penis and Cross, and Freud devoted his considerable talents to the exorcism of the latter. The good doctor and his followers were not, of course, the first atheists, or the first sect that rejected the legitimacy of the church. They were, however, as Thomas Szasz has noted, the first to insist that the church was an instance of mental disorder—of madness.[49] John McNeill wrote in the early 1950s that Socrates "was and wished to be *iatros tes psuches,* a healer of the soul." These Greek syllables are the etymological roots of the word *psychiatrist.* "But Socrates," McNeill suggests, "would hardly recognize the medical psychiatrist as a member of his fraternity. Scientific psychiatry indifferent to religion and philosophy is a new and strange phenomenon."[50] As Szasz pointed out later, the therapeutic culture was not at all "indifferent" to religion but was rather "implacably hostile to it."[51]

Equally fateful was Freud's critique of the culture's emphasis on restraint and self-denial. He provided a powerful scientific gloss to the modern aversion to those fixed and stable institutions that had been under attack since Rousseau had launched his campaign of human liberation in the eighteenth century. Now the family and church could be seen not merely as politically and socially repressive but as unhealthy, as carriers of mental disability, as actually pathogenic. In 1938, Freud wrote that "the ultimate ground of all intellectual inhibitions and all inhibitions of work seems to be the inhibition of masturbation in childhood."[52] But by then childhood had already been transformed into a mental fever ward of complexes, traumas, and psychic injuries. In the therapeutic culture, Brigitte and Peter Berger note, the family is at best "reduced to being one of the many freely chosen and freely disposable mechanisms whose purpose is the fostering of the individual's project of self-attainment." At worst, it becomes the chief villain, first among those institutions responsible for distorting the original purity of the human character in the infernal mills of modern society.

But where Freud was, at bottom, a bourgeois thinker who acknowledged the need for socialization, many of the new psychologies

---

*In *The Future of an Illusion,* Freud wrote of religious faith: "All of them are illusions. . . . Some of them are so improbable, so incompatible with everything we have laboriously discovered about the reality of the world, that we may compare them . . . to delusions."

of "human liberation"—notably those propounded by Abraham Maslow and Carl Rogers—take a far more hostile view of social reality. Freud saw the healthy individual as one who has adapted himself to society, the Bergers point out, but the new psychologies "substitute rebellion for adjustment."[53]

Stripped of its transcendent basis, unsure of its moral standing, bourgeois society was especially unable to withstand an attack that cloaked itself in the mantle of science. The bourgeois had eagerly embraced both reason and science as instruments with which they could open the world by displacing magic and superstition. Too late, they learned that these tools could in turn be applied to society itself, undermining the very institutions which had brought them to preeminence.

FOUR

Psychologically Correct

If the psychologization of American life transformed our expectations and our understanding of morality, its influence on politics was no less thoroughgoing. It is difficult to know whether to speak of the psychologization of politics or of the politicization of psychology, for the processes were so closely intertwined that it has become almost impossible to disentangle cause from effect. But the fateful consequences of the transformation clearly included a shift in the nature of public debate from a political to a therapeutic idiom; the stigmatization of a host of attitudes and practices not merely as politically "incorrect" but as psychologically *diseased*; and the redefinition of political and psychological health, setting an extraordinarily demanding standard of emotional and ideological conformity. This change predates the upheavals of the 1960s, although its consequences would not be apparent until afterward.

Perhaps the most influential landmark in the rise of the new psychopolitics was the publication in 1950 of *The Authoritarian Personality*, written by Theodor Adorno and a gaggle of fellow researchers.[1] Its most memorable contribution was the creation of the so-called F-scale, which purported to measure incipient fascist tendencies by means of a psychological profile that measured "anti-democratic" attitudes. Anti-Semitism, ethnocentrism, and other forms of prejudice, the authors argued, were all forms of a psychological disorder with its roots in a specific personality structure they called "authoritarian." And this form of aberrant personality was the result not of reflective choice or reasoned decision making but of a weakness of the ego that was caused by society at large.

The Authoritarian Personality is an uncompromising indictment of bourgeois civilization, with the twist that what was considered merely old-fashioned by previous critics was now declared both fascistic and psychologically warped. This stance was certainly the flip side of a therapeutic culture that had raised human expectations of happiness and preached tolerance for so many types of behavior. In his own critique of the psychotherapeutic culture, Thomas Szasz has repeatedly taken note of the temptation of the new science to discredit opposition at will. "Since the Freudian revolution," he writes, "and especially since the Second World War, the secret formula has been this: If you want to debase what a person is doing, call his act psychopathological and call him mentally ill; if you want to exalt what a person is doing, call his act psychotherapeutic and call him a mental healer."[2] With the advent of psychopolitics, the full fury of political therapy was turned on the middle class.

The foundations of bourgeois civilization had been loyalty to family, belief in a higher power, and a strict moral code. But in the hands of Adorno et al., those values underwent a remarkable transvaluation. Far from being upheld as the basis of stable culture, the bourgeois verities were now transmogrified into a variety of pathologies variously labeled "conventionalism," "authoritarian submission," "authoritarian aggression," "anti-intraception," "superstition and stereotypy," "destructiveness and cynicism," and "projectivity."

Adorno and his team hardly bothered to conceal their biases. "It is a well-known hypothesis," they wrote, "that susceptibility to fascism is most characteristically a middle-class phenomenon, that it is 'in the culture' and, hence, *that those who conform the most to this culture will be the most prejudiced.*"[3] [Emphasis added.] Although equating fascism with middle-class values is here stated merely as a "hypothesis," it is an assumption that runs throughout *The Authoritarian Personality* and never for a moment loosens its grip on the authors' methodology. The weaknesses of their approach should have been obvious. The first, and most glaring, is the question of causation. It is true that some members of the middle class have in the past been fascists. But was that *because* of bourgeois values or, perhaps, *in spite of* them? The Adornoites ignore, for example, the role that middle-class values had played in the rise of democratic society and in the expansion of human freedoms. Nor did they take into account that much of the antifascist movement in World War II was solidly bourgeois, as was the bulk of the Western Alliance. Adorno and his compatriots simply dismissed the possibility that the terrors of the twentieth century might be due more to the *breakdown* of traditional values than to their persistence.

Adorno and Co. began their study of the fascist personality with an analysis of "conventionalism," which they define, with due obeisance to Freud, as the strong, "rigid" adherence to conventional values. Among the attitudes the researchers felt would point to the "potential anti-democratic personality" was a belief that "obedience and respect for authority are the most important virtues children must learn."[4] Anyone who believed that "if people would talk less and work more, everybody would be better off"[5] was also seen as an example of a potentially anti-democratic personality. Although many of the questions posed to subjects seemed to be consciously designed to distort the definition of middle-class values to suit the researchers' agenda, Adorno and his colleagues occasionally stated their bias with admirable clarity. In an early version of the F-Scale, the opinion that "What a man does is not so important so long as he does it well"[6]— a classic statement of the bourgeois work ethic —was included among the measures of protofascistic conventionalism.

Even a lack of faith in the totalizing knowledge of science made one suspect to Adorno and his confederates. It was a sign of fascist tendencies, according to the researchers, to believe that while science has its place, "there are many important things that can never possibly be understood by the human mind."[7] This was taken as a sign of "authoritarian submission."* So too was the opinion that "every person should have complete faith in some supernatural power whose decisions he obeys without question."[8] The belief in a biblical God was labeled "compulsive and highly punitive."† (This probably should

*"Submission to authority, desire for a strong leader, subservience of the individual to the state, and so forth, have so frequently, and it seems to us, correctly, been set forth as important aspects of the Nazi creeds that a search for correlates of prejudice had naturally to take these attitudes into account." T. W. Adorno et al., *The Authoritarian Personality* (New York: Harper & Brothers, 1950), 231.

†The beliefs labeled "compulsive and highly punitive" were:

My belief is that, just as according to the Bible, there is a God—the world has gone alone and needed a Savior, and there was one born, lived, died, risen again, and will come back some time; and the person who has lived according to Christianity will live forever—those who have not will perish at that time.

It is perhaps worth noting that at the time of this interview (the late 1940s or early 1950), this view represented the overwhelming consensus of the Christian churches and the orthodox doctrine of the major denominations.

not have been surprising, given Freud's hostility to religion. But Freud did not attempt to Nazify it.)

Building their larger case, the authors linked the submission to authority (including teaching "obedience and respect for authority" to children) with the tendency they called "ethnocentrism," which included identification with one's family or faith (jargonized as the "in-group"). For example, the belief that "there is hardly anything lower than a person who does not feel a great love, gratitude, and respect for his parents" was labeled an example of "authoritarian aggression," which was linked to the "ethnocentric rejection of such groups as zootsuiters, foreigners, other nations. . . ."[9]

Adorno's study demanded an unusual level of conformity to the demands of the therapeutic culture—specifically that everyone adopt its doctrines of "openness" and "sharing."[10]* In Adorno's F-Scale, anyone who, for example, thought that "when a person has a problem or worry, it is best for him not to think about it, but to keep busy with more cheerful things" was clearly someone with a weak ego, "afraid of genuine feelings," and thus a potential reactionary.[11] The same opprobrium fell on anyone who felt that "Nowadays more and more people are prying into matters that should remain personal and private" or who happened to feel that a businessman or a manufacturer might possibly be "more important to society than the artist and the professor."[12]

One can be forgiven, I think, for seeing a bit of special pleading here. After all, Adorno was apotheosizing psychologists, social workers, artists, and academics—the entire array of the New Class and the "helping professionals." Wearing his best scientific regalia, Adorno filled the role of priest-cum-enforcer. Anyone who failed to recognize the essential value of the therapeutic callings, or declined to give them due respect, was automatically labeled not merely a boor but a bent one.

THE GENUINE LIBERAL

This portrait of creeping, insensitive facism was contrasted with considerable dramatic flourish (by social science's rather restrained

*The Adornoites did so by labeling any opposition "to the subjective, the imaginative, the tender-minded" as a form of incipient fascism which they jargonized as "anti-intraception." They defined "intraception" as "the dominance of feelings, fantasies, speculations, aspirations—an imaginative human outlook."

standards) to what Adorno and his associates call the "genuine liberal." In their view, this type "has a strong sense of personal autonomy and independence."

> He cannot stand any outside interference with his personal
> convictions and beliefs, and he does not want to interfere with
> those of others either. . . . One of his conspicuous features is
> moral courage, often beyond his rational evaluation of a
> situation. He cannot "keep silent" if something wrong is being
> done, even if he seriously endangers himself. Just as he is
> strongly "individualized" himself, he sees the others, above all,
> as individuals, not as specimens of a general concept. . . . He is
> little repressed and even has certain difficulties in keeping
> himself under "control." However, his emotionality is not
> blind, but directed towards the other person as a *subject*. His
> love is not only desire but also compassion—as a matter of fact,
> one might think of defining this syndrome as "the
> compassionate."[13]

Whereas Christian faith was dismissed as "compulsive" and "punitive," the liberal's attitudes were "centered in the idea of Utopia."*
The liberal was sympathetic to minorities, and on sex his or her
attitude was one of "precarious restraint." ("She thinks that friendship should precede sexual relations, but [her boyfriend] thinks that
sex relations are a way of getting to know each other better.")[14]

Perhaps predictably, the researchers insisted that the dominant
factor in determining the outstanding qualities of the tolerant, coura-
geous liberal was the family, in this case "the open-mindedness of
the parents and the great love [that the] subject's mother bore all her
children. . . ."[15] The fight against fascism was thus a fight to be
waged in the bosom of the family itself. "If this can be generalized,
and consequences be drawn for high scores [on the F-Scale], we
might postulate that the increasing significance of the fascist character
depends largely upon basic changes in the structure of the family
itself."[16]

This was a bold thrust, for it not only conflated therapy with
politics but sought to shift the entire focus of social policy from
politics to psychology. In time, this was to be decisive for the devel-

---

*"The gist of [the liberal's] religion is contained in the statement: 'Perhaps we will all be
saved.' " Adorno et al., *The Authoritarian Personality*, 783.

opment of "political correctness." By redefining prejudice as a "social disease," Adorno's pronouncement substituted a medical idiom for a political one and relegated an increasingly wide range of issues to the clinic. "This procedure," writes Christopher Lasch, "had the effect of making it unnecessary to discuss moral and political questions on their merits."[17]

Naturally, the notion that an entire society was "sick" inspired the attractive possibility of running an entire country like a psychotherapeutic ward. One need not debate the strictures of family identity or religious faith or sexual morality when they could simply be dismissed as products of the "authoritarian syndrome." An unsophisticated, traditionalist, or backward-looking populace hardly needed to be argued with when it could be *cured*. "The task is comparable to that of eliminating neurosis, or delinquency, or nationalism from the world," the authors wrote. *"These are the products of the total organization of society and are to be changed only as that society is changed."* [Emphasis added.] They add, with becoming modesty, that "it is not for the psychologist to say how such changes are to be brought about." That decision should be left to "all social scientists." But they clearly saw an opportunity. "All that we would *insist upon* is that in the councils or round tables where the problem is considered and action planned the psychologist should have a voice."[18]

This would be mere overambitious therapeutic marketing were it not for the scope of *The Authoritarian Personality* and its tremendous influence. By defining personality attributes as potentially fascistic, the book insisted that the very existence of certain attitudes and practices posed an imminent threat to freedom and dignity, and might even constitute an act of potential, if not actual, oppression. This turned the world upside down.

Everyday life—especially family life—was demonized, while attacks on the social structure were redefined as therapeutic. It was now not only possible but scientifically respectable to equate sexual repression, the bourgeois family, religious faith, and conventional morality with . . . Hitlerism.

Some conservative critics have made much of the Marxist tinge to much of Adorno's work. But as Christopher Lasch notes, Adorno's attack on the bourgeois worldview "fitted comfortably into a liberal consensus that condemned the allegedly repressive family patterns typical of working-class and lower-middle-class milieux. . . ."[19] Its real importance, he writes, "lay in its contribution to the redefinition of liberalism as a cultural as well as a political impulse." Writes Lasch:

By identifying the "liberal personality" as the antithesis of the authoritarian personality, [Adorno and his associates] equated mental health with an approved political position. They defended liberalism not on the grounds that liberal policies served the ends of justice and freedom but on the grounds that other positions had their roots in personal pathology. They enlarged the definition of liberalism to include a critical attitude toward all forms of authority, faith in science, relaxed and non-punitive child-rearing practices and flexible conceptions of sex roles. This expansive, largely cultural definition of liberalism made it easy to interpret adherence to liberalism as a "psychological matter."[20]

Adorno's work was also a decisive development for the other-directed society, adding a new dimension to the potential for anxiety. It was one thing to be out of step with the advanced and enlightened political consensus, quite another to inadvertently fall into a pathological state of fascism manqué. "The replacement of moral and political arguments by reckless psychologizing not only enabled Adorno and his collaborators to dismiss unacceptable opinions on medical grounds," Lasch notes, "it led them to set up an impossible standard of political health—one that only members of a self-constructed cultural vanguard would consistently meet. . . . It was not enough to have liberal ideas; one has to have a liberal *personality*."[21]

But what was the liberal *personality* and how did it differ from liberalism itself? *The Authoritarian Personality* provided some intriguing clues—but not necessarily the ones the authors had intended. The authors emphasized the passionate idealism of the "genuine liberal," buttressed by references to "his personal convictions and beliefs" and his "moral courage." But they were also drawing a portrait of a type that edged into self-righteousness and even egoism. Their liberal is the ultimate individualist, with a "strong sense of autonomy and personal independence," who does not hesitate to assert himself or to assume a posture of moral indignation. The overall image was of an attitude being struck. As noted, the liberal "cannot stand" being interfered with, and "cannot 'keep silent' if wrong is being done," even if he puts himself at risk.

But equally important is the emphasis placed on right *feeling*. Traditional liberalism had been founded on strong faith in the powers of reason. But in the description of the "genuine liberal," reason is given short shrift indeed. The liberal's moral courage is "often beyond his *rational* evaluation," he has trouble keeping himself "under 'control,' " and his relationship to others is described by the word *emotionality*. The word *justice* never appears. In its place is *compassion.*

But on one level, this emphasis was beside the point, because the portrait of righteousness, emotionality, and impulsiveness did not really represent the historic liberal at all, or, for that matter, any discernible political position; instead, Adorno and his colleagues had drawn a picture of *adolescence.*

THE YOUTH CULTURE

This accent on youth would become decisive in the 1960s, when the various streams of politics, therapy, alienation, and self-indulgence would meet in the confluence known as the counterculture.

The movement certainly did not lack for its theorists or its apologists. Foremost among them was Kenneth Keniston, who claimed that society was witnessing "the emergence on a mass scale of a previously unrecognized stage of life," a transition stage that connected adolescence and adulthood. He called it "youth." The major themes of this newly minted stage of life, Keniston argued, were "the tension between self and society" and alternations between the apparent polar opposites of "estrangement" ("feelings of isolation, unreality, absurdity and disconnectedness") and "omnipotentiality" ("the feeling of absolute freedom, of living in a world of pure possibilities, of being able to change or achieve anything").*[22]

Keniston also argued that the "refusal of socialization and acculturation"—a rejection of history and social norms—was a characteristic of youth, as was a passion for "movement" and "the consequent abhorrence of stasis," and a "fear of death."[23]

But Keniston's description was notable for its lack of anything that marks youth as a distinctive stage of life—or that distinguishes it at all from the general condition of modern man in a technological, impersonal, therapeutic world. Although Keniston had accurately described the crisis of the modern and the mores of the therapeutic

---

*"Omnipotentiality and estrangement are obviously related: the same sense of freedom and possibility that may come from casting off old inhibitions, values, and constraints may also lead directly to a feeling of absurdity, disconnectedness, and estrangement." Kenneth Keniston, *Youth and Dissent* (New York: Harcourt Brace Jovanovich, 1970), 9.

culture, he had mistaken them for a generational phenomenon. In truth, feelings of alienation and estrangement were by no means invented by the baby-boom generation, nor was the notion of limitless possibilities. Only a radically ahistorical view could have imagined that they were.

Keniston's analysis seemed to suffer from the same shortcoming as that of Adorno and his colleagues in *The Authoritarian Personality*. Adorno had imagined he was describing the "genuine liberal" when in fact he was describing adolescence. Keniston imagined he was describing youth when he was describing modernity itself. What are we to make of this?

Perhaps we might choose to envision the "youth culture" not as a culture of young people but as a culture that refuses to grow up. A culture of innocence, of limitless expectations, of the perpetually new, will always be one that holds the process of maturation at arm's length. And a culture that disdains the processes of self-control and restraint, celebrates impulse and *immediate* self-gratification, and insists upon the unlimited indulgence of its eccentricities will always have a soft spot for adolescence. Even though Adorno and Keniston declared that they were describing something quite new, they were actually describing something that had been around quite a long time. "The sensitive individual turned inwards," remarked Richard Weaver of an earlier age's adolescents, "and there discovered an appalling well of melancholy and unhappiness, which was attributed to the perverse circumstances of the world. . . . The young romantic Goethe in *Werther*, and Shelley crying, 'I fall upon the thorns of life, I bleed,' continue the indulgence in egocentric sensibility."[24] Adorno and Keniston were re-presenting roughly the same phenomenon, but in their zeal to transform egoism into idealism, they chose only to change its name. The youth culture was essentially an attack on adulthood itself.

Every society of the past had its own coming-of-age rituals to welcome the young into the larger community of shared responsibilities. Adulthood represented the ceding by the individual of his selfishness in favor of society's rules and norms; this was the process of growing up. Maturation was the process of moderating impulses, adjusting the claims of childhood to the realities of the world. It was the focusing of choice into the channels of the possible; it was the socialization of the young into a recognition of the consequences of those choices. With the rise of the youth culture, this process fell into disrepair.

A society that embraces the egoism of youth and spurns maturity is essentially a youth culture, even if it is getting baggy around the eyes. So perhaps it is not surprising that the theorists of social change would mistake adolescence for "genuine liberalism," or modernity for youth. Increasingly they were one and the same. Hence the domination of the insistent child, who wants everything and wants it *now*, who holds its breath until it turns blue, and insists "It's not fair" whenever it doesn't get everything it demands. Hence a society, moreover, that would come to recognize the tantrum as a legitimate form of public discourse.

All of this had been latent in the culture for generations. What was new in the 1960s was the articulation of an ideology that captured these impulses and the presence of an audience eager to embrace it.

SECTION THREE

The High Noon
of Victimism

FIVE

"I Have a Dream . . ."

The 1960s will be remembered as the height of the youth culture. There were, after all, so many of them, the fruits of the baby boom come of age. But the crisis of the young tended to overshadow the less dramatic but equally fateful crisis of their elders. They had, in effect, created a new world for their children by dismantling the repressive structures of the past. They had challenged obsolete notions of character and rejected outmoded ideas of morality. And they had raised the banner of human happiness at the very center of the dour bourgeois power structure. Lionel Trilling was to give a name to the impulse of modernism, which he called the "adversary culture." In literature, the adversary culture saw its mission as "detaching the reader from the habits of thought and feeling that the larger culture imposes, of giving him a ground and a vantage point from which to judge and condemn and perhaps revise the culture which has produced him." This tendency had become so pervasive throughout the arts that Trilling speculated that historians of the era "will take virtually for granted the adversary intention, the actually subversive intention, that characterizes modern writing."[1]

Because the modernist critics of bourgeois culture refused to define themselves in terms of a specific social program or agenda, the dissatisfaction of the adversary culture was a permanent fixture. Irving Howe wrote that "the modern must be defined in terms of what it is not . . . an inclusive negative." It was, Howe said, "an unyielding rage against the official order."

In politics, this adversarial stance was reflected in the intelligentsia's lingering romance with Marxism. Among the cultural avant-garde, the goal of the modernist was to shock sensibilities and to discomfit bourgeois complacency. This turned out to be remarkably easy; and further, no one arose to defend the bourgeoisie. Nor did the bourgeois always cooperate by assuming their allotted role of indignant philistine. As the adversary culture scrambled for ways to *épater les bourgeois*, the bourgeois too often failed to be shocked. Worse, they often seemed to *like* it. This lack of outrage was the nagging and apparently insoluble dilemma of modernism. Because it defined itself only by what it was not, modernism required a social order that embraced it enough to support and subsidize its activities, but that also resisted its impulses—or even better, repressed them. The result was a cultural anxiety that would loom large in the later development of political correctness and victimism. Howe stated the problem directly: "Modernism must always struggle, but never quite triumph, and after a time, must struggle in order not to triumph."[2]

The acquiescence of the bourgeoisie in its own pillorying meant that modernism was forced to escalate constantly its outrageousness or be haunted by the fear that it would itself become a social order, a tradition—as Howe put it—that had "acquired wrinkles and a paunch." The most shocking departures in art became staples of advertising and mass entertainment; the radical became routine, the modern housebroken.*

Daniel Bell wrote:

> Today, each new generation, starting off at the benchmarks attained by the adversary culture of its cultural parents, declares in sweeping fashion that the status quo represents backward conservatism or repression, so that in a widening gyre, new and fresh assaults on the social structure are mounted.[3]

---

*Consider the frustration of artist Karen Finley, whose act consists in part of pouring green gelatin into her camisole, smearing chocolate on her breasts and legs (to represent feces), and shoving alfalfa sprouts into the crotch of her underwear—and who insists that the failure of the federal government to subsidize her act would lead to the "end of all art in America." Her dilemma is complex: she must simultaneously shock, offend, demand society's ratification, and declare herself a victim of oppression.

An entire cultural movement now had a vested interest in a state of permanent aggrievement—a condition rendered more piquant by the lack of suitable targets for indignation.

By the 1960s, the modernist insurgents were "no longer outcasts, or a bohemian enclave in the society," Bell pointed out. They dominated the cultural, artistic, and intellectual life of the nation.*[4] They had attacked the mainstream only to *become* the mainstream. Lionel Trilling described this process as "the socialization of the anti-social . . . the acculturation of the anti-cultural . . . the legitimation of the subversive."[5]

This created its own crisis. As early as 1959, Bell described the gnawing unease of the cultural/intellectual classes. "The young intellectual," he wrote, "is unhappy because the 'middle way' is for the middle-aged, not for him; it is without passion and is deadening. . . . In the search for a 'cause' there is a deep, desperate, almost pathetic anger."[6] In 1960, Norman Podhoretz, then the new editor of *Commentary*, detected "a hunger for something new and something radical" among intellectuals.[7]

In the 1960s, they would find what they were looking for.

A MORAL COMMUNITY

The world changed the night a Montgomery, Alabama, bus driver named J. F. Blake told Rosa Parks to give up her seat. The courage of the early civil rights workers, the sit-ins at lunch counters, and the appeals for basic human rights were part of a riveting moral drama in which the issues were drawn with unusual clarity.

But the movement's significance transcended politics. For many, the moral resonance of the campaign for civil rights came from its promise to restore a sense of community in a society whose centrifu-

---

*"In both doctrine and life-style, the anti-bourgeois won out. This triumph meant that in the culture antinomianism and anti-institutionalism ruled. In the realm of art, on the level of aesthetic doctrine, few opposed the idea of boundless experiment, of unfettered freedom, of unconstrained sensibility, of impulse being superior to order, of the imagination being immune to merely rational criticism. *There is no longer an avant-garde, because no one in our postmodern culture is on the side of order or tradition. There exists only a desire for the new—or boredom with the old and the new.*" [Emphasis added.] Daniel Bell, *The Cultural Contradictions of Capitalism* (New York: Basic Books, 1976), 53.

gal force had seemed irreversible. The movement would be the defining moment in their lives, indelibly shaping their view of morality
and justice because it provided *something* to believe in. Robert Nisbet
has described the quest for community as the dominant theme of the
age. That search led many to embrace a variety of failed ideologies;
ultimately, none had provided the sense of *meaning* and moral order
that define a genuine community.

The civil rights movement, however, insisted on a decisively moral
vocabulary, a system of ethical obligations to others, and an acknowledgment of communal purpose that seemed the antithesis of a culture
of self-assertion. The most enlightened religious leaders recognized
the potency of the new movement. Writing in the mid-1960s, Philip
Rieff noted the hope that the movement would "serve, providentially, to revitalize the moral demand system in the white American
culture."[8]

Historically, this had been the pattern of moral renewal, as a class
or religious group—such as the Puritans in their time—defined itself
as the instrument of moral regeneration. From the start, the civil
rights movement seemed to carry such aspirations. And especially
noteworthy in this regard were its religious leadership and its self-
consciously middle-class value system.

The latter is now largely forgotten, but the Southern black leadership of the early movement was very much a part of the bourgeoisie.
Despite the depredations of slavery and segregation, the black family
had remained relatively stable and its integrity was jealously guarded.
Church attendance was stressed, and the work ethic was preached
from the pulpit. The goal of the campaign for integration was not
the destruction of middle-class life, but simply the demand that blacks
be allowed to share in it as full participants.

Although the civil rights movement is now obviously central to
any account of victim politics, this was not always inevitably so. In
his early days of leadership, Martin Luther King, Jr., resisted the
pressure to fall back upon victimization as the defining experience of
the American black or to use it to justify or explain deviant behavior.
Although his aide Stanley Levison urged that all references to self-
help and character be deleted from his writings,[9] King nevertheless
insisted: "We must not let the fact that we are the victims of injustice
lull us into abrogating respect for our own lives." He did not hesitate
to stress self-reliance as a remedy for poverty. Significantly, King
did not join other black leaders in attacking Daniel Patrick Moynihan's report that focused attention on the crisis of the black family,

nor did he join the chorus which claimed that an emphasis on family values as a cause of poverty was a form of "blaming the victim." "Nothing," King argued, "is so much needed as a secure family life for a people to pull themselves out of poverty."[10]

King's philosophy blended elements of Old Testament righteousness, New Testament forgiveness, the nonviolence of Mohandas Gandhi, and the theology of Reinhold Niebuhr, whose realism and acknowledgment of sin as "an inevitable fact of human existence" moderated the utopian optimism of the so-called social gospel. King later credited Niebuhr for showing him "the complexity of human motives and the reality of sin on every level of man's existence."[11]

Unlike many religious liberals, Niebuhr was under no illusion that society's problems would gradually disappear as it became morally enlightened. Change would not come so easily. It was absurd, Niebuhr thought, for American blacks to expect full emancipation "merely by trusting in the moral sense of the white race."[12] He rejected the extreme pacificism of those who, following the lead of Tolstoyan spirituality, refused to resist evil in any form or by any means. Instead, he urged a more active engagement with the immorality of society, through nonviolent resistance. He regarded "modern man's loss of confidence in moral forces" as the tragedy of modernity.

Niebuhr also recognized the danger inherent in campaigns based on moral indignation. He warned strongly against "moral conceit" and urged a "spiritual discipline against resentment." He did not, however, mean to condemn resentment against injustice. Southern blacks had reason enough to feel such resentment, even bitterness and hatred, but to Niebuhr, this justifiable enmity argued all the more strongly for the renunciation of victimhood. A sense of moral superiority that permitted answering injustice with injustice, and violence with violence, he argued, would merely perpetuate the "endless cycle of social conflict." Resentment was "merely the egoistic side of the sense of injustice."[13] Inevitably, the egoism of resentment merely aroused the egoism of the oppressor.

The alternative was what Gandhi had called "soul force," a nonviolence not merely of tactics but of a "spirit of moral goodwill." For Gandhi, Niebuhr wrote, this involved "freedom from personal resentments and a moral purpose free of selfish ambition."[14] The key to this was the affirmation of the humanity of both victim and oppressor. "One of the most important results of a spiritual discipline against resentment in a social dispute," Niebuhr wrote in *Moral Man and Immoral Society*, "is that it leads to an effort to discriminate between the evils of a social system and the individuals who are involved in it."[15] The abolitionist William Lloyd Garrison, for instance, had simply solidified Southern support for slavery by his personal attacks against the slave owners. In contrast, Niebuhr noted that Gandhi "never tire[d] of making a distinction between individual Englishmen and the system of imperialism which they maintain[ed]."[16]

Writing in 1936, Niebuhr had looked ahead optimistically to a campaign for equal rights for blacks because of what he said were "the peculiar spiritual gifts of the Negro." He envisioned a movement that would blend the aggressiveness of young blacks with the "forbearance" of their elders.[17] To avoid disaster, he insisted, it was essential that the movement be governed by restraint and Gandhian charity. Niebuhr envisioned nothing less than the re-creation of a moral community, even among foes.

> The discovery of elements of common human frailty in the foe
> and, concomitantly, the appreciation of all human life as
> possessing transcendent worth, creates attitudes which transcend
> social conflict and thus mitigate its cruelties. It binds human
> beings together by reminding them of the common roots and
> similar character of both their vices and their virtues. These
> attitudes of repentance which recognize that the evil in the foe is
> also in the self, and these impulses of love which claim kinship
> with all men in spite of social conflict are the peculiar gifts of
> religion to the human spirit.[18]

It was clear that King had embraced this morally complex position even as a young minister, when he rose to national prominence as a leader of the Montgomery bus boycott.* "What we are preaching," King told one correspondent, "is best described by the Greek word 'agape,' " a sort of redemptive love. While the fight in Montgomery was between "light and darkness," he made it plain that it was not between blacks and whites. "While I will fight him to get out from

---

*Christopher Lasch remarks upon King's combination of "militancy and moral self-restraint." The civil rights movement, Lasch writes, "had to declare war on segregation . . . without appealing to [blacks'] history of victimization in order to claim a position of moral superiority. That King should have come to see that racial hatred feeds off self-righteousness and acquiescence alike testified to his capacity for spiritual growth." *The True and Only Heaven* (New York: W. W. Norton, 1991), 393.

under his subjugation," he said of the white man, "I will also try to understand him and I will not try to defeat him."[19]

King's embrace of nonviolence and passive resistance—as well as his emphasis on moral restraint and forgiveness—created an irresistable momentum for the civil rights movement, which reached its apogee in August 1963 when he delivered his most famous speech in Washington, D.C. The tone was not one of accusation, but of biblical justice, redemption, and forgiveness. He envisioned "the sons of former slaves and sons of former slave owners" sitting down together "at the table of brotherhood." In his vision, even the state of Mississippi, "a state sweltering with the heat of injustice, sweltering with the heat of oppression, will be transformed into an oasis of freedom and justice."

> I have a dream that my four little children will one day live in a nation where they will not be judged by the color of their skin but by the content of their character. I have a dream today!
>
> I have a dream that one day, down in Alabama, with its vicious racists, with its governor having his lips dripping with the words of interposition and nullification, one day, right there in Alabama, little black boys and black girls will be able to join hands with little white boys and white girls as sisters and brothers. I have a dream today!

It was an extraordinary moment, both for the movement and as a reaffirmation of faith. People who would have regarded a white preacher with disdain—and a white Southern Baptist preacher with fear and loathing—listened to King with tears in their eyes, deeply moved by a moral appeal they would otherwise have regarded as impossibly alien to a modern worldview.

In the early years of the campaign for civil rights, King was obviously aware of the short-term potency of asserting moral superiority. But he also recognized the limitations such a strategy would impose on his attempts to build a broad-based coalition. He was right. As the movement shifted from an interracial moral coalition to strident and radicalized black-power advocacy, the broad consensus he had helped to shape fragmented. "No one knew it at the time," one historian later noted, but King's "I Have a Dream" speech was "the valedictory of the southern movement."[20]

In time, faced with the loss of his leadership position, King adopted an accusatory stance, denouncing white society for "psychological and spiritual genocide" and demanding not merely fairness but "compensatory treatment" for centuries of victimization. Before northern audiences, King began to downplay the middle-class roots of the movement. Even so, he was increasingly shoved aside by more insistent voices, who found that by playing the victim they could force the acquiescence of the white power structure to their most outrageous demands. Violence, whether it was organized and purposeful or random and brutal, was now explained as the bitter fruit of victimization, and justifiable as righteous payback to the oppressors.

By the late 1960s, the idea that the civil rights movement should be built on *agape* was greeted with derision. In place of appeals to justice and American fair play, the movement now played upon emotions of fear, pity, guilt, and ideologically tinged "compassion." Instead of equality of opportunity, the rhetoric of the movement now demanded "reparations." And where King had originally stressed the work ethic, strong families, and faith, the new voices rejected those values as instruments of repressive racism itself. Fatefully, their denunciation was echoed by many of the movement's most influential white supporters. The rich potential of the movement to re-create a sense of moral community was shattered in the increasingly vitriolic and shrill demands of the antagonists.

One of the persistent puzzles of the civil rights era is the question of why the movement was so successful in the backward and traditional South but foundered as it moved to the more flexible and tolerant North. The answer, in part, is that the move was more than merely geographical—it was a fundamental shift in cultural milieus, a transition between eras and cultures. In the South, both black society and white society still clung to the vestiges of middle-class ideals. Underlying the ugliness of southern racism was a shared moral culture that would enable an ultimate resolution of racial conflicts. But those same values had little traction in the society as a whole, especially in the North. The middle-class worldview was badly battered in the inner city, not because the black community was irresponsible, but because it was being acculturated into the values of the larger society. As Christopher Lasch has noted, when Martin Luther King moved to the northern urban areas, he "no longer addressed a constituency that cared to hear about self-help, the dignity of labor, the importance of strong families, and the healing power of *agape*."[21] When King abandoned the middle-class values of his early campaigns, Lasch argues, "he lost any chance to forge a biracial coalition based on ideas of responsibility and self-help. . . ." In all probability,

King would have had no better luck among the white cultural elites.* His influence faded among white academics, who embraced the Black Panther movement with far more zeal than they displayed for the preacher of nonviolence in his latter days.

A common theme among explanations of the era is the role played by white liberal guilt and fear in ratifying the moral terrorism of the black-power movement. And it is certainly true that white liberals gave in to radical demands because they felt complicit in the oppression and brutalization of blacks in the United States. Consider an enduring image of the 1960s: the capitulation of terrified college administrators before the demands of black-power radicals. While it is easy to see the alacrity with which they caved in as simple gutlessness, this does not explain the *enthusiasm* with which they acted or the sense of complacency and moral self-congratulation with which they justified themselves. The counterculture of the 1960s was hardly compatible with the reassertion of values celebrated by King in his early days. But it saw the movement as a powerful weapon with which to strike out against a smugly repressive, materialistic, soulless society. Appropriating the civil rights cause, the new cultural revolution could marry its own resentments with moral purity and fervor: The combination would be irresistible. This point needs to be stated explicitly: The politics of racial resentment was not a grass-roots phenomenon of the black masses but an ideology of a cultural elite. In 1966, while white radicals were already declaring King an anachronism, the preacher received the approval of 88 percent of black Americans; in contrast, black-power advocate Stokely Carmichael won the approval of only 19 percent. "Among the black masses," historian Allen J. Matusow writes, "the classic liberal ideal . . . never lost its appeal."[22]

But set against that ideal was the new figure of the Victim.

---

*The traditional values did, however, continue to resonate among lower-middle-class white ethnics who had originally been part of the civil rights coalition. They were alienated from the movement, which came to regard them with undisguised contempt and their attempts to preserve their neighborhoods and schools with outrage and contumely.

SIX

The Rise of
the Victim

However much it may have elaborated on the idea, the notion of the morally potent victim is not an invention of the twentieth century. In its religious formulations, this idea is as old as Western civilization, but its modern incarnation can be traced to the late eighteenth and early nineteenth centuries. Throughout the nineteenth century, the moral imagination of American society was increasingly focused on the downtrodden and the oppressed, both foreign and domestic. Indignation at the wrongs suffered by Greek, Polish, and Russian peasants was matched by growing horror over the condition of the urban poor, malnutrition among the young, child labor, and the abuses of the working class in the nation's factories.

Society could no longer regard such conditions as givens; nor was it in any mood to approach suffering with an attitude of resignation. Neither God nor fate provided a credible explanation for human unhappiness. In the increasingly secular nineteenth century, such explanations came to seem archaic and beside the point, if not crass and unfeeling. Suffering no longer seemed the inevitable lot of man.

The mastery of nature by modern society and the advance of technology and science made these conditions all the more intolerable. Indeed, the seemingly endless train of human progress made the persistence of such misfortune appear increasingly outrageous. If a later age would see landing on the moon as a sign that society could solve any problem, the nineteenth century regarded its own achievements with no less triumphalism.

Sewerage systems were improved, nutrition enhanced, and diseases ranging from tuberculosis to typhoid fever and cholera were attacked with vigor and success. "Disease, sickness, and pain," writes Joseph Amato in *Victims and Values*, "were no longer accepted as a matter of fate. They were now understood to be problems to be broken down, analyzed, and solved."[1] If man could wrestle with and defeat disease and death, if he could begin to erect battlements against chance and disaster, then all things were possible. Progress in medicine appeared to be matched stride for stride with advances in economic and political enlightenment; mastery of nature seemed to lead ineluctably to man's mastery over his own fate. The nineteenth century's optimism and compassion inevitably turned to the problem of suffering.

Intellectually, the culture had long been prepared for this embrace of compassion. But here we come to a source of confusion and misunderstanding. More than one tradition claimed compassion as its legacy, even though each represented a different worldview. Throughout the nineteenth century, the Christian tradition provided much of the moral vocabulary for social improvement and reform. But the rise of what would become victimism paralleled the gradual decline of specifically Christian faith. Perhaps this was a sign of the secularization of Christian ethics; the injunction to care for the poor survived the loss of its metaphysical basis.

But to understand the cultural impulse that would later become victimism, we need to recognize the antitradition of secular compassion that arose not out of Christian bourgeois culture but as part of a bitterly hostile attack on that ethos.

ROUSSEAU AND THE ROMANTIC VICTIM

The impressive intellectual armory of the Enlightenment was first turned on the bourgeoisie by Jean-Jacques Rousseau, who was to do so much to transform the middle class into an object of derision and hatred for both the right and the left. For Rousseau, the bourgeois was "unpoetic, unerotic, unheroic, neither aristocrat nor of the peo-

ple; he is not a citizen and his religion is pallid and this-worldly."[2]
He was, in short, despicable and embarrassing at the same time.
Culture, liberation, and dignity all required that man cast off the
shackles of the philistine interlopers and their vulgar morality.

Rousseau did much more, however, than simply hoist the banner
of antibourgeois passion. He was the first to link the assault on
middle-class culture with both the championing of the untrammeled
self *and* the call for compassion. This trinity of attitudes—hostility
toward the bourgeoisie, faith in the self, and the embrace of compassion—was to be the formula for modernity's attitude toward culture,
society, and politics. Allan Bloom argues that Rousseau "single-
handedly invented the category of the disadvantaged." Before Rousseau, Bloom writes, "men believed that their claim on civil society
had to be based on an accounting of what they contributed to it.
After Rousseau, a claim based not on a positive quality but on a lack
became legitimate for the first time."[3]

Rousseau's approach to compassion bore little resemblance to that
of the Christian tradition. Of course, given Rousseau's emphasis on
the liberation of the self, the two views could hardly be compatible,
even though the rhetoric would often seem indistinguishable.

In Christian bourgeois society, charity, like work, was an opportunity to win salvation or (depending on the tradition) to demonstrate
that one had already been saved. A mother of illegitimate children,
a drunkard, the chronically unemployed, and the bankrupt spendthrift all had a moral claim on those who were better off to the extent
that they were in need. But it would have seemed incomprehensibly
alien to the religious middle class to suggest that such misfortune
conferred a special moral character on the downtrodden themselves.
Still less would they have seen a remedy for the plight of the needy
in efforts to raise their self-esteem. And all would have regarded as
madness an ideology insisting that the avoidance of pain was the
preeminent obligation of society. Although Nietzsche would later
argue that Christianity had inverted the healthy moral order by ex-
alting the meek over the strong, martyrdom was a status reserved
for the morally strong. The saint suffered for his faith, and such
suffering was redemptive. Like Christ, he offered himself as a victim,
one—it was to be hoped—without spot or stain. But the saintliness
of these victims did not thereby make all victims saints.

Rousseau—and the Romantics after him—saw compassion very
differently.

Compassion, in their view, was seen not as a sacred duty owed to

God or man but as a way of refining one's sense of self-identity and self-awareness. "Self-satisfaction of egalitarian man is what Rousseau promotes," notes Bloom. The sense of moral satisfaction that concern for the downtrodden engendered was, for Rousseau, an essential element in the development of *amour propre*, and thus had to be cultivated. Rousseau was actually rather pragmatic in the matter. If men were to think themselves worse off than others, they would develop base and vindictive passions. The only way to avoid this debasement was to find others who were more wretched. This would engender pity, and a sense of moral freedom and satisfaction to boot. Compassion and pity were not, however, absolutes for Rousseau. They would never, for example, stand in the way of self-preservation. Rather, they were passions meant to counterbalance other, more ugly, passions. To the extent that man sees that he potentially shares the fate of the more wretched, his compassion develops a social bond with the less fortunate. Rousseau imagined that such compassion would "dampen the harsh competitiveness and egotism of egalitarian political orders," and that such amiable sentiments, rather than self-interest, could bind society together.[4]

But his approach, which Bloom calls "a hardheaded softness," could—and did—lend itself to self-indulgent posturing. For the Romantics of the early nineteenth century, concern for the downtrodden and with human suffering became not only fashionable but a form of self-therapy and elaborate self-indulgence. Abstracted from the moral order, pity became contagious, turned first on a lengthening and shifting list of putative sufferers but ultimately back upon the self.

Goethe's Young Werther was only the first among many Romantics to throw himself upon the thorns of life and bleed. "Suffering itself became a vehicle for self-identity and expression" among the Romantics, notes Joseph Amato.

> Sorrow, misery, and suffering provided fertile material for self-dramatization. Identifying oneself with suffering was a way to assert one's own sincerity and profundity. It served many as a shortcut to "originality." To suffer, as Jean Jacques Rousseau, founder and master of the art of self-cultivation, taught, made one sensitive, serious, interesting, something other than a superficial, materialistic, and vulgar member of the middle class, whom artists and bohemians from Baudelaire's time on condemn with such righteousness and spleen.[5]

From the beginning, then, obsession with the self and compassion for others had been inextricably bound—and confused—in the modern sensibility. This linkage did not in any way detract from the moral weight and authority of genuine concern for the downtrodden; nor did it discredit real empathy with the unfortunate. But it did mean that what had once been a path to salvation was now also a means to self-realization; genuine moral concern had become virtually indistinguishable from aesthetic posturing.

By the beginning of the twentieth century, a revolution of sensibilities had occurred. Through much of the previous century, James Turner wrote, "sympathy was a tenuous, fitful, and often superficial response to the distress of others. By 1900 compassion for suffering was second nature." Describing what he calls the "expansion of the human heart" in the nineteenth century, Amato remarks:

> By 1900 great numbers of the Western upper classes took the possibility of the elimination of suffering to be a moral imperative. . . . By 1900 an awesome horizon of problems and victims, on the one hand, and possibilities, and dreams, on the other, had been assembled before the Western conscience for deliberation and action. . . . People now felt responsible for more than they ever had before. This new sensibility exceeded any specific form of conscience, any particular claim to justice, any special cause, movement, or program. Dominating so much of the Western conscience, rhetoric, and politics, this sensibility determined the moral assumptions of a whole civilization.[6]

THE NEW MARTYRS

This new sense of moral obligation provided the moral and emotional basis for the metastasis of victim politics in the twentieth century, beginning with the proletariat and spreading outward, ultimately embracing the civil rights movement.

But the ethos of compassion had little patience for the counsels of caution and moral restraint advanced by leaders like King and Niebuhr. In part, the change in the moral compass of the civil rights movement can be traced by its shift in emphasis from seeking equality under the law to a focus on the vague and volatile concept of racism. In its original form, civil rights had guaranteed legal protections and had barred specific acts of discrimination. Antiracism, however, goes much deeper. "To fight against racism," notes Julius Lester, "divides humanity into an us against a them. It leads to a self-definition as 'victim,' and anyone who defines himself as a victim has found a way to keep himself in a perpetual state of righteous self-pity and anger. . . ." But the shift to racism had other advantages, which Lester recognized. The buzzwords of *racism* and *victim* were "designed to make blacks feel self-righteously indignant over real and imagined wrongs, designed to make whites feel eternally guilty as the perpetrators of those wrongs."[7]

With passionate eloquence, author James Baldwin endowed victimization with the mantle of both moral power and transcendent insight, arguing that the oppressed actually had a clearer, purer vision of the world. They saw more and their testimony was incontrovertible.

> That man who is forced every day to snatch his manhood, his identity out of the fire of human cruelty that rages to destroy it knows, if he survives his effort, and even if he does not survive it, something about himself and human life that no school on earth—and, indeed, no church—can teach. He achieves his own authority, and that is unshakable.[8]

The victim-as-martyr theme proved so potent that it transformed the rules of victim politics. "One no longer had to fear the charge of self-pity when detailing the suffering of one's group," critic Stanley Crouch recalls. "Catastrophic experience was elevated. Race became an industry. It spawned careers, studies, experts, college departments, films, laws, hairdos, name changes, federal programs, and so many books. Blessed are the victims, the new catechism taught, for their suffering has illuminated them, and they shall lead us to the light, even as they provide magnets for our guilt."[9]

Victimism obviously *worked*. But it worked not merely because of guilt or fear. It worked because society *needed* victims. They had become the irreplaceable currency of self-identity and self-justification.

THE IDEOLOGY OF OPPRESSION

The impulse to regard society as a series of oppressions required more than the mere disposition to be outraged. Although the impressive armory of the therapeutic culture was at hand, an ideology was required. As the civil rights movement relocated from South to North, Gandhi, Christ, and Niebuhr were replaced by theorists of a radically different bent. Black-power advocates turned instead to Frantz Fanon and the French writer Albert Memmi to provide the intellectual apologia for their undertakings. Fanon was to become a counterculture pinup and a mainstay of victimist university curriculums into the 1990s, while Memmi created a universal theory of "total" oppression that argued the existence of a privileged revolutionary morality.

What made Memmi's contribution so valuable was his radical modification of Marxism's insistence that *class* was the only relevant division of society and that the primary sources of oppression were economic. Memmi took a far more expansive view of oppression. He added to the list of certified oppressed victims blacks, Jews, colonials, French Canadians, the proletariat, women, and domestic servants. He was also a harbinger of the crucial shift from material to psychological measures of oppression. "Oppression," he wrote, "is like an octopus; it is hard to tell which of its arms has the tightest stranglehold. Injustice, insults, humiliation and insecurity can be as hard to bear as hunger."[10]

Victimization could not be judged by any objective standard, he insisted, because even the apparently well-off could claim victim status. "It is clear that no one is oppressed in the absolute, but always in relation to someone else, in a given context. In such a way that, even if one is fortunate in comparison with others . . . one may perfectly well be living in a state of domination. . . ."[11]

Memmi's second contribution was to blur the distinctions between these forms of victimization. All victims, he insisted, look essentially alike. "Their own peculiar features and individual history aside, colonized peoples, Jews, women, the poor, show a kind of family likeness," he wrote; "all bear a burden which leaves the same bruises on their soul, and similarly distorts their behavior."[12]

And finally, Memmi presented the doctrine of universal *guilt*. He declared: "*Everyone, or nearly everyone, is an unconscious racist*, or a

semi-conscious one, or even a conscious one." [Emphasis in original.] Racism was spread by literature and religion, and was "as intimate a part of the child's familial and social upbringing as the milk
he sucks in infancy."[13] Put in this light, racism was a charge that
could never be disproved; it had been endowed with an immanent
and metaphysical quality.

Racism was also different from overt and provable acts of discrimination. *Racism* did not necessarily refer to behavior, but to a state of
mind. Equitable *conduct* was no longer enough to prove one's innocence; one's innermost thoughts could now be brought to trial.
Memmi was ready with the guilty verdict.

Memmi seems to have been something of a late convert to the
recognition that American blacks deserved to be classified with other
victims of oppression. If this lag seems surprising, it is perhaps well
to recall that Memmi's attitude was informed by the comparative
sufferings of Jews in the Holocaust and colonials who lived in abject
poverty and were denied even basic human rights. Writing in 1963,
Memmi confessed a "slight hesitation" in placing American blacks
among the ranks of the genuinely oppressed. But he made up for his
slowness with incomparable zeal.

Writing the introduction to the French edition of James Baldwin's
The Fire Next Time, Memmi rejected all half measures. "It is the
whole of American society that excludes, martyrizes and kills the
black man," he insisted. American blacks were the subject of "total
oppression," which Memmi defined as "a state which affects the
human being in all aspects of his existence, in the way he sees himself
and in the way others see him. . . ." There was "no one aspect of
his life, no single action of his, that is not thrown off balance by this
fundamental aggression."

As if this might not be sufficiently persuasive to his French audience, Memmi went even further, drawing a direct link between the
Holocaust and the treatment of American blacks. "*In the final analysis
what the white hopes for is the annihilation of the black,*" Memmi wrote.
[Emphasis in original.] "There is no reason why the Americans
should not one day attempt against their blacks what the Germans,
another white, Christian nation, attempted against the Jews."[14]

Not surprisingly, such views would lead Memmi to reject Martin
Luther King, Jr.'s, conception of American society and his tactics.
By 1965, he could scarcely conceal his contempt for King while
penning tortured apologias for Malcolm X. Memmi saw King's paci-
fism as a mere way station on the road to the inevitable "total revolt"

embodied in Malcolm X's militarism. King, Memmi wrote, was pursuing a "restful," feel-good approach, "a kind of collective Yoga, a lesson in relaxation and self-control. . . ." Memmi all but called King an Uncle Tom, adding that the civil rights leader was, deep down, "still the victim of oppression who persists in wanting to resemble his oppressor." Memmi also noted that King "no longer has any authority in the North."

In sharp contrast, Memmi was fascinated by Malcolm X, whom he portrayed as the inevitable successor to King. "The one is called forth by the other, follows on from it and rounds it off," he wrote. In the rise of Malcolm X, Memmi detected "a new and fascinating chapter" in the history of oppression. He took note of Malcolm X's demagoguery, his bizarre racist mythology, and even his anti-Semitism. But though he recognized Malcolm X as "the poisoned fruit of the black's hatred," Memmi shrugged off his shortcomings (he dismissed his anti-Semitism as an "illogicality"), insisting that "Malcolm is a genuine revolutionary, and the true spokesman of the black American revolt."[15]

Memmi believed that the righteous rage of the oppressed permitted the suspension of morality and, apparently, of logic. Even as he denounced Malcolm X's demagoguery and rejected his reliance on "scandalous" and "incredible" myths of black racial superiority, Memmi asked, "But where could a better source of self-respect be found than in these folk fables?" Fully recognizing the falsity and potential evil of this new pantheon of white devils and black angels, Memmi embraced the mythology of victimism. "The greater his past wretchedness, the more the black's *negritude* must now be made to appear desirable," Memmi wrote, adding that the "myth-image of negritude is a driving force in this revolution."

If we are less charitable than Memmi, we might imagine that he is proposing the doctrine of the Victim Lie—a falsehood that advances the cause of the oppressed no matter how scurrilous it might be.

> These are myths, to be sure! A sort of mass delirium, as
> disastrous as those of the oppressor! That much is certain. . . .
> But if we are dealing with myths, they are more correctly
> counter-myths, the crazed reaction to the accuser's own folly.

Thus, if whites had turned blacks into monsters, Malcolm X was only returning the favor. After all, what choice did he have? Memmi denied that King's approach was a real alternative. "King's policy of love is scarcely less myth-inspired than Malcolm's open violence."[16]

Memmi's counterreality was also a counterjustice, in which the retaliation and violence of the victim "must transcend all justice."*[17]

Having relativized truth for victims, Memmi proceeded to relativize all morality. "Total revolt," he wrote, "means also immoral, or rather amoral, warfare, fought under the one standard left: that of liberty. It is an unprincipled war, for principles have too long been used to mystify and grind down the oppressed."

Even the "most evil deeds" are allowed to the victim. "For what is the meaning of 'evil'?" Memmi asked. "The underdog was never asked his opinion of these fake definitions. The search for new standards and for a new order can begin after the cataclysm."[18] Here Memmi echoed Frantz Fanon, who was an even more explicit and enthusiastic advocate of revolutionary terrorism. The victim of oppression, Fanon wrote, "is ready for violence at all times."[19] Fanon had also rejected the moral order of society for its creation of "an atmosphere of submission and inhibition" among colonized natives.[20] The victim of oppression "laughs in mockery when Western values are mentioned in front of him. . . . [The masses] insult them, and vomit them up."[21]

The first value to go in Fanon's world was individualism. "Henceforth," he declared, "the interest of one will be the interests of all, for in concrete fact *everyone* will be discovered by the troops, *everyone* will be massacred—or *everyone* will be saved."[22] He drew no distinction, for instance, between the official roles of the colonizers and the individuals themselves. All were marked for death. "As far as the native is concerned, morality is very concrete; it is to silence the settler's defiance, to break his flaunting violence—in a word, to put him out of the picture."[23]

But if all principles are discarded, all morality scrapped, on what basis can new standards ever be found? This is a question neither Fanon nor Memmi addresses. Nor do they explain how liberty can survive the wreckage of values (including justice) to retain a privileged status in the victim's universe. But the rejection of any appeal to shared values or accepted notions of justice is one of the central tenets of victimist politics. The victim defined by Fanon and Memmi

---

*It is perhaps worth noting that Memmi wrote with full awareness of the price civilization had paid for the Big Lie, and for the distortion of truth for ideological ends. His position cannot be explained by naïveté.

disdains all use of reason and persuasion; he employs only the weapons of demand and force. He is entitled to whatever he can grab.

But if the victim is beyond all moral judgment, he is equally beyond moral appeal. Having condemned "principles" as an agent of oppression, he cannot then invoke the principles of equity or fairness on his own behalf. Nor, having adopted the immorality of his oppressor, does he seem to have any other fate than to become an oppressor himself. This is precisely what Niebuhr had warned against, also noting that dehumanization was an inevitable part of victim politics.

Memmi insisted that one's status as a victim must transcend all other human characteristics and loyalties. Victimhood must define one's humanity as totally as the total oppression one sees everywhere. Memmi chided author Richard Wright for insisting, "I am first of all an American!" and condemned Wright's declaration of a nonoppressed identity as the embracing of an illusion, an aspect of "self-hatred."[24] But as one critic noted, seeing oneself solely as a victim— irrespective of other identities—changes one's "victimhood from accident to essence. It expands the category of victim until it swallows the whole person."[25]

The countermorality of Fanon's and Memmi's victimism begins by taking away the humanity of the oppressor, and ends by denying it to the oppressed himself.

SEVEN

The Revolt of
the Kids

By almost any measure, the generation that came of age in the 1960s was the most pampered and doted upon in history. Its economic advantages had been extraordinary, its prospects exceptionally bright. The children of the baby boom were raised with scientifically approved methods, dressed with care, and educated far beyond the dreams of any previous generation. They were rewarded for their precociousness with the adulation of their elders. Even after some of them trashed Columbia University, a committee headed by Archibald Cox extolled them as "the best informed, the most intelligent, and the most idealistic [generation] this country has ever known." So it was both striking and puzzling when this golden generation descended into a decade-long funk from which they would never fully emerge. It was equally remarkable that this privileged generation would so emphatically declare itself a victim of social, familial, governmental, and educational repression.

There was no shortage of explanations.

American society may well have been on the verge of becoming the "affluent society," argued Abraham Maslow, but the young suffered from what he portentously called "intrinsic-value starvation." Their basic physical needs had been more than met, but the new generation now craved "self-actualization" and needed to become "more fully human."

"How could the young people not be disappointed and disillusioned?" Maslow asked. "What else could be the result of *getting* all the material and animal gratifications and then *not being happy*, as they were led to expect, not only by the theorists, but also by the conventional wisdom of parents and teachers, and the insistent gray lies of advertisers."

True to the tenets of the therapeutic culture, Maslow declared that the failure to achieve self-actualization and full "humanness" was not merely unfortunate, it was an *illness*. This "illness," Maslow declared, was a "metapathology." Maslow made no attempt to hide his medicalization of an essentially existential problem. The "illness" was the deprivation of "the spiritual life, the highest aspiration of mankind." But he dismissed organized religions, as well as most spiritual traditions, as "non-human, non-natural sources" and a "denial of human nature."

In Maslow's view, then, the "frustrated idealism" of youth was the result of a psychologically sick society. Maslow's place in the pantheon of the therapeutic culture was assured by his insistence that the "value life" of humans was actually rooted in their biological makeup and that medical science could annex the entire area of spiritual crisis as a "hot research topic."[1] Since existential doubt was now *sickness*, the role of the priest could be assumed by the psychotherapist.

And, perhaps, by the political activist.

LIKE PARENTS, LIKE CHILD

At least originally, the campus upheavals of the 1960s were very much an elite affair. The struggle against the allegedly repressive social order did not arise from students whose families were disadvantaged or poor. Protestors were often the most gifted and successful students. "The higher the student's grade average," wrote Kenneth Keniston, "the more outstanding his academic achievement, the more likely it is that he will become involved in any given political demonstration." The revolutionaries were overwhelmingly "recruited from among those young Americans who have had the most socially fortunate upbringing."[2]

But their identity was not simply a matter of economic or social class. Many of them were the children of what could be called the New Class or the Knowledge Class—they were the heirs to the adversary culture, distinguished not so much by their financial status as by their cultural impulses.* Dominant in the arts, literature, academia, and heavily represented among the opinion-making elite, this New Class tended to see liberalism less as a matter of political principle than as a collection of cultural and psychological positions, all of them in tension with the dominant (as they saw it) bourgeois ethos.

Describing the New Class, Daniel Bell wrote: "They function institutionally as a group, bound by a consciousness of a kind."[3] For counterculture guru Charles Reich, this consciousness was "not a set of opinions, information, or values, but a *total configuration in any given individual, which makes up his whole perception of reality, his whole world-view.*"[4] [Emphasis added.] Reich was setting a remarkably high standard for political/cultural/psychological health and conformity. Reich insisted that it was easy to determine any individual's "total configuration" simply by knowing his position on a single issue. "Ask a stranger on a bus or airplane about psychiatry or redwoods or police or taxes or morals or war," Reich argued, "and you can guess with fair accuracy his views on *all the rest of these topics and many others besides,* even though they are seemingly unrelated." [Emphasis added.] If, for example, someone favored developing wilderness areas, Reich took that as a reliable sign that "he is quite likely to favor punitive treatment for campus disruptions." Following the same logic, Reich insisted that anyone who "is enthusiastic about hunting wild animals" could reliably be counted as someone who "believes that the American economic system rests on individual business activity." And anyone who believes these things, opined Reich, surely also "has an aversion to people with long hair."[5]

Reich could justify such non sequiturs by asserting that "an individual's opinions, understanding, and values are all part of some invisible whole" that apparently could be readily discerned only by the politically/culturally/psychologically enlightened. Despite his lack of any empirical evidence to support his position, Reich *was* describing a genuine cultural reality—at least for his own cultural milieu. One's opinions *were* a constant barometer of moral and political rectitude, and the slightest deviation could be taken as a sign of corruption in the "invisible whole" and the "total configuration" of

---

*Keniston added: "Similarly, student activists come from families with liberal political values; a disproportionate number report that their parents hold views essentially similar to their own, and accept and support their activities. Thus, among the parents of protestors we find large numbers of liberal Democrats, plus an unusually large scattering of pacifists, socialists, etc."

the individual. The Sixties counterculture was the high-water mark of other-directedness, as well as a precursor of what would become known as "political correctness."

While the counterculture encouraged every sort of idiosyncracy, it left remarkably little room for individual thought or dissent from the cultural "consciousness." Fail to show sufficient sensitivity to redwoods and you were the moral equivalent of the National Guardsmen who gunned down four students at Kent State; hunt deer on weekends and you became the cultural equivalent of a redneck or a hard hat. Reich acknowledged the implicit absolutism of his position. "An argument between people who are on different levels of consciousness often goes nowhere," he wrote; "there is no common ground on which they can meet."[6] Absent any rational grounds for resolving disagreements, the demands of this consciousness led to the development of an increasingly rarefied aesthetic built upon a complex range of sensibilities finely attuned to the merest shades of injustice.

Writing in the early 1950s, Randall Jarrell captured some of the anxiety of liberal cultural conformity in his novel *Pictures From an Institution*. Most of the faculty members of Jarrell's fictional Benton College "would have swallowed a porcupine, if you had dyed its quills and called it Modern Art; they longed for men to be discovered on the moon, so that they could show that *they* weren't prejudiced towards moon men. . . ."[7]

This baroque aesthetic of compulsory progressivism also helped to refine perceptions of the crudity and insensitivity of the nation's culture. Such infra dig embarrassments as LBJ, Richard Nixon, and Dwight Eisenhower not only conjured up images of banality and hypocrisy but also symbolized the barrenness of the middle classes, who were tone-deaf to the complicated symphony of grievance around them.

John Updike recognized an element of cultural snobbery in the passionate antiwar sentiments of his East Coast intellectual acquaintances: "Cambridge professors and Manhattan lawyers and their guitar-strumming children thought they could run the country and the world better than" Lyndon Johnson—"this lugubrious bohunk from Texas." This privileged class, he wrote, "was full of disdain" for its own defenders.[8]

Such disdain was not easily contained. The 1960s was to witness a constant jockeying for moral superiority and for sneering rights in the elaborate hierarchy of moral righteousness.

LITMUS TESTS

Crucially, the younger generation had inherited from its parents the same nagging anxiety about psychological and political health that was making life miserable for so many aging liberals. The notion of a "generation gap" tends to obscure this vital continuum. Many of the activists of the 1960s, Kenneth Keniston argued, did not reject their parents' values at all, but rather were "concerned with *living out expressed but unimplemented parental values.*"[9] [Emphasis added.] They were taking their parents' political and cultural subversiveness at face value; what Mom and Dad had only talked about, their children acted upon.* As Daniel Bell noted, the radical movement of the 1960s "found the values of the adversary culture—the attack on society through such themes as mass society, anomie, alienation—as the Ariadne's thread which allowed it to emerge into a new radical period."[10]

Because of their privileged status, the militant young did not expend their passions in fighting injustices that they themselves felt. "For example," Keniston pointed out, "one of the apparent paradoxes about protests against current draft policies is that the protesting students are selectively drawn from the subgroup *most* likely to receive student deferments for graduate work."[11] Instead, theirs was a sort of proxy outrage in which they appropriated the grievances of eminently draftable blacks to strike a moral pose of their own, one that became an essential part of their self-identity and was all the more gratifying since they could then imagine themselves sharing in the oppression and struggle of their brothers. Undoubtedly, blacks *were* genuine victims of repression; and the moral duality of their struggle with the white racist establishment inspired the response of the affluent young radicals. Because the issues were so clear, the

---

*Family backgrounds were also decisive for the group of disaffected young labeled by Keniston the "culturally alienated." Less interested in politics and less hopeful of change, the "alienated" student tended to stress his nonconformity in his private life and dress. He was also more likely to reject his parents' values. "In particular, he is likely to see his father as a man who has 'sold out' to the pressures of success and status in American society; he is determined to avoid the fate that overtook his father." But this should not be read as an all-out rejection of the family's values. Keniston added that the alienated student was likely to be quite close to his mother, whose values he had imbibed as a counterbalance to those of the disdained paterfamilias. "The most common family environment of the alienated-student-to-be," wrote Keniston, "consists of a parental schism supplemented by a special mother-son alliance of mutual understanding and maternal control and depreciation of the father."

black struggle also provided the long-sought litmus test of moral correctness. Much in the same way that Calvinists once sought means to give outward proofs of their salvation, the children of the fading adversary culture needed to prove their political rectitude. And in the 1960s, the stakes were constantly being raised. Ratifying the demands of the civil rights movement, and later of the black-power movement, provided the proof positive of psychological/political health. Solidarity with black militants (along with opposition to the Vietnam War and support for sexual liberation) became a metaphor for the rejection of society's values and the idealistic basis of what was, by now, a generalized grudge against the social order.

However much the elder generation celebrated their children's outbreak of idealism, what followed was not necessarily what they had had in mind. While the acolytes of modernism had prided themselves on their outrageousness, Daniel Bell pointed out, their insurgency, "no matter how daring, played out its impulses in the imagination, within the constraints of art." Their children recognized no such limits, trampling over the barriers that had separated art from life. In this postmodern world, Bell said, "Impulse and pleasure alone are real and life-affirming; all else is neurosis and death."[12]

James Q. Wilson was to describe the difference between traditional liberalism and the new revolutionary faith as the tension between justice and benevolence. Clutching their totems of idealism and embracing a politics of sincerity, right feeling, and compassion for society's victims, the young radicals had little patience for the liberals' faith in the bloodless ideals of "justice—the rule of law, equality of opportunity, democratic voting." None of these, Wilson wrote, could "easily or for long withstand an aroused sense of benevolence."[13] Too long out of the habit of insisting on fixed standards of moral judgment, the liberals put up only a feeble resistance against the forces that Sidney Hook was to describe as the "barbarism of virtue."[14]

"Sincerity" had its own rules, and idealism conferred its own immunities; neither suffered delay or opposition. It was a powerful and heady brew, because it conferred an undeniable moral authority that justified the most outrageous self-assertions.

Wilson noted the paradox at the heart of what would become victim politics. When frustrated, he wrote, the politics of benevolence "often turns to rage and those who celebrated the virtues of compassion may come to indulge sentiments of hatred."[15]

The transition from the liberal faith in justice to the barbarism of virtue was captured in the devolution of the Students for a Democratic Society, which declared in 1962 that it regarded "men as infinitely precious and possessed of unfulfilled capacities for reason, freedom and love. . . ."

"Within a few years," Wilson would write, "this organization, including many of those who signed this statement . . . were attacking universities, harassing those who disagreed with them, demanding political obedience, and engaging in deliberate terrorism. Nothing could have been more liberal than the 1962 statement of the SDS; nothing could have been less liberal than its subsequent history."[16]

Their elders were not far behind.

EIGHT

Victim Chic, Victim Therapy

Leonard Bernstein's fete for the Black Panthers, immortalized by Tom Wolfe, merely hinted at the potential of victimist chic. Bolstered by Roquefort cheese morsels rolled in crushed nuts, asparagus tips in mayonnaise dabs, and *meatballs petits au Coq Hardi*, Bernstein and the New York culturati shivered with the excitement of their daring—a thrill Wolfe described as a "rogue hormone" that ran through Bernstein's fashionable duplex. Unlike the moderate might-as-well-be-white leaders of the civil rights movement—unlike Martin Luther King, Jr., for example—the surly and beleathered Panthers represented the genuine article. In a culture that valued sincerity and authenticity, they were *real*.

One can only imagine what the Panthers in attendance made of it all. They were surely savvy enough to recognize that they were being patronized. And they no doubt found the fawning servility of their hosts amusing. But they must also have reveled in their success and obvious power. Even when the Panther "field marshal" described the Party's shakedown of Jewish merchants for contributions, "which they *should give*, because they are the exploiters of the black community," no one registered a single demurral. The Panthers had carte blanche.[1]

The tendency of the New Left to use protest as a form of self-therapy was first remarked upon by Nat Hentoff in 1967. Commenting on a dramatic antiwar protest that erupted during a high mass at Saint Patrick's Cathedral in New York, Hentoff questioned the demonstration's effectiveness. Didn't unfurling a poster of a maimed Vietnamese child merely widen the gap between the protesters and their audience? "If the intent was to speak to all those who would see or read about the demonstration, what actually was the effect on *them*?" Hentoff asked. Most likely it was "resentment and anger." Rather than focusing attention on the Vietnam War, the protesters had shifted the focus onto themselves.

Hentoff suggested that this may have been the point all along. "I would suggest," he wrote, "that their act's essential effect was to make *them* feel relevant, to make *them* feel that some of their guilt as Americans had been atoned for by this witness. I am all for self-therapy, but if that's what it is, let us call it that."[2]

For obvious reasons, the movement was loath to follow Hentoff's call for candor. But seeing the New Left as an exercise in self-therapy is helpful in explaining events like the "New Politics" convention held in Chicago in 1967. I recall it with particular affection, since I attended it (at age thirteen) with my father, who was then heading up Senator Eugene McCarthy's presidential campaign in Wisconsin.

Although the organizers of the conference had envisioned a "dream" presidential ticket of Martin Luther King, Jr., and Benjamin Spock, the event ultimately degenerated into a repudiation of King's philosophy. Even as King addressed the conference, appealing for "a new coalition of conscience," militants marched outside, chanting, "Kill Whitey." But this was merely prologue. Historian Ronald Radosh vividly recounts what followed, a scene he calls "a numbing charade of revolutionary politics."[3] The conference attempted the fusing of the counterculture New Left with the black-liberation movement, gathering together black militants from SNCC, CORE, and SCLC, members of the Socialist Workers and Communist parties, and anxious bourgeois radicals eager to accommodate the others' every demand. It ended as one of the decade's classic set pieces, illustrating the power of white self-therapy but also demonstrating its reciprocal effect on the burgeoning black-power movement.

Throughout the conference, the black caucus met in secret sessions, guarded by shaven-headed bodyguards who taunted whites "as they solicited contributions for 'our black brothers in the jails.'" According to Radosh, the caucus was divided between those who wanted to take a strictly separatist path and those who were willing to work with the white radicals. Eventually, they settled on a test of the whites' tolerance: a thirteen-point nonnegotiable program including "acceptance of a black armed militia, the right of blacks to revolt when they deemed it necessary, and a dialogue for partitioning the United States into two separate nations, one black and one white." Their program also condemned Israel for its victory in the Six Day War, which it called an "imperialistic Zionist war."

The response of the white delegates was the apogee of victim politics. Instead of debating the demands, the whites accepted "their own responsibility for centuries of oppression" and voted three-to-one to endorse the entire litany of the black caucus's demands. Radosh quotes one Jewish leftist screaming: "After 400 years of slavery, it is right that whites should be castrated." The ease of their success emboldened the black caucus to up its demands even further. As it turned out, both sides had developed a taste for humiliation: one in inflicting it, the other in experiencing it.

The process of self-castration continued when the black caucus (which represented only about a third of the participants) demanded half of the votes at the convention. Again, the white radicals quickly acquiesced. One white delegate explained his rationale for supporting the putsch: "We are just a little tail on the end of the very powerful black panther, and I want to be on that tail—if they'll let me."[4]

Despite such enthusiastic kowtowing, the blacks were not mollified. Their caucus staged a noisy walkout, denouncing the white radicals. In his account of this debacle, Radosh quoted Fred Siegel's remark that Black Power was "the social therapy of self-assertion." But the self-flagellation of the white radicals was equally therapeutic, if ultimately self-destructive.

EGOISM AND IDEALISM

Among the most extraordinary aspects of the 1960s was the bizarre menagerie of gurus and pop prophets whose fulminations were, for a time, actually taken seriously. Many were probably weirder than Charles Reich, but few were more influential. Reich's book *The Greening of America* became a top best-seller and something of a cult classic; it was even treated as a reputable intellectual treatise. Senator George McGovern called it "one of the most gripping, penetrating and revealing analyses of American society" he had ever read. Supreme Court justice William O. Douglas declared that it was "challenging and provocative—a first-rate piece of creative thinking," while William McPherson, writing in *The Washington Post*, gushed that it was "a brilliant synthesis of contemporary ideas."[5]

In retrospect, Reich's enthusiasm for free and frequent sex, for the mind-expanding capabilities of drug use, and his fervid defense of bell-bottom pants as a revolutionary symbol make the book something of an embarrassment. "Bell bottoms," Reich wrote earnestly, "have to be worn to be understood. They express the body as jeans do, but they say much more. They give the ankles a special freedom as if to invite dancing right on the street. They bring dance back into our sober lives. A touch football game, if the players are wearing bell bottoms, is like a folk dance or a ballet."[6]

This passage and others like it might lead readers to conclude that Reich was as good as his word when he insisted elsewhere in the book that "one of the most important means for restoring dulled consciousness is psychedelic drugs. . . . The term 'getting stoned' is confusing; it implies losing consciousness, rather than a higher awareness. But . . . using marijuana is more like what happens when a person with fuzzy vision puts on glasses. Listening to a familiar piece of music . . . the mind is newly conscious of the bass line; listening to a conversation, the mind is more aware of the nuances of each voice. . . . Grass is a subtle and delicate experience . . . not too different from the heightened awareness that an unusually sensitive artistic person has."[7]* For sure.

In the 1960s, Reich's notion of a "revolution by consciousness" provided a vision to the insurgent culture and a manifesto for postmodernism. It also marked the passage of unabashed egoism into idealism.

The early Americans, Reich argued, had been characterized by what he called Consciousness I, which represented the Puritan ethos of industry, self-restraint, and self-reliance. Consciousness II arose out of the "disastrous failure of Consciousness I." This second stage, Reich argued, was the "consciousness that created the Corporate State" because it extolled the virtues of the organization over the individual.

"The foundation of Consciousness III," wrote Reich, "is liberation. It comes into being the moment the individual frees himself from automatic acceptance of the imperatives of society and the false consciousness which society imposes." Individuals could create their own philosophies, life-styles, and culture "from a new beginning."[8]

---

*Having read the above passages, reread the endorsements of Reich's book quoted earlier. I think you'll pretty much understand the 1960s.

First, however, everyone had to recognize how thoroughly they were being oppressed.

Reich was nothing if not creative in his critique of the victimized consciousness of the young. He described one infernal machine as creating "a constant and total atmosphere of violence." The prisons? The military? The police? Actually, the answer was none of the above.

Reich was talking about *high school*.

And he was not referring to physical violence. "We mean," he wrote, "violence in the sense of any assault upon, or violation of, the personality." At first blush, this was a radical expansion of the notion of "violence," but Reich proceeded quickly to expand it even further, multiplying the ways in which teenagers (who feel that way anyway) could feel themselves abused and repressed. "An examination or test," he insisted, "is a form of violence. Compulsory gym, to one embarrassed or afraid, is a form of violence." Reich kept upping the ante of victimization: "The requirement that a student must get a pass to walk in the hallways is violence." Everyone covered by now? Not at all. Reich continued: "Compulsory attendance in the classroom, compulsory studying in study hall, is violence." In fact, Reich concluded, "the amount of violence in high school is staggering."[9]

"THE ONLY TRUE REALITY"

Reich insisted that Consciousness III was a caring, sharing, sensitive kind of thing. But he also stressed that at its heart was the self. "Consciousness III starts with the self," declared Reich. In contrast to the bourgeois consciousness, "which accepts society, the public interest, and institutions as the primary reality," the postmodern sensibility "declares that the individual self is the *only true reality*." Reich even appropriated the tradition of Walt Whitman for his cause. Consciousness III, he insisted, "returns to the earlier America: 'Myself I Sing.' The first commandment is: thou shalt not do violence to thyself." In particular, this meant not allowing oneself to be compromised by society's requirements. "It is a crime to allow oneself to become an instrumental being, a projectile designed to accomplish some extrinsic end, a part of an organization or a machine." It was a crime, in other words, to get a job.

It was also a crime "to be alienated from oneself, to be a divided or schizophrenic being, to defer meaning to the future."[10] It was thus a crime to plan for the future, to defer gratification, to sacrifice for a long-term goal.

To his credit, Reich appears to have glimpsed the contradiction between the alleged altruism and compassion of the insurgent and his almost Nietzschean celebration of self. "To start from the self," Reich insisted, "does not mean to be selfish" and is, moreover, perfectly compatible with "a deep personal commitment to the welfare of the community." Reich notes that "this may sound contradictory to those who wrongly equate the premise of self with selfishness. But there is no contradiction." Even though the self does not "accept the goals or standards set by society," it has a strong feeling for other individuals, and therefore, "for the sake of the welfare of individuals, [the self] is committed to the improvement of society."[11] This suggestion of community spirit is pretty weak tea, however, especially since it necessitates the willingness of the self to cede some of its independence in the cause of social betterment. And how likely is that if the self is the dominant reality, whose needs come before any possible community need or definition of public welfare?

Reich attempted to bridge the gap between social compassion and the free, primal, and obligationless self by proposing what he called "independent consciousness." To achieve it, the self must cultivate "by whatever means are available, including clothes, speech mannerisms, illegal activities, and so forth, the feeling of being an outsider." One of the ways "the new generation struggles to feel itself as outsiders," Reich wrote, is to identify "with the blacks, with the poor, with Bonnie and Clyde, and with the losers of this world. . . ."[12]

But this implied that identifying with "losers" is merely *tactical*—a *therapeutic* posture adopted to enhance the insurgent's desired self-image as well as provide proof of his political, emotional, and mental health. Compassion for the downtrodden was urged not for the benefits it might confer on the victim but for its effectiveness in developing outsiderhood. It was also a way of identifying with and thus acquiring some of the moral standing of the genuinely downtrodden. This impulse could trace its lineage to Rousseau, who saw compassion as an element of amour propre, and to the Romantics, who saw suffering as a shortcut to self-dramatization, originality, sincerity, and profundity.

When young middle-class whites claimed that students were the niggers of the university system, they were declaring themselves to be both compassionate *and* victims in their own right—presumably with the same right to assert their moral superiority as any real victim. The very argument against self-ishness becomes an instance of psychological self-indulgence.

Strip away the rhetoric of Consciousness III and what is left is a catalog of immanent grievance and infinite self-assertion.

NINE

Blaming the Victim

As the 1960s degenerated into Reichian self-indulgence, the politics of victimism increasingly replaced mere compassion with
ratification. It was no longer enough to simply sympathize with
victims; one had to suspend judgment and embrace them, no matter
what their demands or their conduct. The new sociology of victimhood had unseated the culture of consequence. The stigma that
had once been attached to certain forms of conduct was replaced by
a stigma on judging such conduct.

But this was not always a matter of self-indulgence. Behind the
politics of victimhood lay a reservoir of honest intentions and goodwill. Many of the most important figures in the movement would
rather have been strangled with their own bell-bottoms than linked
with Charles Reich, and some of them were not at all far from
a religious tradition that emphasized human compassion on more
substantial grounds than those imagined by Reich.

There were, however, two legacies of the 1960s that were to dominate the development of social policy. The first was moral optimism,
the belief that people would continue to behave with decency and
self-restraint even if the established norms of society were discarded.
Richard John Neuhaus notes that among the progressive thinkers of
the era were men and women who were "born into a very Protestant
society and spent a lifetime drawing on its taken-for-granted moral
capital."[1] This resulted in something of a paradox.

"To be progressive," Neuhaus says, "was to rebel against an assumed moral establishment, *while continuing to assume that that establishment would provide the habits of virtue that would prevent liberation from turning into libertinism.*" [Emphasis added.] Neuhaus noted that Joseph Fletcher's influential *Situational Ethics,* an attack on traditional and fixed views of morality and ethics, was "redolent with the confidence that almost everybody is like Joe Fletcher—fundamentally decent, ever so enlightened, eminently reasonable, and eager to do the right thing."

While naïveté always has its charm, it is usually a poor basis for—if not downright deadly to—the development of social policy. Fletcher simply could not imagine the way his ideas might take flesh among the urban underclass.

Closely related to this moral optimism was the tendency to treat compassion as self-therapy. From Rousseau and the Romantics through Charles Reich, assuming a compassionate posture had been a crucial element in one's self-definition and self-realization. But self-involved compassion could easily turn good intentions into absolutes. Increasingly, social policies and programs were judged not on their actual results but on their benign intentions—not by how they affected the poor and the downtrodden but by how they made their proponents feel. "Who cares more?" tended to obscure "What works best?" Of course, the important thing was to attack poverty, racism, and inequality with moral fervor. The morally fervid, however, could be quite intolerant of the cautious and moderate, especially those who tried to point out that despite the best and most compassionate of intentions, many undeniably moral policies had either failed or had tragic and unintended consequences.

THE WAR OVER THE FAMILY

One of the decisive debates of the era centered on a 1965 paper entitled *The Negro Family: The Case for National Action,* written by then White House aide Daniel Patrick Moynihan.[2] Moynihan surveyed the success of the civil rights movement in sweeping aside the legal barriers to equality of opportunity: The Civil Rights Act had mobilized the power and authority of the federal government against racial discrimination, and the most notorious manifestations of white racism had been struck down. But even with the legal barriers gone, blacks still lagged far behind whites in the competition for jobs and economic success. Worse, the gap seemed to be widening despite the movement's achievements.

This was the puzzle of 1960s liberalism. Poverty had proven far more intractable than the social engineers had imagined; welfare rolls grew at dizzying rates as the stigmas of the dole and illegitimacy seemed to lose their power. Between 1958 and 1968—years of unprecedented affluence when minorities made considerable economic, social, and political strides toward equality—violent crime had risen by 100 percent. In the larger cities, the picture was especially bleak: The rate of violent crime rose from 293.7 crimes per 100,000 population in 1960 to 773.2 crimes per 100,000 in 1968.[3]

As James Q. Wilson and Richard Herrnstein later noted, the same years saw a sharp increase in other forms of social breakdown, including suicide, divorce, illegitimacy, alcoholism, and drug abuse. "It is hard to imagine that each of these changes could have been caused by economic problems," they wrote. "It is not hard to imagine that each was influenced by familial and cultural factors."[4]

This was precisely the area that Moynihan chose to explore in *The Negro Family*. He argued that the social fabric of the black community was being destroyed, especially the family, which was "approaching complete breakdown." A wave of illegitimacy, desertions by fathers, welfare dependency, the surge in youth-related crime, all constituted a daunting barrier to the realization of full equality for blacks, Moynihan wrote.

> At the heart of the deterioration of the fabric of Negro society is the deterioration of the Negro family. It is the fundamental source of weakness of the Negro community at the present time. . . . Unless this damage is repaired, all the effort to end discrimination and poverty and injustice will come to little. . . .[5]

Nearly three decades later, Moynihan's analysis hardly seems controversial; the link between single-parent households and black poverty is difficult to ignore. The relationship between the breakup of families, the high birthrate among teenage girls, the loss of male role models, and ignorance, crime, and unemployment seems clear enough. There is a new social fact: the black underclass.

But when Moynihan's report was released in August 1965, it unleashed a wave of denunciation. Moynihan ran directly into the "new mood of self-assertion and black pride taking hold" in America's inner cities, historian Allen Matusow later wrote.[6] James Farmer of CORE accused Moynihan of trying to shift the attention of the civil rights movement to "Negro mental health," while others accused him of trying to impose white middle-class values on the black community.[7] Nor was this criticism limited to militant fringe groups. In November 1965, a civil rights meeting convened by religious groups asked President Johnson to eliminate the issue of the Negro family from an upcoming White House conference.

At a planning meeting for the conference (which ultimately was never held), one of the speakers joked, "I have been reliably informed that no such person as Daniel Patrick Moynihan exists." Indeed, one of the legacies of the controversy was to put an effective end to public debate on the status of the family in the black community for more than a decade. Even after James Coleman's study of American education essentially concluded that the key determinant of educational success was a functioning and motivated family, discussion of the "family question" fell under an extraordinary intellectual taboo that was to have appalling consequences for social policy.*

One of the decisive shots in the battle came from a white Boston sociologist named William Ryan, who charged that Moynihan was the purveyor of an insidious new "ideology" that blamed the victims of poverty for their condition. In 1971, Ryan followed up his attack with an influential book expanding upon his theme. His *Blaming the Victim* not only gave victim politics its rhetorical theme but elaborated in great detail the doctrine that victims should not be held responsible for their conduct or their choices.[8]

Ryan flexed the explanatory muscle of the word *racism*—and found it exceptionally serviceable. For Ryan, being a victim of racism meant never having to say you're sorry or suffering the consequences of your misdeeds. Even in the cases of men who fathered illegitimate children or deserted their families, there was *always* someone else to blame. With considerable vigor, Ryan read out of the progressive/liberal movement anyone who did not embrace this position.

Ryan aimed his book not at conservatives but at liberals who might be wavering on the issue of personal responsibility or who might begin to acknowledge that some social problems have their roots in the specific attitudes and behaviors of the purported "victims."

The new "blame the victim" ideology, Ryan acknowledged, was very different from open prejudice and reactionary racism. "Its ad-

*In 1985, single-parent families were twice as common as they'd been in 1965.

herents include sympathetic social scientists with social consciences in good working order, and liberal politicians with a genuine commitment to reform," who, Ryan declared, had been duped by a doctrine that was the moral equivalent of the "vulgar Calvinism and crude racism" of another era. Whereas the racist believed that individuals were defective because they were "born that way," the emphasis on character and personal responsibility attributed the problems of minorities to "the malignant nature of poverty, injustice, slum life, and racial difficulties."[9] But, Ryan noted, these explanations still located the stigma of defect *within* the victim rather than focusing attention on eradicating racism—the true and only source of victimization. Any attempt to change the behavior or conduct of the victim was thus part of the overall pattern of victimization because it ignored the genuine causes.

Ryan's refusal to distinguish racism from distinctions based on personal conduct ignored the abyss that separated biological determinism from free will. But his popular success should not be puzzling: His argument was aimed at the tenderest spot in the liberal psyche; he challenged its sincerity, its authenticity, and (to use Theodor Adorno's term) its genuineness. As a psychologist, Ryan was able to draw upon his analytic skills to deny that liberals who believed in responsibility had arrived at their position in a "logical, rational, conscious way." Instead, he described what he called a "highly-charged psychological problem" facing the charitable liberal who had to balance self-interest with humanitarian impulses. The ideology of "blaming the victim," Ryan wrote, "is a process that takes place far below the level of sharp consciousness. . . ."[10]

Even more aggressively than Adorno had in *The Authoritarian Personality*, Ryan set impossibly high standards of psychological and political health. Suggesting that inner-city residents had certain disabilities was part of what Ryan called "the art of savage discovery." By labeling inner-city blacks as problematic, they were marked as "different," and therefore as "strangers." With typical victimist flourish, Ryan quickly evoked potential genocide. "Automatically labelling strangers as savages, weird and inhuman creatures (thus explaining difference by exaggerating difference) not infrequently justifies mistreatment, enslavement, or even extermination of the Different Ones."[11] All this in response to attitudes even Ryan admitted were generally benign and philanthropic!

The real crime of the wavering liberals, Ryan insisted, was the attempt to "revamp and revise the victim. . . . They want to change his attitudes, alter his values, fill up his cultural deficits, energize his apathetic soul, cure his character defects, train him and polish him and woo him from his savage ways."[12]

There was very little difference between this approach, Ryan declared, and the ugliest form of social Darwinism. The idea that blacks suffered from a "culture of poverty," for instance, was merely an updated, tricked-out, newfangled version of old views of black inferiority. All of this, he asserted, was part of a "dreadful war against the poor and the oppressed."

One was guilty of waging such a war by focusing on minorities' lack of job skills and education; by emphasizing "better values" and "habits of thrift and foresight"; by discussing the impact of "apathy," "ignorance," and "deviant low class cultural patterns."[13] When Catherine Chilman ventured a modest, even apologetic, defense of middle-class values in *Growing Up Poor*, noting that middle-class lifestyles seemed "to be more in harmony with present-day economic realities" than the culture of the poor, Ryan thundered that her ideas were "nefarious."[14] Poverty had nothing to do with character, skills, or indeed with any characteristic of the poor themselves, Ryan declared: Poverty "is most simply and clearly understood as a lack of money."[15]

Ryan mounted a search-and-destroy operation for any program that even hinted at changing or "improving" the behavior of the downtrodden. He was particularly exercised about educational programs whose aim was to "make up for the deficiencies in [students'] backgrounds which cause them to fail on the kindergarten and primary level. . . ." He quoted a school superintendent who noted:

> A victim of his environment, a ghetto child begins his school
> career, psychologically, socially, and physically disadvantaged.
> He is oriented to the present rather than the future, to
> immediate needs rather than delayed gratification, to the
> concrete rather than the abstract. He is often handicapped by
> limited verbal skills, low self-esteem, and a stunted drive toward
> achievement.[16]

Even Ryan admitted that the superintendent was "conscientious and committed." But this statement Ryan also covered with his malediction, as part of the "dogma" of cultural deprivation.

The problem the superintendent described was not in the children, Ryan insisted. The real problem was the false expectations of the schools, which, he charged, were "tailored for, and stacked in favor of, the [white] middle-class child."[17] Poor children think and learn differently, Ryan argued. Middle-class kids are comfortable with words as words, he explained, while poor children are "more comfortable with words as they relate to actions, feelings." Ryan asked: "Is it important for children going to school to be able to define 'caboose'?" It is important, he answered, only "because teachers make simple-minded judgments" about students' verbal skills.[18]

Here then was a statement of the educational ideology that would become so fashionable—and destructive—as one urban school district after another turned away from skills and toward "feelings" and self-esteem. The argument that it was unfair to black children to require of them verbal facility contributed mightily to the epidemic of functional illiteracy that ravaged a generation of inner-city children.

When sociologist James Coleman found that family background was the single most important factor in educational success and that variations in school quality tended to have a negligible effect on educational outcome, Ryan howled with indignation. Coleman had noted that black parents showed a high interest in educational achievement, but that "this interest often does not get translated into action which supports the child's work in school." Despite the high levels of motivation and concern, Coleman found, there was a glaring gap between the aspirations of black parents and their actual follow-through. He noted that many black families seemed to approach the requirements of achieving an education with a "lack of realism."[19]

Sputtered Ryan: "Is this or is this not, a clear case of blaming the victim?"[20] It was not. Rather, it was a sober work of social research that has since become the basis for educational reform efforts across the country. But it clashed with Ryan's ideological worldview. "The task to be accomplished," Ryan intoned, "is *not* to revise, and amend and repair deficient children, but to alter and transform the atmosphere and operation of the schools to which we commit these children."[21]

There *was* some merit in Ryan's position. Schools in the nation's cities were, and are, notorious for their crumbling infrastructures, lousy curriculums, and nonexistent discipline. Students subjected to a system with appallingly low standards can hardly be held solely responsible for their failure to learn. But here Ryan detoured into a logical dead end. He raked the schools for their low expectations of ghetto children, but what could he say about the possibility of genuinely toughened standards and heightened academic expectations?

Wouldn't they merely reflect middle-class values and standards? Would these expectations include verbal skills (even if their introduction resulted in a disproportionate number of minority failures)?

And what did Ryan have in mind when he wrote about transforming the atmosphere of the schools? Presumably, he envisioned schools that would be better able to serve students by compensating for the former deficiencies in their education. But if we are required to deny the deficiencies and to repudiate the idea of repairing or changing the child, then what exactly is the function of Ryan's new "quality" schools? His argument leads into an ideological hall of mirrors in which we recognize the ambivalence and ultimate impotence that has overtaken urban education.

Ryan's approach to the question of family breakdown and illegitimacy followed the same black-as-victim line. He ruled out personal choice, character, or the moral climate of the community as having anything to do with the problem. The culprit was, by now, familiar: "The 'problem' of illegitimacy is not due to promiscuity, immorality, or culturally-based variations in sexual habits; it is due to discrimination and gross inequities between rich and poor, and more particularly between white and black."[22]

Interestingly, Ryan rejected the notion that the deficiencies of the black family are a product of slavery—a victimist canard that had achieved surprisingly wide acceptance. In truth, the black family had proven remarkably resilient. In 1940, 76 percent of black families were headed by both a father and a mother. This lagged behind the proportion of white families with both parents (85 percent), but the proportion of intact black families remained relatively stable until the 1960s. Ryan made the provocative point that liberals were eager to blame slavery for the problems of the black family because they were, in effect, "copping a plea."

> As the murderer pleads guilty to manslaughter to avoid a conviction that might lead to his being electrocuted, liberal America today is pleading guilty to savagery and oppression against the Negro of one hundred years ago in order to escape trial for the crimes of today.[23]

Despite the growing frequency of divorce and illegitimacy among blacks at a time of increasing prosperity, Ryan continued to insist that the breakdown of the black family could be completely explained by evoking poverty and discrimination. Perhaps because this was obviously a weak hand, Ryan downplayed the negative consequences of broken families. The absence of a father, wrote Ryan, "is really not quite the disaster it is sometimes made out to be."[24] A young black man raised without a father "is really not deprived of the basic information that boys play baseball and girls jump rope," Ryan wrote. "He gets this message from his mother, relatives, friends, teachers, newspapers, television, schools and every institution he encounters."[25] The role of fathers in socializing their sons, in nurturing values and responsibility, was thus casually dismissed by Ryan as a nonproblem.*

Ryan takes roughly the same approach to the question of illegitimacy, which he insisted was exaggerated and completely unrelated to the rapid growth in AFDC (Aid to Families with Dependent Children) reliance in the 1960s.

Summoning all his ideological imagination, Ryan also minimized crime as a major problem in the inner city. He labeled the following propositions as examples of "blaming the victim" ideology: "that crime is dramatically more prevalent in the slums and among the poor"; that "the criminality of the poor is a result of social conditions which, in effect, warp their character and behavior"; and "that these lower-class criminals make up a distinct subgroup in the population."[26] Ryan called these observations "the most outrageous collection of non-facts imaginable" and proceeded to explain how "the mugger, the purse-snatcher, the thug who beats up our neighbor in Central Park" could be considered victims in their own right.

In attacking these "non-facts," Ryan began by rejecting most of the *known* facts about urban disorder. With joyful abandon, he dismissed police reports of crimes and called the FBI's Uniform Crime Report "the most preposterously non-factual document" ever published. Of course, statistics provide the main support to any empirical analysis of crime; but free of them, Ryan was able to ridicule the idea of "some separate group of criminals" by arguing that this notion addressed only criminals who had actually been arrested. And because (Ryan continued) the police were so thoroughly racist, they tended

---

*In 1960, only 22 percent of black families were headed by women. Over the next twenty-five years, that proportion would double. In 1969, 58 percent of poor black children lived in female-headed households. By the mid-1980s, 75 percent of them lived in female-headed households. National Research Council, *A Common Destiny* (Washington, D.C.: National Academy Press, 1989), 276.

to arrest mostly black people. Whites were probably committing crimes just as often as blacks, Ryan implied; they just got away with it more frequently.[27]

This accusation did contain a nugget of truth. Racial bias in urban police departments has proven to be tenacious. But that hardly means, as Ryan seemed to argue, that inner-city crime is therefore a *myth*. He also ignored that blacks in the inner city are themselves the most vulnerable to crime and the most likely to be victimized. Downplaying the prevalence of crime, Ryan dismissed one of the primary factors in the impoverishment and isolation of the inner city.

Ryan's belief in the pervasiveness of racism also colored his analysis of the Sixties' urban riots. He denied that the rioters were to blame; they were, again, victims. Their random looting, for example, may have looked bad, but Ryan declared: "In almost all cases, the stores being looted were white-owned and, in a substantial number of cases, were defined by members of the community as exploitative and oppressive."[28]

Ryan's comparisons of the rioters and the police invariably favored the rioters, who seem almost humanitarian in his telling, urban Fabians with just a touch of impatience. "The predominant focus of violence by residents is against property, rather than persons. . . . Instant, rather than creeping socialism, if you will. The forces of law and order, on the other hand, were truly violent to a homicidal degree."[29]

Ryan did take note of what he called "so-called sniping" but insisted that the police and National Guard were "almost a mirror image" of random violence. "In most civil disorders," Ryan charged, "the police and the troopers appeared to concentrate on the task of shooting black people and they were remarkably successful."[30]

Far from being acts of random violence and rampage, the riots were, according to Ryan, acts of "resisting and trying to drive out the police—the forces of repressive control—and 'taking back' from cheating and exploiting businessmen."[31] In other words, the rioters merely acted in self-defense. Echoing Albert Memmi, Ryan declared that although claims of racial genocide by black militants might sound like a paranoid fantasy, "there is a core of reality in the vision. . . ."[32]

With the exception of that final point, Ryan's views were far from extreme in the climate of the early 1970s. Many of his arguments came close to becoming conventional wisdom, at least in sophisticated opinion. It is worth recalling that the Kerner Commission, convened in the wake of the riots, accepted their "protest character" and blamed them on what it called "institutionalized racism."[33] More important was the climate of elite tolerance, which effectively stigmatized discussions of personal responsibility and of policies aimed at preserving the traditional structures of the community. (The only people who talked about "pulling oneself up by the bootstraps" were rednecks; the American opinion aristocracy preferred to discuss "root causes.")

Ryan's approach was very much in tune with the temper of the times. Certainly, one of the central lessons of the 1960s was the relative nature of victimization. Ryan himself recognized as much. In the second edition of *Blaming the Victim*, published in 1976, Ryan described his revised conviction that the number of victims in American society was actually much larger than he had originally believed. In fact, he wrote, almost everyone could be a victim, since "perhaps three-fourths of us are relatively poor compared to the standards of the top 10 or 5 percent."[34]

There were, of course, voices raised in dissent. The idea that society should continually suspend its moral judgment of the poor was derided by Midge Decter as a "very liberal and very racist idea: that being black is a condition for special moral allowance."[35] That notion was also met with uneasiness and outright opposition by much of the general public. Ryan himself bemoaned the continuing resistance to "welfare rights" by people who "seem unable to rid themselves of the ingrained belief that getting money without working for it— no matter how worthy and touching the recipient may be—is illicit, slothful and vaguely criminal."[36]

But the reaction of urban liberals was often very different. Jim Sleeper notes that many of them "mistook the vertigo of young blacks whose families and communities had been shattered for the freedom they themselves sought from upbringings and responsibilities they found too stable and confining."[37]

No account of the rise of victimism would be complete without noting the dramatic growth of what would come to be a full-fledged "compassion bureaucracy" as the welfare state was expanded and social scientists and litigators were enlisted in the cause. Increasingly, the bias of society favored public—and professional—solutions to what had once been strictly private problems.

Thus, what began as a strictly elite attack on social norms quickly

spread throughout the lower ranks of society by means of the therapeutic ethos of the helping professions, who had become politicized
as well as publicly funded. Although this was not a result of radical
politics alone, the politics of liberation added impetus to a tendency
already well under way. The professionalization of family life was
clearly abetted by the belief that both society and the family itself
were "sick."

When Kate Millett demanded the liberation of children from what
she called "the ancient oppression of the young under the patriarchal
proprietary family," she saw the helping professions as potentially
crucial allies. She insisted on the "attainment of the human rights
presently denied" to underage children, but also on "the *professionalization* and therefore improvement of their care."[38]

The uneasiness with which adults regarded the need to manage
their own lives and the anxiety with which they approached parenthood created an opening which was quickly filled. The increased
clout of the helping professionals changed the cultural landscape. No
longer was the assault on the traditional family led only by radicals
on the fringes of society. By the 1970s, Brigitte and Peter Berger
have noted, demands for sweeping changes in social policy regarding
families were now supported by "activist sectors of the religious
community, politicians and, most important, the professional com-
bines regarding the family as a field of expertise." In effect, this led
to the institutionalization of much of the cultural revolution of the
1960s.[39]

By the time the Carter White House held a conference on the
American family at the end of the 1970s, it was more or less taken
for granted among the professional/political class that the traditional
family of an intact marriage and children was "myopic and limiting."
Instead, the conference adopted a paper that called for a recognition
of the "diversity" in acceptable living styles.

"It is important to note here," the Bergers comment, "that the
empirical fact of diversity is here quietly translated into a *norm* of
diversity. In other words, norms and values, as well as the wishes
and hopes of many people, are simply bypassed by this definition.
Put simply, *demography is translated into a new morality.*"[40] But this
was not a policy in and of itself; it merely reflected the shift in the
culture away from traditional norms, toward a posture of moral
laissez-faire. The refusal of personal responsibility also accorded with
the growing no-fault culture of American society. Nowhere were
the results more tragic than in inner-city schools.

THE YOUNGEST VICTIMS

The suspicion that minority academic achievement has been held hostage to racist policies is more than plausible: It has a demonstrable basis in fact. In the South, schools were segregated by law; in the North by custom. The separation of the races has been mirrored by dramatically different levels of spending on predominantly white or predominantly black schools and by a persistent gap in the aptitude and achievement levels of black and white students. "By any measure of academic achievement," the superintendent of Milwaukee's largely nonwhite public-school system declared within weeks of taking office in 1991, "[this district] is a failing system." In 1990, less than a third of the black students in Milwaukee's schools graduated from high school; Hispanic graduation rates were only slightly better. At some high schools, the *average* grade point for black students was *F-plus*. More than half of the city's black students flunked basic core courses.[41]

Recriminations, not surprisingly, are bitter and emotional. Attributing the continuing failure of urban education to lingering racism, critics have attacked efforts to implement standardized achievement tests or tighten graduation requirements—arguing that such measures would disproportionately penalize black students. Efforts to toughen disciplinary standards have been criticized as insensitive to minority cultures (as if disruption were a form of cultural expression). Traditional rigorous curriculums have been scrapped in favor of offerings that stress the need to adapt to "differences" in the way minority students learn. Reflecting the ascendancy of therapeutic approaches, self-esteem rather than analytic thinking has emerged as urban education's premier obsession. The actual results are ironic.

By the 1990s, American students lagged pathetically behind much of the rest of the world in academic achievement—but consistently ranked on top when asked to rate their own performance. This is not surprising when one considers how deeply ingrained in the educationist culture is the idea that schools must constantly hand out positive reinforcement and "feedback." "Elementary school teachers are taught," reports education expert Rita Kramer, "to concern themselves with children's feelings of self-worth and not with the worth of hard work or of realistically measured achievement."[42]

Kramer's revelation was cited in a recent survey of teacher reports on student progress conducted by Chester Finn. In terms of actual academic performance, Finn writes, "almost never did I encounter any comment designed to alarm parent or child about the youngster's performance to date. There were no statements calculated to stop them in their tracks, to rattle their complacency, or to demand—with all the authority of teacher and school looming in the background—that a whole new leaf must be turned immediately. To the contrary. It was as if teachers had practiced how to avoid giving offense, raising blood pressure, or causing Mom and Dad to confront Junior about the sorry state of his schoolwork."[43]

Reality often comes as a rude and quite unwelcome shock. One survey of Chicago-area families found that minority parents and children alike had "high evaluations" of their children's achievement, but "the [children's] self-evaluations of their skills in reading and mathematics were unrelated to their actual level of achievement."

Finn calls this "unholy marriage of low expectations and high marks . . . a poisonous brew of humanitarianism and condescension."[44] One exception is Los Angeles math teacher Jaime Escalante, whose extraordinary success in teaching inner-city youths was portrayed in the movie *Stand and Deliver*. His critique of the victimist/therapeutic culture of inner city schools is blunt and chilling:

> Our schools today . . . tend to look upon disadvantaged
> minority students as though they were on the verge of a mental
> breakdown, to be protected from any undue stress. . . . Ideas
> like this are not just false. They are the kiss of death for
> minority youth and, if allowed to proliferate, will significantly
> stall the advancement of minorities.[45]

Even so, one example of the persistent notion that the stress on personal accountability was a form of "blaming the victim" was the reaction to Education Secretary Lauro Cavazos's 1990 comments that Hispanic parents should take greater responsibility for their children's educations. Noting that Hispanic culture had always placed a premium on quality education, Cavazos lamented that "somewhere along the line we lost that. . . . I think in part we Hispanics have not acknowledged that problem. . . . I think that's been one of our problems in America today. We really have not cared that youngsters have dropped out of school. . . . We must have a commitment from Hispanics, from Hispanic parents especially, that their children will be educated. That is the vital first step."

Cavazos was roundly denounced for this bit of heresy. The director of one educational program in Texas declared: "He's wrong to say the families are at fault, when society is at fault for not supporting families that are overwhelmed by economic problems." Congressman Jose Serrano was even more direct: "How can you blame the victim?"[46]

Commented former Assistant Education Secretary Chester Finn: "In our no-fault society, it is acceptable to be a victim but not to be held responsible for one's own situation or for that of one's children."[47]

TEARING UP THE
MORAL CONTRACT

Before the mid-1960s, it was taken for granted that the liberal vision of integration and equality was based on shared middle-class values. But by the end of the decade, a determined coalition of civil rights litigators, welfare rights activists, and social workers had mounted a full-scale assault on those social norms. To a remarkable extent, they succeeded in institutionalizing their ideology in social policy and legal guarantees.

Rules that limited access to public housing projects to stable families and to those without criminal records, for example, were attacked by civil rights lawyers as racist. The result was the exodus of whites from the projects and the slow deterioration of public housing as it was taken over by criminal elements and gangs.[48]

Social scientists also rushed forward with victimist "explanations" of youth crime and social disorder. The usual suspects were rounded up. Sociologist Douglas Glasgow argued that what seemed to be rampant street crime among inner-city black males was really the reflection of what he called a "survival culture." The behavior of inner-city blacks, he wrote, was the direct result of a racist society. Glasgow explained the life-style of ghetto youth as "consciously propagated via special socialization rituals that help young Blacks [sic] prepare for inequality at an early age." Ignoring the devastating consequences of gangs, drug use, street crime, and educational failure, Glasgow insisted: "With maturity, these models of behavior are employed to neutralize the personally destructive effects of institutionalized racism."[49]

While there are some ideas so bizarre that only a tenured professor of sociology could believe them, such notions had legs. Given the poor quality of their education, ghetto youngsters should have been immune from the influence of such advanced social "science," as well as from the larger cultural transformation in the country. "But," writes Nathan Glazer, "one could hear from young delinquents the very explanations and excuses that social psychologists and sociologists were making for behavior that damaged society—and themselves."[50]

Inevitably, the consequences on the street were tragic. Like every other community, Christopher Jencks notes, the black community had been held together by a moral demand system in which "censoriousness and blame" were the principle weapons in holding the society together. This included "blame for teenage boys who steal from their neighbors, blame for drunken men who beat up their wives, blame for young women who have babies they cannot offer a decent home, blame for young men who say a four-dollar-an-hour job is not worth the bother, blame for everyone who acts as if society owes them more than they owe society."

What had happened, Jencks writes, amounted to tearing up "the moral contract." The abandonment of social norms and stigmas by the larger society left the inner city particularly vulnerable. Given this retreat on values, Jencks says, the "respectable poor" could no longer carry on their twilight struggle "against illegitimacy and desertion with their old fervor. They still deplore such behavior, but they cannot make it morally taboo. Once the two-parent norm loses its sanctity, the selfish considerations that always pulled poor people apart often become overwhelming."[51]

But the impact of victimism was not limited to the poor.

THE REVOLUTION OF RISING VICTIMIZATION

In the 1960s, the political and moral stature of the victim was transformed and made attractive to an increasingly wide array of groups who rushed to grab a piece of the action for themselves. This rush was accelerated by the creation of an elaborate array of programs, privileges, and entitlements that were specifically attached to various groups' victim status. Besides its moral cachet, victimhood conferred specific economic and legal benefits. Sociologists have described the Sixties as a "revolution of rising expectations," but as Nathan Glazer points out, the decade also saw a "revolution of equality," which set off a chain reaction of new demands and expanded grievances.

"Rising expectations continually enlarge the sea of felt and perceived misery, whatever happens to it in actuality," Glazer writes. "And just as there is no point at which the sea of misery is finally drained, so too, there is no point at which the equality revolution comes to an end, if only because as it proceeds we become ever more sensitive to smaller and smaller degrees of inequality."

Glazer is echoing Tocqueville, who predicted more than a century ago that sensitivity to inequality would generate more sensitivity as grievance expanded exponentially.* Even so, the demand for "equal" treatment, Glazer notes, does not always mean genuine equality. As demands for more equality grew increasingly shrill in the 1960s, such claims "drove the expansion of social policy, only to create new inequalities that other advocates could seize on to demonstrate mistreatment (welfare clients versus the working poor? social security recipients versus social security tax payers? government employees versus private sector employees? and on and on). Social policy thus, in almost every field, created new and unmanageable demands."[52]

Equally fateful was the extension of this new egalitarian ethos from the political and economic realms into what Robert Nisbet calls the "smaller, more intimate and subjective areas of family, marriage, and other close personal relationships." "The great difficulty with equality as a driving force," he writes, "is that it too easily moves from the worthy objective of smiting Philistine inequality, to the different objective of smiting mere *differentiation* of role and function."[53]

Increasingly uncomfortable with distinctions based on individual success—distinctions that challenged the egalitarian ethos—society paradoxically multiplied distinctions of victimization.

As the political landscape fragmented into competing special-interest groups and the law adjusted itself to accommodate these new

---

*"It is possible to conceive of men arrived at a degree of freedom that should easily content them. . . . But men will never establish any equality with which they can be contented. . . . When inequality of conditions is the common law of society, the most marked inequalities do not strike the eye; when everything is nearly on the same level, the slightest are marked enough to hurt it. Hence the desire for equality always becomes more insatiable in proportion as equality is more complete." Tocqueville, *Democracy in America* (New York: Alfred A. Knopf, 1945), Vol. II, Book 2, Chapter 13.

categories, a lucrative market sprang up for the continued metastasis of victim groups who would also demand special protection.

"The power to be found in victimization, like any power," writes Shelby Steele, "is intoxicating and can lend itself to the creation of a new class of super-victims who can feel the pea of victimization under twenty mattresses."[54]

Metaphor played a crucial role in expanding the definition of victimhood. The civil rights movement had drawn upon the imagery of the Holocaust to portray the plight of blacks in the South; in turn, the new oppressed groups defined themselves in terms of the civil rights movement's struggle for liberation. This process of verbal and moral inflation meant that relatively mundane dissatisfactions could now appropriate the cloak of injured innocence. This too was a legacy of the therapeutic culture, which metaphorically applied the language of disease to a variety of phenomena that had not hitherto been regarded as medical. Would-be victims were now armed with both the vocabulary and the moral indignation of victimism. Disappointment could now be transformed into grievance, which in turn could be blamed upon newly discovered "diseases" or upon a malignant social order. Or both.

SECTION FOUR

The New Victims

TEN

The Rights Revolution: *E Pluribus Victim*

In the wake of the civil rights movement, the first group to exploit the metaphorical power of victimism were the feminists. Blending a call for political action with psychological liberation, leaders like Juliet Mitchell declared that women (rather than blacks, for example) were "the most oppressed of all people." Kate Millett insisted that "sexist oppression is more endemic to our society than racism," while Yoko Ono made the metaphor more explicit by calling woman "the nigger of the world."[1] Shulamith Firestone went even further, comparing the life of a suburban housewife to a victim of the Nazi Holocaust. ("Why should a woman give up her precious seat in the cattle car . . . ?")[2] But the drive to enshrine women as victims was only one aspect of the revolution of the 1960s and early 1970s.

Perhaps the decisive tactical shift of civil rights activists in the late 1960s was their flight to the judiciary to enforce and expand the rights of the poor and of minorities. "More and more dependent on the courts," Fred Siegel writes, "liberals forgot how to talk to most Americans. . . ."[3] By fleeing to the courts, the movement had substituted the language of litigation for the grammar of moral appeal. Over the last two decades, the civil rights movement has been defined less by overarching principles of human rights than by court briefs, injunctions, and class-action suits. Instead of positioning minorities as fellow citizens seeking to obtain equal standing, the shift to litigation transformed them into a special class seeking "protection." "The transformation of American political culture they effected," writes Jim Sleeper, "was nothing short of astonishing."

> In twenty-five years, government moved from ensuring that people were not formally categorized on the basis of race to ensuring that they are so categorized, whether they want to be or not. . . . The shift increasingly constrains individuals to think of themselves primarily as members of persecuted groups as defined by color.[4]

The abandonment of the political playing field for the courtroom certainly contributed to the sleight of hand with which the left dealt with the internal contradictions of their new politics. The notion that skin color should carry specific entitlements was clearly at variance with the liberal tradition of personal responsibility and fairness. That ideal had been, at best, only imperfectly and sporadically realized, but it *was* the vision of true equality that had gripped Martin Luther King when he spoke of his children being judged not on their race but on their characters. Scrapping that goal changed not only the course of civil rights but the nation's political culture.

As Tom Bethell pointed out in the mid-1970s, "Once affirmative action programs were in place . . . it was foreseeable that the remainder of the population would soon devise ways of sectoring itself up into further minorities, so that they, too, could make a plausible claim upon the public conscience."[5]

Following quickly on the heels of Black Power and the feminist insurgency came the raucous parade of gays, Native Americans, the elderly, the handicapped, consumers, children, animal-rights activists, and environmentalists.

Not by coincidence, they all tended to display a passion for litigation and for the shrill rhetoric of unconditional demand. The new language, called "rights talk" by Harvard law professor Mary Ann Glendon, was distinguished by its "penchant for absolute, extravagant formulations, its near aphasia concerning responsibility . . . and its unapologetic insularity."[6]

Until the 1950s, constitutional law had primarily been concerned with the relations between the states and the federal government. Now concern for individual rights came to dominate the constitutional agenda, and the multiplication of such rights was rapid. "To a great extent," Glendon notes, "the intellectual framework and the professional ethos of the entire current population of American lawyers have been infused with the romance of rights."[7] At the heart of the new assertiveness was the assumption that "if rights are good, more rights must be even better, and the more emphatically they are stated, the less likely it is that they will be watered down or taken away."[8] This inevitably led to a new attitude toward litigation. Where lawsuits had traditionally been viewed as an avoidable but perhaps necessary evil, law schools and courts now embraced a far more benign view of the lawsuit as an acceptable and even desirable weapon in the protection and extension of basic rights.

But the rise of the litigator in American society also reflected a larger social phenomenon. Before the twentieth century, people had more or less accepted the vagaries of fate. Sudden reverses could ruin farmers or businessmen; death, disease, and accident were familiar presences. Faith cushioned many of the shocks, but it could do nothing to eliminate them. But with the decline of religion and the rise of technology and science, society began to lose its belief in both the inevitability of suffering and the need for stoicism in the face of adversity. In his book *Total Justice*, Lawrence Friedman describes what he calls a "major revolution in legal culture as well as in the social order." Advances in technology had not merely changed the world, they had reduced uncertainty. In time, this changed the public's attitude toward the law and toward government. The "reduction in uncertainty in one area of life leads to demand for reduction of uncertainty in others. . . . Disasters still occur—fires, floods, earthquakes—but now there are programs of disaster relief. People still lose jobs . . . but unemployment insurance acts as a cushion. People still have accidents at work, but workmen's compensation provides a floor of benefits. . . . [People] still grow old and feeble, but pensions guarantee a basic income, and there are special programs (housing for the elderly and, very notably, medicare) that grant benefits in kind. And so it goes . . ."[9]

Over time, the public's expectation of what government could accomplish blended with its expectations about life in general. "Slowly people have come to expect more out of government, out of law, out of life," Friedman has observed. "At the end of the process, what people come to expect is a higher level of justice—social justice, life justice."[10]

And if they didn't get it, there were always lawyers and the courts.

SO SUE ME

In the mid-1970s, the courts were flooded with allegations of discrimination. In 1970, the Equal Employment Opportunity Commission had received fewer than 15,000 complaints; by 1973, the number had risen to 48,900; by 1977, the number topped 79,000. This new spirit pervaded the whole of society. As recently as 1950, the United States had only about 200,000 lawyers. In the 1960s alone, that number grew by a third; between 1970 and 1975, admissions to the bar rose by 91 percent. In the 1990s, law schools will turn out 40,000 new attorneys a year. "At this rate," quips Friedman, "unless something happens to save the nation, at some point in the distant future every living soul in the country will be a member of the bar."[11]

Although it is easy to blame the glut of lawyers for the carnival of litigation, the litigators were clearly responding to society's demand; the lawsuit boom was as much a product of the Zeitgeist as a shaper of the new ethos. The new culture of rights, with its prickly absolutism, reflected a nagging sense of expectations unfulfilled. In the absence of either a social ethos or a transcendent ethic to confront adversity, litigation became both a proxy and a shortcut to innocence, meaning, and justification: If something has gone wrong, *someone must be at fault.* And it is not me.

Consider the legal and cultural climate that inspired the men who were injured while carrying refrigerators on their backs during "refrigerator races" to sue the manufacturer because the appliances carried insufficient warnings of possible injury from such activities. Or the case of the New York man who deliberately leapt in front of a moving subway train—and was then awarded $650,000 because the train had failed to stop in time to avoid mangling him.[12] Or the supreme creativity of San Francisco's Ocie McClure, who sued a cab company for $5 million after he was pinned to a wall by one of its cabs. McClure had knocked down a woman, kicked her, and stolen her purse; the cab gave chase, eventually cornering him. McClure has ample leisure to pursue his litigation, since he was sentenced to eight years in prison for the robbery.[13]

It is the rare doctor who has gone unsued. By one estimate, between 70 and 80 percent of all obstetricians have been served with malpractice suits.[14] "It used to be that if a child was born with birth defects, the presumption was that it was in the nature of things," says Roger Conner, the director of the American Alliance for Rights and Responsibilities. "Now the obstetrician is all too often held responsible for the production of perfect babies. Victimization takes the place of what used to be thought of as acts of God."[15]

While the reaction of distraught parents is certainly understandable, our courts often seem to be swamped by an epidemic of annoyance. Men have sued diet clinics because they sponsor female-only weight-loss programs; the San Francisco Giants are sued for giving away Father's Day gifts to men only; a psychology professor complains that she has been victimized by the presence of mistletoe at a Christmas party, and claims sexual harassment. In the current legal climate, even an attempt to uphold civil rights can become a source of claimed victimization: In Miami, a court ruled that a women be paid forty thousand dollars in worker's compensation benefits after she complained that she was so afraid of blacks that she was unable to work in an integrated office.[16]

Two Marines alleged they had been unconstitutionally discriminated against because the Marine Corps had discharged them for "being chronically overweight." A postal clerk who is left-handed accused the U.S. Postal Service of discriminatory bias in setting up filing cases "for the convenience of right-handed clerks." A twenty-four-year-old Colorado man sued his mother and father for what he called "parental malpractice."[17] In Hawaii, a family of tourists who had been shunted to "less desirable lodgings" by their overbooked hotel not only sued for their economic losses, but were awarded cash for their "emotional distress and disappointment."[18]

In *The Litigation Explosion*, Walter Olson reports the case of a psychic, Judith Haimes, who had conducted seances featuring such metaphysical celebrities as the poet John Milton (who spoke through her), and whose psychic powers, she claimed, were blotted out by a dye used in a CAT scan. Insisting that her doctor had thus interfered with her ability to make a living, she sued. The judge in the case ordered the jury to ignore the claim of psychic damage, but the jurors took only forty-five minutes to return an award of $986,000.[19]

Nothing, apparently, is sacred. The Salvation Army has been sued on the grounds that it violated an employee's right to freedom of religion after it dismissed a woman for using agency equipment to copy materials describing Satanic rituals.

In Michigan, a former brewery worker convinced the state's court of appeals that he was entitled to worker's compensation benefits because he had become an alcoholic while working for the Stroh's Brewery Company. Stroh's did not, of course, require the man to drink, but he nonetheless charged that his drinking problem was aggravated by the jobsite availability of free beer (a benefit that had been demanded and won by the man's union). The court discounted arguments that the man was responsible for his own alcoholism, ruling that the "unique circumstances of the employment shaped the course of the plaintiff's disease, aggravating and accelerating the underlying alcoholic predisposition to the point of uncontrolled addiction, thus constituting a personal injury under the act."[20]

If individuals were no longer to be held responsible for their own drinking, they were understandably reluctant to take responsibility even for their appearance or their size. In Orlando, a man filed a lawsuit as a result of a haircut that he claimed was so bad that it induced a panic-anxiety attack. In his suit, the inadequately coiffed plaintiff alleged that the negligent hairstylist had deprived him of his "right to enjoy life."[21]

THE NEW VICTIMS

One reason for the explosion of litigation was the mushrooming of legal rights and the resulting expansion of the definition of discrimination and victimization. In 1973, Congress passed the Rehabilitation Act, which required any company with a federal contract of more than twenty-five hundred dollars to undertake affirmative action for the handicapped, and which prohibited discrimination against them. The law extended civil rights protections to an entirely new protected class that was not always easy to identify. As one legal scholar noted, the inclusion of "mental impairments" in the law left the definition of who was covered somewhat fuzzy, especially given "the elusive nature of the sciences of psychology and psychiatry."[22]

The Justice Department's guidelines hardly cleared up the matter. They defined a mental impairment as "any mental or psychological disorder, such as mental retardation, organic brain syndrome, *emotional or mental illness*, and specific learning disabilities."[23] [Emphasis added.] But this definition could be used to define an extraordinary number of Americans as impaired. One expert estimated that 20 percent of Americans are "affected by diagnosable psychiatric disorders"; adding that more than 5 percent of Americans suffer from "generalized anxiety"; another 5 to 10 percent from "severe personality disorders"; *another* 5 to 10 percent from "affective disorders"; and that 15 percent will "suffer an episode of severe depression in their lifetime" (not to mention the 1 percent who were full-blown schizo-phrenics).[24] Unwittingly, perhaps, the law created an incentive for litigants and their attorneys to be creative and aggressive in claiming "handicapped" status.

Here, again, distinctions need to be drawn. The Rehabilitation Act was intended to provide opportunity for and protection to the genuinely handicapped—people who suffer long-term disabilities such as blindness or deafness, or who are confined to wheelchairs. The act opened many doors that had been closed to them. No one who has seen the efforts of, for instance, someone with multiple sclerosis performing difficult and painstaking work can doubt the valor of such workers or the direness of the barriers they must surmount to lead productive lives. Of all the groups clamoring for rights, the demands of the physically handicapped are the most compelling. Whatever might be said of other "victims," the disabled bear no responsibility for their condition and thus have a special and undeniable claim on society's goodwill.

Criticism, therefore, of the distortions of what it means to be "handicapped" does not apply to the genuinely disabled. It merely highlights the gross cynicism of a culture of victimism that encourages and allows others to latch onto the moral and legal standing of the disabled for their own advantage.

THE NEW HANDICAPPED

One case involving a medical student expelled by New York University reflected the changing legal climate. Identified only as Jane Doe, the student sued in federal court to win readmission to the NYU Medical School as a handicapped individual protected under the Rehabilitation Act.[25] By any measure, the student was a troubled woman. When she was fourteen years old, she had taken an overdose of sleeping pills; at other times, she had injected herself with a powerful cancer drug, plunged a kitchen knife into her stomach, cut herself numerous times, severing arteries and veins, and taken cyanide. Her violence was not, however, restricted to self-abuse. In particular, she had a stormy relationship with doctors, on several occasions biting them, scratching them with her fingernails, or lunging at them with scissors.

When Jane Doe applied to the NYU Medical School, she concealed all of this history, falsely claiming that she had never had any emotional problems. After she was accepted, however, her history came out during the school's mandatory medical examination. School officials later referred her for psychological tests, which concluded that she had a "grossly detached and alienated personality, with no effective or emotional contact with the world of things or people." Perhaps because this did not seem to be a glowing recommendation for a career in medicine, the school and Doe worked out a "leave of absence." Doe was subsequently hospitalized; on being discharged, she was listed has having shown "no improvement." Later, she applied for readmission to the medical school—claiming that she was a handicapped person covered by federal law, a claim based on a psychological diagnosis that she suffered from Borderline Personality Disorder.

To be covered under the law, Doe had to demonstrate that she suffered significant limitations on "a major life activity." But she testified that her ability to function had never been impaired and that her "handicap" had not affected her academic or work life. (In fact, she had graduated from college, earned a master's degree from Harvard, and had done well in her job with the Department of Health, Education, and Welfare.) This led a demurring psychiatrist to reject the diagnosis of Borderline Personality altogether.

But the federal court ignored the dissent and the internal contradictions in Jane Doe's argument and declared that she should indeed be classified as "handicapped" under the Rehabilitation Act and was therefore "protected."

Court records are filled with similar appeals for "protection":

A man who was fired for sexually harassing his female co-workers sued his former employer, arguing that his employers "should have realized that his conduct constituted an aberration from his normal behavior and qualified him as a handicapped person." Using a similar argument, a male engineer sued his former employer, Boeing, after he was fired for wearing a necklace and using the women's room. He charged that the company did not accommodate his "handicap" (he was preparing for a sex-change operation). The judge in the case concluded that the employee's psychosexual life-style *did* qualify him as handicapped under the meaning of state antidiscrimination laws, but ruled that Boeing did not in fact discriminate against him.[26]

In 1980, a data processor for the Philadelphia School District was fired for being late to work virtually every day he was on the job.

He sued, claiming that chronic lateness should be considered a disability. A Pennsylvania Court of Common Pleas agreed with him, citing the Pennsylvania Human Relations Act. Psychiatrists testified that the man was unable to show up on time for work because of what they called his "neurotic compulsion for lateness," which was a "behavioral aberration that is deeply rooted in his personality and almost certainly had its origins in conflictual interaction with his parents in early life."

One of the psychiatrists testified, "Although I recognize that his lateness is disruptive to an organization that includes a uniform work schedule in its structure, it is a comparatively benign expression of his determination not to be obliterated by a dominating controlling system of which he conceives himself to be a victim." The doctor emphasized what he called "an obvious fact," that the data processor's behavior was almost completely unconscious and literally beyond his control."

Even so, the doctor admitted that he could not come up with a specific diagnostic label for the data processor's condition, except for the general category of "personality disorder." Under cross-examination by the school district's lawyers, this exchange occurred:

Q. Doctor, it's true, is it not, that people with what you have termed a personality disorder exist around us every day in all walks of life; isn't that correct?

A. I'm not sure any of us are spared that diagnosis.

In a burst of sanity, a higher Pennsylvania court reversed the original decision and eliminated "chronic lateness" as a protected disability.[27]

But the record is uneven:

A judge of the equal-rights division of Wisconsin's Department of Industry, Labor and Human Relations ruled in 1991 that "offensive body odor" could indeed be a handicap under the state's Fair Employment Act.[28]

An Illinois man convinced a state appellate court that his paranoia was a recognized handicap. The man, an employee at a Ford Motor Company plant, had exhibited highly unusual behavior at the factory, including "leaving his work area to stare at other employees while they worked, and his refusal to be relieved for his breaks." On one occasion, the man had taunted a co-worker by "waving a white rag at him and carrying a sign which contained derogatory comments

about the co-worker on it." When the maligned co-worker grew
angry and grabbed the man around the neck and shoulders, the man
became "angry and threw shock absorbers at the co-worker and then
chased him down the assembly line."

Ford did not respond by firing the man but rather by placing him
on medical leave for several months. After returning to work, he
was placed on leave again the next year. One psychiatrist concluded
that the Ford employee suffered from a form of paranoia "which
made it difficult for him to assess reality." When Ford was reluctant
to allow the man to return to work, he filed a discrimination complaint with the Illinois Fair Employment Practices Commission.
When the commission dismissed his complaints, he appealed to the
state courts, where he won a reversal of the commission's decision
and won the coveted status of "handicapped."[29]

In 1982, a onetime U.S. Treasury Department employee showed
up in a dress for a job interview with his former employer, and made
it clear that if hired, he intended to wear women's clothes to the
office regularly. The Treasury Department declined to reemploy
him. Charging that he had been discriminated against under the
Rehabilitation Act of 1973, the former T-man filed suit in federal
court, which eventually ruled that the man was not handicapped
under the meaning of the law, but still ruled in his favor because the
Treasury Department had *thought* he was handicapped because of his
sexually ambivalent sartorial preferences.[30]

In Virginia, a special-education teacher sued in federal court after
she had repeatedly failed to achieve the minimum acceptable score
on a standardized national test for teachers that measured "listening,
reading and writing and tests the candidates' ability to understand
and use the elements of written or spoken language." The teacher
failed the test eight times—including two times when she was given
both extra time to complete it and a written transcript of the oral
portion. In her suit, the teacher claimed that she was "discriminated
against solely on the basis of her handicap" because the test did not
accommodate her slowness in understanding written and spoken
information. A federal judge dismissed her suit, but the Fourth Cir-
cuit Court of Appeals overruled the lower court and reinstated the
claim.[31]

Equally as creative but less successful was a Georgia man who had
assaulted his supervisor (and therefore lost his job) and then tried to
convince a federal judge that he suffered from a "maladaptive reaction

to psychological stressor" condition and should therefore be considered handicapped.[32]

In 1983, a labor-relations specialist with the U.S. Department of Agriculture was arrested for shoplifting during an official visit to Fargo, North Dakota. He later pled guilty and was convicted. His employers learned of the conviction only after a whistle-blower complaint was filed. Numerous other shoplifting incidents quickly came to light. In 1984, the man was fired. Undeterred, he filed discrimination complaints with the EEOC and, having failed there, with the U.S. District Court. He claimed that he was handicapped because he suffered from "Borderline Personality Organization with obsessive-compulsive features," and should therefore be given his job back. He lost.[33]

However outrageous, these cases may be only prologue to a starburst of victimist creativity inspired by the Americans with Disability Act, passed by Congress in 1990. The new bill substantially expands the rights of the disabled (the "differently abled," in the new lexicon) beyond the rights already accorded them in the Rehabilitation Act. Humorist P. J. O'Rourke attended the signing of the ADA on the White House lawn. "People in wheelchairs were yelling at the deaf to sit down and the blind were bumping the palsied with their dogs," O'Rourke reported. "In a crueler age some onlookers might have laughed, but we never laugh at misfortune today. In fact we're all trying to get in on it."[34] As is so often the case with the federal government, the reality outpaces even O'Rourke's satire.

The history of the ADA indicates that its authors intended it to cover forty-three million Americans, but even that estimate may be modest. Unlike the Rehabilitation Act of 1973, which covered only the federal government and its contractors, the ADA extends antidiscrimination coverage to all private employers with fifteen or more workers and to state and municipal governments. Moreover, the bill establishes a "disparate impact" standard, barring employers from using qualifications, standards, or other selection criteria that have the effect of unfairly screening out the handicapped unless they can show that the standards are a "business necessity." Since the handicapped are not a homogenous group and employment standards would have very different impacts on a blind applicant and a paraplegic, it is unclear how the courts will interpret this provision.

Nor is it any clearer who exactly qualifies as "disabled" under the bill. The Americans with Disabilities Act specifically excludes from coverage "homosexuality, bisexuality, transvestism, pedophilia, exhibitionism, voyeurism, gender identity disorders not resulting from physical impairment or other sexual behavior disorders, compulsive gambling, kleptomania, pyromania and psychoactive substance use disorders resulting from current illegal use of drugs." Although this may sound reassuring at first glance, that the authors needed to spell out those exclusions was an indication of just how sweeping the definition of *handicapped* is under the new law.

"Given the law's broad coverage, along with its many uncertainties," says attorney Julie M. Buchanan, an expert on the legislation, "it is a nightmare for employers and a dream for lawyers. Nearly everyone has a chance to be a victim now."[35]

ELEVEN

Are We All Sick?

The following notice was posted in a Colorado church:

SUPPORT GROUPS MEET WEEKLY IN THE PARISH
HOUSE AS FOLLOWS:

Sunday
12:00 NOON—Cocaine Anonymous, Main Floor
5:30 P.M. —Survivors of Incest, Main Floor
6:00 P.M. —Al-Anon, 2nd Floor
6:00 P.M. —Alcoholics Anonymous, Basement

Monday
5:30 P.M. —Debtors Anonymous, Basement
6:30 P.M. —Codependents of Sex Addicts Anonymous, 2nd Floor
7:00 P.M. —Adult Children of Alcoholics, 2nd Floor
8:00 P.M. —Alcoholics Anonymous, Basement
8:00 P.M. —Al-Anon, 2nd Floor
8:00 P.M. —Alateen, Basement
8:00 P.M. —Cocaine Anonymous

Tuesday
8:00 P.M. —Survivors of Incest Anonymous, Basement

Wednesday
5:30 P.M. —Sex & Love Addicts Anonymous, Basement

7:30 P.M. —Adult Children of Alcoholics, 2nd Floor
8:00 P.M. —Cocaine Anonymous, Main Floor

Thursday
7:00 P.M. —Codependents of Sex Addicts Anonymous, 2nd Floor
7:00 P.M. —Women's Cocaine Anonymous, 2nd Floor

Friday
5:30 P.M. —Sex & Love Addicts Anonymous, Basement
5:45 P.M. —Adult Overeaters Anonymous, Main Floor
7:30 P.M. —Codependents Anonymous
7:30 P.M. —Adult Children of Alcoholics, 2nd Floor
8:00 P.M. —Cocaine Anonymous, Main Floor

Saturday
10:00 A.M. —Adult Children of Alcoholics, Main Floor
12:00 NOON—Self-Abusers Anonymous, 2nd Floor[1]

One can only marvel at the energetic exertions of the therapeutic clergy—and at the spirit of democratization represented by support groups that encourage participants to stand up and declare, "My name is John, I am a self-abuser. . . ."

The modern American culture of the support group grew out of a single epiphany: Once the language of disease and addiction could be applied to *behavior* rather than merely to biological disorders, almost any aspect of human life could be redefined in medical terms. The Ur-addiction was alcoholism. At best, the scientific search for a definitive physical or biological cause of uncontrollable drinking has been inconclusive. Although some experts insist that alcoholism is indeed genetically based, others, equally adamant, either deny the biological link or insist that it has been greatly exaggerated. Nevertheless, the definition of alcoholism as a disease, trumpeted by a growing network of helping professionals, alcoholic-treatment institutions, and related lobbies, has won widespread acceptance. Declaring drinking a disease, Herbert Fingarette notes, triggers special status in employment, health, and civil law, as well as in health-insurance payments and government and employment benefits.[2]

More important, however, is the power of the disease analogy to change social norms and attitudes. Almost by definition, disease is caused by agents or forces largely beyond the control of an individual—by viruses, microbes, genetic deficiencies, or environmental factors. If someone who drinks excessively is sick, then the notion of personal or moral responsibility becomes highly problematic. Perhaps for that reason, alcoholism-as-disease has proven an attractive model in the new self-help culture. Dr. Stan Katz and Aimee Liu, the authors of *The Codependency Conspiracy,* note that "disease has little or no relationship to the affected individual's personal values or beliefs. The diseased person is cast as a victim of the infectious agents, a person who is powerless over his or her disease and has no responsibility for its onset. The sickness is not viewed as a consequence of choices or actions but as something that *has happened to the affected individual.*"[3] A host of activities that had once seemed to be a matter of choice—and barometers of character—could now be transformed into pathologies. "Sufferers" increasingly defined themselves in terms of their "illness," by seeing their "addiction/disease" as an integral and permanent aspect of their identity.

There are obvious difficulties with this approach, both from a moral and a medical point of view. "Addiction to drink is a 'disease,'" a former president of the American Psychiatric Association declared in 1976, "only in the sense that excessive eating, sleeping, smoking, wandering or lechery can be so classified."[4] This reductio ad absurdum was an attempt to ridicule the notion of behavior-as-illness. But within a few years, disease treatments were developed not only for all the maladies the doctor had listed but, as Dr. Stanton Peele notes in his book *The Diseasing of America,* also for "stealing, overwork, worrying, sadness, fear, incompetence, procrastination, anger, child abuse, forgetfulness, murder, premenstrual tension, television viewing, gambling, shopping, and on and on."[5]

The nation of victims had radically expanded its borders—transforming our relationships to medicine, the family, work, education, and one another.

THE MISSING LINK

The impulse to translate behavior into disease is not without some basis in fact. As Stanton Peele explains, "Everything that humans do—eating, drinking, raising children, learning, having sex, having periods, feeling, thinking about oneself—has a healthy and unhealthy side, sometimes both at the same time or often alternating with one another. By elevating the unhealthy side of normal functioning to the status of disease, therapists and others who claim the mantle of science now *guarantee* the preeminence, pervasiveness, and persistence of sickness in everyday life."[6]

Such ostensibly medical decisions are not, however, value-free; they have a profound impact on norms of social and personal conduct and on the very notion of civilized behavior. Describing behavior in terms of disease/addiction, Peele argues, can "legitimize, reinforce, and excuse the behaviors in question—convincing people, contrary to all evidence, that their behavior is not their own. Meanwhile, the number of addicts and those who believe they cannot control themselves grows steadily."[7]

With such momentum, the title of this chapter is not as fanciful as it may seem. One of the masterstrokes of the new movement was the discovery that even eating could be annexed to the disease industry by treating obesity and a myriad of "eating disorders" as forms of addiction. "Eating is perhaps the ultimate disease," Peele remarks, "in being not only legal but essential, completely approved, and everywhere around us encouraged and invited."[8] The same principle applies to shopping. Insists psychotherapist Marilyn Jacovsky: "The compulsion to use debt and credit is just like any other compulsion— the compulsion to overeat, for example. It is progressive, and it finally gets out of the individual's control."[9]

Although it was surely not Dr. Jacovsky's intention, her diagnosis of debt addiction exposes the machinery of the disease/addiction movement. What is most notable about her analysis is what she does *not* say—what a literary critic might call "the presence of absence." There is nothing especially novel in the idea that people have strong appetites or compulsions. But compulsions do not exist in a vacuum; they are counterbalanced by the social and personal norms of restraint.

The issue is hardly a new one. Aristotle seemed to address it quite directly when he wrote:

> Nor, again, is action due to wealth or poverty. It is of course true that poor men, being short of money, do have an appetite for it, and that rich men, being able to command needless pleasures, do have an appetite for such pleasures; here, again, their actions will be due not to wealth or poverty but to appetite.[10]

The rejection of economic determinism applies equally to psycho-addictive explanations. Debt binging and compulsive gambling are the result not of the availability of credit cards and roulette wheels but of value-laden choices. Not everyone who gambles loses control of himself; people limit their drinking, their eating, and their spending when it interferes with their priorities or threatens to endanger their goals in life.

"Those who overeat or who gamble away their families' food budgets or who spend more money than they earn on clothes and cars or who endlessly pursue sexual liaisons," Stanton Peele writes, "do not necessarily have stronger urges to do these things than everyone else, so much as they display less self-restraint in giving in to these urges."[11]

Personal and family values may explain why certain ethnic groups that place a premium on self-control—conservative Jews and the Chinese, for instance—have such low rates of alcoholism. It may also explain why many problem drinkers seem to outgrow their overuse as their values change and the necessity for making life choices becomes unavoidable. Several studies have found that drinking and drug use tend to decline rapidly after age thirty-five. Even among serious drug abusers, studies have found that while most heroin addicts, for instance, become hooked as adolescents or young adults, nine out of ten are heroin-free by age forty-five. A *Rolling Stone* poll of Americans aged twenty-five to forty-four found that while nearly half had used recreational drugs, roughly half had quit altogether, while another third had significantly cut back on their use. Stan Katz comments: "The deciding factor in their quitting drugs was not treatment, but maturity."[12]

But while "treatment" continues to be a booming growth industry, maturity continues to get a very cold shoulder indeed.

MOMMY AND DADDY DEAREST

By the 1990s, the movement toward "two shrinks in every pot" extended virtually down to infancy. Children as young as age five were being introduced to therapeutic support groups by schools anxious to develop "the rich emotional lives" of unanalyzed youngsters and encourage a shift "away from shame and guilt and toward self-awareness." Apparently, this movement included the abolition of the family's remaining privacy and its independence from school-based therapeutic professionals. Gushed the president of the National Association of School Psychologists: "The beauty of these sessions [is that] they are dedicated to the notion that you don't have to have family secrets." The psyche of modern youth is now considered so fragile that *Newsweek* opines that such support groups for children may now be "a dire necessity."[13]

The most recent—and successful—expansion of the definition of victimization is the codependency movement, which began with children of alcoholics and expanded to cover virtually every form of "dysfunctional" family.

One of the seminal discoveries of codependency is that addictions need not be limited to chemicals or even behavior. *People* could now be redefined as addictions. Melody Beattie, author of *Codependent No More*, defines codependency as "a dependency on people—on their moods, behaviors, sickness or well-being, and their love."[14]

Just being around an addict can be seen as a form of illness. "By its nature," Beattie insists, "alcoholism and other compulsive disorders turn everyone affected by the illness into victims—people who need help even if they are not drinking, using other drugs, gambling, overeating, or overdoing a compulsion."[15]

Nowadays, it is no longer necessary even to be around an *actual* addict to be part of the codependency movement. "People who didn't come from alcoholic homes," Elizabeth Kristol has observed, "liked the idea that their current unhappiness could be laid at the feet of their folks, who, while they might not actually have abused alcohol or drugs, were sufficiently obnoxious in other respects as to cripple their children emotionally and, well, keep them from being all that they could be." The result was a new category for Those Who Identify, fellow travelers in the world of familial dysfunction; seekers of treatment and recovery. The cofounder of Minnesota's Children Are People organization declared that you did not "have to be the son or daughter of an alcoholic to be a co-dependent. Any critical parent will do."[16] So the "adult child of alcoholics" has become, simply, the "adult child," a sweeping classification that includes everyone who was in any way traumatized by their parents' shortcomings, a list that stretches from alcoholism and drug abuse to "rushaholism," "careaholism," "negaholism," and "rigid religious beliefs."

Codependent caretaking behavior, for example, can include thinking and feeling responsible for other people, feeling "anxiety, pity and guilt when other people have a problem," and anticipating "other people's needs."[17] One author describes a woman who likes to stay at home with her children, for whom she cares deeply, as a classic sufferer of codependent caretaking behavior.[18] Anne Wilson Schaef, a leader of the movement, describes codependents as "servers . . . the people who hold society together, who set aside their own physical, emotional, and spiritual needs for the sake of others."[19] Another theorist of codependency calls this concern for others a "crippling emotional, mental and physical disease . . . which is more contagious than AIDS."[20]

Codependency shows every sign of being an epidemic completely out of control. One leader of the codependency movement puts the number of "adult children" at more than 230 million—higher than the nation's actual *total* adult population.[21]

Almost any of the anxieties and failings of adult life can now be attributed to a toxic or unenlightened upbringing. One leading psychologist argued on "The Phil Donahue Show" that "much of what we consider normal parenting is actually abusive," while a best-selling book warns of the dangers of Toxic Parents.[22]

What are the signs of parental toxicity? Psychologist Susan Forward asks: "Do you have a hard time knowing who you are, what you feel, and what you want? . . . Are you a perfectionist? Is it difficult for you to relax or have a good time? Despite your best intentions, do you find yourself behaving 'just like your parents'?"[23]

Undoubtedly, many people who do not feel abused or injured by their parents would answer yes to these questions. But because it is an essential part of the therapeutic culture to define otherwise normal feelings as problems, Forward insists that affirmative responses constitute warning signs of one's parents' "hurtful legacy." She even anticipates objections from prospective clients who might ask whether or not they should feel some personal responsibility for their own problems. "By now you may be thinking, 'Wait a minute, Susan. Almost all the other books and experts say I can't blame anybody else for my problems.' Baloney. Your parents are accountable for what they did. Of course, you are responsible for your adult life, *but that life was largely shaped by experiences over which you have no control.*" [Emphasis added.][24]

Another tack is illustrated by Letty Pogrebin's *Growing Up Free*, which challenges virtually every aspect of family life on both therapeutic and political grounds.

"My intention," she wrote, "is to question everything we do with, to, for, and around children—our speaking habits, living styles, adult relationships, household chores, academic standards and our way of dealing with punishment, privilege, religion, television, sex, money, and love." Included in her jeremiad are: "Ten Commandments for Non-Homophobic Parenthood," "Twelve Dos and Don'ts for Promoting Free-Flowing Gender-Blind Alliances," and specific techniques "to countermand sexist sex education." The urgency of this agenda is underlined by Dr. Benjamin Spock's warning on the cover of the book that sex stereotyping should now be considered a "crippling disease."[25]

Failure to follow any of these new prescriptions is thus a new and quite virulent form of victimization.

Unfortunately, despite its popularity and appeal, the codependency movement has little if any scientific basis. The National Institute on Alcohol Abuse and Alcoholism, for instance, recently sponsored a study that found no evidence to support the contention that people can develop "a personality disorder on the basis of their family membership."[26] Donald Goodwin, a leading researcher on the inheritance of alcoholism, is even blunter. Goodwin labels much of the "adult children of alcoholics" movement a hoax. Despite the movement's claims to the contrary, Goodwin notes, children of alcoholics are "about like adult children of everybody else with a problem." Goodwin charges that professional addiction therapists "invented" the concept of "adult children" so as to be "able to sell this concept to the public and [become] eligible for reimbursement from insurance companies. In short . . . it was a way for therapists to tap into a new market and make money."[27]

But if we cannot point to science as the basis of this extraordinary phenomenon, then what accounts for the numbers who have embraced codependency? Once again we come to the role of the youth culture in American society and, in particular, to its influence on the development of the Imperial Self.

One of the most powerful unifying themes of the new movement is the emphasis on returning to infancy—or beyond—to discover the source of human unhappiness and dysfunction. John Bradshaw and other practitioners of this version of pop Freudianism have made the endlessly injured "inner child" a virtual household word. Bradshaw, who insists that as many as 96 percent of American families are dysfunctional in one way or another, is the author of several books, a frequent daytime talk-show guest, and has been featured in a PBS series in which he passionately proclaims the necessity of healing our "inner children."

Repeating slogans such as "Embrace the pain" and "You can't heal what you can't feel," Bradshaw insists that "We are all infants with needs." And those needs *must* be met, even if that means returning to the womb. As recipients of Bradshaw's "treatment," grown men and women sit around holding teddy bears, listening to a maternal heartbeat, while Bradshaw urges them to imagine themselves back in the womb and as infants. His message is whispered to the inner child over and over: "You are perfect in every way/We love you just the way you are/Welcome to the world, I'm so glad you are here/ I've been waiting for you and I've prepared a very special place for you/I love you just the way you are/You have all the time you need to have your needs met."

This sort of affirmation is undoubtedly comforting. It represents man's immemorial search for comfort and surety. At times, Bradshaw's description of the womb sounds surprisingly like traditional visions of heaven. But Bradshaw has no truck with theological notions. On his TV show, he gets one of his biggest laughs when he ridicules the nuns who instructed him in grade school, who claimed to have an "actual picture of hell." However amused they may be by such religious flummery, Bradshaw's audiences nonetheless accept without question his equally mystical vision of the womb and of infancy, in which all needs are met, all demands satisfied, all anxieties allayed. Nor do they show much levity when he ends one show by promising that next time he will show them how to "reclaim [their] toddler self."

They seem to accept such notions easily because they take for granted the centrality of the infant/toddler self, and submit to the absolute necessity of meeting every demand of that self. In a very real sense, the grown man holding a teddy bear and imagining himself as an infant is the logical culmination of several of the cultural impulses I have been discussing here—from the therapeutic self to the flight from adulthood. At the heart of the matter is an attitude toward maturity.

Saint Paul may have put aside the thoughts of a child when he reached manhood; Bradshaw wants to reverse the process.

Rather than seeing maturity as a cure for the endless demands and frustrations of the inner child, gurus like Bradshaw proclaim the necessity of turning inward and backward into the absolutism of the mythical and perfect womb life. This seems a peculiar way to restore an individual's sense of dignity and self-worth. Seeing the individual as an eternal inner child who is victimized by his unmet needs permanently infantilizes the subject. But this is not an illogical development in a movement whose concern is increasingly inward-looking.

Here, however, self-absorption is no longer enough; what Bradshaw demands is absorption and obsession with the infant self, whose polymorphous demands must be met by the adult if he is to achieve Bradshawian self-actualization. Not only the demands of the ego are given priority, but also the demands of the *infant ego*, the most extreme possible formulation of the doctrines of the Imperial Self as codified by the youth culture.

Such attitudes have profound social consequences. Absorbed by the needs of the inner child, adults can hardly be expected to have much emotional or moral capital left over for suffering children in the real world. Upper-middle-class professionals who refuse to give handouts to the homeless (or donations to charities) because they do not want to become "codependents" are doing more than adopting fashionable therapeutic jargon. They are placing the health of their own inner child ahead of the needs of others. In effect, the victimology of codependency has come full circle. If victimism originally thrived on idealism and a concern for others, its latest manifestation has turned back upon itself, declaring that caring and compassion can be forms of disease. Ultimately, it is the quintessence of self-ishness.

THE ABOLITION OF SIN

Inevitably, the repeal of personal responsibility has undermined society's ability to call wrongdoers to account for their behavior. In the criminal courts, where the illness excuse has become the sine qua non of a sophisticated defense, the extent of this sea change is depressingly obvious. From Michael Deaver (alcoholism) to John W. Hinckley (insanity) to San Francisco Supervisor Dan White (Twinkies) to murderer Robert Alton Harris (fetal alcohol syndrome), our therapeutic culture has an explanation and a defense at hand.

Although the nuances and intonations differ, the plaintive cry is always the same: *I am not at fault. [Fill in the Blank] made me do it.*

Employing the full armory of deconstructionism and moral relativism for the forces of social psychology, Swarthmore College psychology professor Kenneth J. Gergen argues that traditional ideas of the "self," "responsibility," and "voluntary decision making" simply don't cut it anymore. When a suburban Philadelphia woman dressed in army fatigues went on a shooting rampage in a shopping mall, killing and wounding several people before being captured, Gergen insisted that society should apply a "postmodern" concept of justice to the case. In Gergen's view, that means recognizing that the "concept of the individual who chooses 'wrong' loses tenability." Thus, blame "should not be attributed to the individual alone but to the array of relationships in which he or she is a part," or what Gergen euphemistically calls the "complicities of daily life."[28]

Providing an intellectual gloss to the it's-not-my-fault culture, Gergen writes: "As the traditional concept of 'immoral decisions' becomes moot, the issue is not to extend the boundaries of guilt. Rather, it is . . . to vitally expand the sensitivity to the network of relations in which we participate"—and which network, he might have added, we can sue whenever anything goes wrong. He notes with satisfaction that in the case of the mall gunwoman, "lawyers have broadly extended the network of responsibility, bringing suit against mental health officials who knew of her distraught condition, the local police department . . . the shopping mall . . . the shop which sold her a weapon, and so on."[29] While postmodern politics declares everyone guilty, postmodern psychology lets almost everyone off the hook for just about anything.

Critics of the psychotherapeutic culture have long denounced what Garth Wood sees as a "conspiracy to extend indefinitely the boundaries of mental illness" and to undermine the idea of personal responsibility. Wood states the relationship between medicalization and moral responsibility directly: "If we are not ill then we are well, although we may be unhappy." Later he adds, "If we are not ill, then we are well—and responsible for our predicament."[30]

Nor has medical science always served a useful purpose by creating new categories of psychopathology or sociopathology to explain deviant behavior. "We already have a perfectly good concept to explain and describe . . . moral bankruptcy," Wood says. "*It is the notion of evil.* Extreme wickedness is no surer indicator of mental illness than is extreme goodness, and we would do well not to confuse evil with disease."[31] At stake here is not so much science as the age-old debate over the nature of man and whether or not he is a free moral actor exercising an autonomous will. The idea that man should be held responsible for his choices implies such free will. If, on the other hand, his actions are the product of impulses or unconscious causes, the free-will approach makes no sense and might actually be regarded as inhumane and barbarous.

In the novel *Satan*, by Jeremy Leven, the archdemon expresses anxiety about the spread of psychotherapy: "It keeps turning evil into neuroses and explaining away people's behavior with drives and complexes. . . . Modern psychiatry is putting me out of business."[32] But the Enemy's enemy is not so much psychiatry per se as the general therapeutic bias against applying any *moral* standards where *clinical* ones would do as well. "It has become the fashion of late," Garth Wood writes, "to consider that the development of an unsatisfactory personality should carry with it no implications of blame [and] should not occasion feelings of guilt. . . ."[33]

This belief in utter blamelessness is of course, the inversion of the Puritan ethos that regarded man as, by nature, depraved. In the new ethos, man is restored to his original *innocence*. He is not evil but merely *distorted*, bent by a sick-making social order. The yearning for a return to such innocence antedates the therapeutic ethos, but never before has it had such powerful "scientific" weapons at its disposal. The bad boy becomes the misunderstood child; the brutal killer becomes a sociopath in need of therapy. In criminal justice, incarceration falls from favor as treatment centers and programs of all sorts blossom in the rich soil of the postmoral therapeutic age. In this world, guilt is little more than a hopeless archaism. What relevance, after all, does it have if an individual's conduct is really the fault of society, of his parents, of his biology, or of the dark impulses of his unconscious?

In some (though not all) of its forms, psychotherapy is only one of several doctrines of determinism. Some are ideological, some scientific. But whether they apply a mechanistic metaphor to the process of choice or account for human behavior by employing racial, economic, or social explanations, they share the conviction that we are the products, rather than the masters, of circumstance.

Although it has not always done so explicitly, the therapeutic culture tends to minimize the role of choice and free will. If a man's action is not the result of his economic status, it is a product of childhood traumas or addictions or unresolved conflicts of the id. At its most behavioristic extreme, this mind-set comes close to abolishing mind altogether. The therapeutic culture has thus created the same sort of double bind that characterizes the larger phenomenon of victimism. If a person is really a bundle of impulses and traumas, he can be absolved of guilt and responsibility for his actions. But this absolution lasts only as long as the "illness" that causes the actions. Once cured, one can no longer avoid responsibility; only by clinging to the disease is one free from moral claims.

But the embrace of illness is also the embrace of helplessness and incompetence. Responsibility means choice, which means the possibility of human dignity and even of change and reform—all options seemingly foreclosed for the impaired. "We pay a terrible price for our absolution," Wood writes, "for how can we have self-respect if we are not responsible for what we are?[34]

"If our personalities are not our own creative act, the most fundamental reflection of our essence, of our hopes, and ambitions, what are we but machines . . . ? For if we are not allowed to blame the psychopath for his actions, then we are not free to praise and admire his antithesis," those who refuse to "succumb to temptation, wickedness and evil. This is the depressing legacy of such outwardly loving and caring attitudes."[35]

NOT GUILTY, JUST SICK

Encouraged by the medicalization of wrongdoing, defendants charged with murder, rape, and robbery have cited PMS, alcoholism, drug use, junk food, excessive television watching, and "lovesickness" in their defenses. Mothers who kill their infant children have claimed that they suffered from postpartum depression, a defense that even proved successful for a pediatric nurse who suffocated two of her babies and attempted to smother a third.[36]

In Maryland, Governor William D. Schaefer cited the "battered woman syndrome" in commuting the sentences of eight women convicted of killing their husbands; in Ohio, outgoing governor Richard Celeste commuted the sentences of twenty-five "battered" women on the same basis. Afterward, Celeste explained, "These cases had in common a woman who was a victim of an identifiable battered woman's syndrome." However, *The Columbus Dispatch* later reported that fifteen of the twenty-five women had denied being sexually abused, "six had discussed killing their boyfriends or husbands, sometimes months before doing so, and two had tracked down and killed husbands from whom they were separated."[37] In Maryland, one of the women freed by Schaefer had hired someone to kill her husband so she could collect a $22,000 life-insurance policy. Another testified that her husband had never struck her before the night she killed him, while yet another had threatened to kill a potential witness against her.[38]

By claiming that he was emotionally distraught, Yale student Richard Herrin avoided a first-degree murder conviction even though he had beaten in his girlfriend's skull with a hammer. He was convicted only of manslaughter.[39] Other violent crimes have been defended on the basis that their perpetrator suffered from "posttraumatic stress disorder," which blames violent acts on traumas caused by other violent acts. As Stanton Peele notes, this has become an increasingly popular, if not automatic, excuse for virtually every accused criminal raised in a "violent subculture," where killing, drug dealing, and child abuse are common. "In short," writes Peele, "we have opened up violence as an excuse for perpetual violence without, however, showing any societal tendency to reduce violence or the conditions that lead to it."[40]

Indeed, in Milwaukee, a defense attorney announced that she might use a defense of "cultural psychosis" on behalf of a teenage girl who had shot and killed another girl in a fight over a coat. Her defense, the lawyer said, would argue that the murder was a result of the generalized trauma of inner-city life—a trauma that affects thousands of city residents.[41] Such defenses have become so sweeping that Stanton Peele grimly concludes, "We are in the process of rejecting the idea that people can be responsible for their behavior when they are in a bad mood."[42]

The criminal-justice system's obsession with psychological diagnoses occasionally has tragic consequences. In 1989, a Milwaukee judge who was immersed in the therapeutic mentality ignored warnings from prosecutors and pleas to keep Jeffrey Dahmer in jail on a sex-abuse charge. "The reality is that treatment within the community is just plain not going to work," an assistant district attorney told the judge. "The reality is that his track record exhibits that he is very likely to reoffend." The lawyer noted that Dahmer's offenses— second-degree sexual assault and enticing a child for immoral purposes—were serious and that he showed neither remorse nor any willingness to cooperate.

Instead of jailing Dahmer, the judge put him on probation, permitting him to serve a one-year sentence on a work-release plan. His main concern, the judge told Dahmer, "was therapy, and I'm really concerned that we don't have a program in prison right now. . . .

This is the kind of thing . . . that the prosecutor would just ask the judge to throw away the book and the judge would say 10 [years] and 10 [years] consecutive and good-bye. But if there is an opportunity to salvage you, I want to make use of that opportunity."[43]

Two years later, Dahmer was arrested for murdering and dismembering more than a dozen young men, including the older brother of the boy Dahmer had been charged with molesting in 1989.

TWELVE

Pick a Disorder, Any Disorder

The bible of the psychological enterprise is the *Diagnostic and Statistical Manual of Mental Disorders, Third Edition, Revised*—known affectionately as *DSM-III-R*. Published by the American Psychiatric Association, the book has become "the common language of mental health clinicians and researchers" and the Rosetta stone for the therapeutic culture's interpretation of the human psyche.[1]

Given the role of psychological "disorders" in criminal justice, civil law, and the Americans with Disabilities Act, the book's enumeration of recognized disturbances is of more than merely academic or clinical interest. With a sense of prudence that does not always inform the rest of the book, *DSM-III-R* opens with a list of cautions and caveats. Conditions not mentioned in the book can be real problems, it assures readers, while those that are included "may not be relevant" in settings outside of "clinical or research settings," such as courtrooms.[2]

DSM-III-R also makes no secret of its political nature. The decision to include or exclude various disorders is often controversial and the subject of lobbying and maneuvering. In the introduction, the editors admit that there was considerable debate about several candidate disorders, especially those like "Late Luteal Phase Dysphoric Disorder," known to laymen as premenstrual syndrome. Faced with accusations that some categories "had such a high potential for misuse, particularly against women," the editors compromised, listing "Late

Luteal Phase Dysphoric Disorder" in an appendix, under the heading "Proposed Diagnostic Categories Needing Further Study," along with "Self-Defeating Personality Disorder" (once known as "Masochistic Personality") and "Sadistic Personality Disorder" (once known as being a mean son of a bitch).[3]

The editors also pay homage to cultural diversity, noting that psychologists should be cautious in applying the various diagnoses of disorders to non-Western cultures, should not be "insensitive to differences in language, values, behavioral norms, and idiomatic expressions of distress," and should always be watchful for "the presence of distinctive cultural patterns and [sensitive] to the possibility of unintended bias because of such differences."[4] It is nowhere made clear why this concern for cultural diversity is limited to non-Western cultures and why similar sensitivity is not urged for other distinctively human reactions to the challenges posed by life. In *DSM-III-R*, the idea of the general diversity of human experience seems vaguely alien.

Consider, for instance, what *DSM-III-R* calls an "identity disorder," defined as "severe subjective distress regarding inability to integrate aspects of the self into a relatively coherent and acceptable sense of the self." That may sound ominous, but as the diagnosis continues, it begins to sound somewhat more familiar: "There is uncertainty about a variety of issues relating to identity, including long-term goals, career choice, friendship patterns, sexual orientation, and behavior, religious identification, moral value systems, and group loyalties. . . . Frequently, the disturbance is epitomized by the person's asking, 'Who Am I?' "

But is this a psychological disorder or a description of existential angst? Is this illness or man faced with the disorder of modern life? Is this sickness or the crisis experienced by adolescents in general? Remarkably, the editors of *DSM-III-R* seem to acknowledge that what they are describing is less a psychological phenomenon than a reflection of the way society and its values have changed in this century. Admitting that they have no information about the prevalence of the identity disorder, they note, "The disorder is apparently more common now than several decades ago, *perhaps because today there are more options regarding values, behavior, and lifestyles and more conflict between adolescent peer values and parental or societal values.*" [Emphasis added.][5]

The editors acknowledge that the identity crisis is a ubiquitous feature of postmodern society. *DSM-III-R* simply redefines it as a disorder.* In *DSM-III-R*, little that is human escapes therapeutic redefinition. Ground in its mill, egotism, selfishness, envy, grandiosity, and a "sense of entitlement" can become the "Narcissistic Personality Disorder."[6] An individual who is indecisive and unable to make decisions "without an excessive amount of advice and reassurance from others, and will even allow others to make most of their important decisions," is not merely weak or indecisive—he might suffer from what *DSM-III-R* defines as a "Dependent Personality Disorder." The afflicted would include an adult who would "allow his or her spouse to decide where they should live, what kind of job he or she should have, and with which neighbors they should be friendly." A child might be suffering from this disorder if he permits his parents "to decide what he . . . should wear, with whom to associate, how to spend free time, and what school or college to attend."[7]

While not always pleasant or free of stress, some of these aspects of the "Dependent Personality Disorder" were once considered part of what it meant to be a family.

On the other hand, an assertive, thoroughly obnoxious person who is frequently argumentative, loses his temper, swears, and is "often angry, resentful and easily annoyed by others" is no longer merely a jerk—his "pattern of negativistic, hostile, and defiant behavior" can now be classified as "Oppositional Defiant Disorder."[8]

Likewise, anyone who experiences a divorce, business setback, chronic illness, natural disaster, "persecution based on social, religious, or other group affiliation," or simply the stress associated with going to school, getting married, becoming a parent, losing out on a promotion, or retiring can suffer from what *DSM-III-R* calls "Adjustment Disorders." Blandly, the book notes that the "disorder is apparently common."[9]

No wonder. *DSM-III-R* enumerates the "Adjustment Disorder with Anxious Mood," "Adjustment Disorder with Depressed Mood," "Adjustment Disorder with Disturbance of Conduct," "Adjustment Disorder with Mixed Disturbance of Emotions and Conduct," "Adjustment Disorder with Mixed Emotional Features," "Adjustment Disorder with Physical Complaints," "Adjustment

---

*DSM-III-R tries to distinguish the full-fledged disorder from "adolescent turmoil" and "midlife crisis" by insisting that the disorder is accompanied by "severe distress and impairment in occupational or social functioning," but these subjective judgments fall well short of the definitive status the book seems to claim for them.

Disorder with Withdrawal," "Adjustment Disorder with Work (or Academic) Inhibition," and even "Adjustment Disorder Not Otherwise Specified."[10]

One can imagine that a natural disaster like a hurricane or the death of a parent might result in what *DSM-III-R* calls an "inability to write papers or reports." But grief and preoccupation are something different than psychological disorder. We can only imagine what the authors of *DSM-III-R* would have made of Hamlet. I would suspect "Adjustment Disorder with Mixed Disturbance of Emotions and Conduct" or perhaps "Identity Disorder." Queen Gertrude might be covered by the "Dependent Personality Disorder." Would Ophelia, however, be a candidate for "Late Luteal Phase Dysphoric Disorder"? Would Lady Macbeth? Or would she fall under "Oppositional Defiant Disorder" or, perhaps, "Sadistic Personality Disorder"?

But all of these illnesses are being overshadowed by a newly discovered epidemic known as the obsessive-compulsive disorder, defined as "a pervasive pattern of perfectionism and inflexibility."[11] In 1988, the National Institute of Mental Health conducted a survey of mental disorders and found that obsessive-compulsiveness was far more prevalent than had been thought. "[Like] other stigmatized and hidden disorders in the past," the NIMH study concluded, "[the obsessive-compulsive disorder] may be ready for discovery. . . ."[12] Researchers have been quick to follow up on this invitation to bring to light a once-invisible disease. One ad placed in a Madison, Wisconsin, newspaper by the University of Wisconsin Hospital reflects the aggressive marketing of obsessive-compulsiveness:

OBSESSIVE-COMPULSIVE
DISORDER

If you can answer yes to any of these questions, you may have Obsessive Compulsive Disorder.

- Do you avoid using public telephones or restrooms because they might be dirty or "germy"?
- Are you often late because you have to check things over and over before leaving the house?
- Do you feel the need to do things symmetrically so that they are "evened up"?

Over 5 million people in this country suffer from this disorder. Often these people suffer in silence, afraid of being weak or "crazy." But help IS available. [The University of Wisconsin] is conducting studies of medications for the treatment of obsessive-compulsive disorder. All treatment is confidential and free of charge. . . .[13]

The scientific validity of this particular advertisement can be measured by its claim that a *single* "yes" answer is evidence that one may suffer from obsessive-compulsive disorder. (Has the author of this ad ever *seen* a bus-station bathroom?) But as a marketing tool, it is effective: It defines as symptoms traits that are not exceptionally unusual, creates anxiety about them, and promises help. That formula, repeated over and over, is the mark of the therapeutic culture and the foundation of the addiction-recovery industry.

Another previously undiscovered malady waiting in the wings for its moment in the spotlight may be something called "Epidemic Psychogenic Illness," in which large numbers of people in the same building all decide that they are sick at the same time for no apparent reason. "Schoolchildren and workers in routine, monotonous jobs," *Psychology Today* reports, "seem to be the most frequent victims."[14] A psychiatrist who estimated that thousands of schools are hit with the "epidemic" every year told the magazine, "Once one kid gets sick, it's OK for the others to get sick." Although a layman might suspect that the sudden sick-in was simply a neat way to skip school or get out of work, the psychiatrist straight-facedly attributed the syndrome's outbreak to stress "in situations that didn't allow for an emotional reaction like crying."

Similarly, the contagion of so-called environmental illnesses that appeared to rampage through the 1980s turned out, on closer examination, to have less to do with the environment than with people's psyches. This was bad news for the new helping professionals known as chemical ecologists, who had claimed that chemicals, food additives, or environmental conditions were attacking the immune system, causing everything from nausea and dizziness to rashes, fatigue, and breathing problems. But researchers reported in 1990 that "some, if not all, symptoms of environmental illness, from fatigue to headaches, confusion to nasal congestion, are probably the results of a mental disorder."[15] It turned out that many of the patients who had originally been diagnosed as suffering from chemical sensitivity also fit the definitions for depression, anxiety, and obsessive-compulsive disorder.

MY JOB IS DRIVING ME CRAZY

Nearly a decade ago, a poll of psychotherapy experts predicted a "boom in occupational specialization"—the identification and treatment of specifically job-related stresses. Not surprisingly, the experts were right, in part because the therapeutic community has itself aggressively expanded and endlessly refined the nuances of psychological occupational hazards.

It was once taken for granted that many jobs were merely compensated drudgery. That the boss was a jerk, the work tedious, the social milieu isolated, and appreciation and affection in short supply was simply regarded as a fact of life—not as the seed of mental breakdown.

Such attitudes changed with the evolving expectations of work. The insistence that employment—like marriage, sex, and parenthood—be meaningful, personally fulfilling, and self-actuating *as well as* remunerative raised the stakes considerably. Something, of course, had to give. Invariably, the therapeutic culture was on hand to offer comfort, counsel, and a plausible diagnosis.

In 1980, less than 5 percent of occupational disease cases were stress related. In just three years, that number doubled and has since been steadily rising as lawyers and therapists joined forces in fashioning creative new causes of action. In 1986, *U.S. News & World Report* described a flood of "cases of psychological illness [that] are becoming a nightmare for employers, insurance companies and state governments alike."

"The American workplace," the magazine reported, "is being swamped with claims ranging from job burnout, or mental fatigue from tedium and stress, to chronic and severe anxiety, manic depression, nervous breakdown and schizophrenia."[16]

Every profession, it seems, has its own way of driving you crazy. A 1989 article in *Psychology Today* sketched out the emotional pitfalls of more than a dozen professions.[17] Clergymen, who are supposed to be selfless, the magazine reported, often burned out "by ignoring their own needs and giving too much of themselves to others." Cops could suffer from the "Rambo complex" if they were not "willing to admit to fears and vulnerabilities." Lawyers could "crumble under the weight of . . . responsibility and fear [of] making a mistake." (Stressed-out attorneys, the magazine noted, made up 25 percent of one New Jersey psychologist's clientele.) Teachers tended to "exaggerate their powerlessness and fear confronting authority." Dentists can develop "fairly exacting personalities [that] project their problems onto the people around them. . . ."

Government workers who are rewarded for not screwing up, *Psychology Today* warned, run the risk of developing "lethargic automaton behavior." Inflexible and technocratic computer programmers may lack spontaneity and thus find "relations where flexibility is essential" to be difficult. Middle managers who crave job security find they need "a stable work life to maintain their equilibrium." (Fascinating insight!) Actors, musicians, and dancers may suffer existential angst, haunted by the "empty feeling of 'Is this all?' "

Politicians may begin to believe their own propaganda and develop "trouble separating their public and private lives and thus get no relief from job pressures." (Gary Hart, call your office.) Physicians who develop exaggerated ideas of their talents can burn out in the face of pain, disease, and death. Air-traffic controllers are "often uncomfortable with the ambiguity of human relations."

Even therapists have their own form of professional stress. "They sometimes have trouble dropping the interpretive and restrained professional role and letting their hair down with friends and family," *Psychology Today* acknowledges, adding, "Some therapists also run the risk of becoming grandiose."

All of this is certainly true. In fact, it is little more than a restatement of the normal vagaries and strains of adult life. In another time, the litany of job-related hang-ups would inspire little more than: "So what else is new?" Uptight lawyers? Socially awkward computer wonks? Angst-ridden artists? Cops who aren't in touch with their feelings? Lethargic government bureaucrats? Hardly the sort of revelations to challenge penis envy as the discovery of the century.

But dressed up in the language of therapeutic anxiety, routine disappointments have become the cornerstone of a new legal/therapeutic/sick-making industry.

HANDICAPPING FOR DOLLARS

The contagion of new illnesses and disabilities has other social and economic consequences as well. One in eight children—approximately 119,000—in New York City public schools is now classified as "handicapped" at a cost of hundreds of millions of dollars to the struggling school district. In the last decade, the number of "disabled" students has more than doubled. One quarter of New York's school budget is now devoted to special education.[18]

Those numbers say less about the disabilities of New York's youngsters than they do about the economics of victimism in modern society.

In 1975, Congress created a national network of educational programs for the handicapped, the learning disabled, and the emotionally disturbed. Over the years, those programs have gradually expanded, shielded by a wall of state mandates and court rulings from the cutbacks felt by many other programs. Even when New York's schools were forced to make more than half a billion dollars in cuts in 1991, special-education programs remained sacrosanct. While regular classrooms bulged, children in special education were guaranteed classes of no more than twelve students; often there were as few as six children in a class. All students in the program, moreover, were assured access to a wide range of services, including speech therapists, psychologists, and physical therapists. New York spends $16,746 a year on each special-education child, compared with $7,107 per child in regular classes. "What you had was a road that was falling apart," a former director of special education and education dean of Long Island University in Queens told The New York Times, "and right alongside, they were building a superhighway called special education, which provided no end of money."[19]

Born from compassion and generosity, the program unfortunately had dramatic, if unintended, consequences. By overfeeding special education and starving regular classrooms, the system created an almost irresistible incentive for disability.

The disparities in funding tempted educators to shift many of the system's problem children—kids who were disruptive or unusually demanding or had minor learning problems—into the special-education system. To do so, they merely had to relabel children as "handicapped." *The New York Times* quoted critics of special education as saying that in the last decade and a half, the system "has run wild." Any child who learns differently or has a special need runs the risk of being labeled "learning disabled." One Brooklyn school psychologist told the *Times* that what determines whether a child is placed in special education is how badly a teacher wants to be rid of him. "We try to get the teachers off the principal's back, and the kid is the victim."[20]

Indeed, despite the extra spending and cornucopia of therapeutic services offered to the newly disabled students, the system is doing them no favors. Only one out of twenty students assigned to New York City's special-education programs ever returns to mainstream classrooms. Fewer than one in five ever graduates from high school. "Once labeled handicapped," a mayoral commission concluded, "virtually all students stay in special education the remainder of their school careers, often isolated from their peers and subject to lowered expectations of achievement, fewer educational opportunities, and depressed self-images."[21]

THE VELVET MANACLES

The embrace of disability has implications far beyond mere occupational malaise or the allocation of public money. Nor is it easily confined to the realms of psychology or law. If the therapeutic culture had decisively changed the relationship between the self and others, the multiplication of infirmities has provided the backdrop to the rise of a new political style notable for its reliance on insecurity and hypersensitivity, as well as for its absolutism.

Over a century ago, Alexis de Tocqueville wrote of the "vague dread" that tormented Americans who were "apt to imagine that their whole destiny is in their hands. . . ." In our own time, Robert Nisbet echoed him, writing: "When the individual is thrown back on his own inner resources, he loses the sense of moral and social involvement with others, he becomes prey to sensations of anxiety and guilt."[22] Those sensations now have tangible shape as well as tangible consequences.

"It is when a people loses its self-confidence," British author and parliamentarian John Buchan wrote in the 1930s, "that it surrenders its soul to a dictator or an oligarchy. In Mr. Walter Lippmann's tremendous metaphor, *it welcomes manacles to prevent its hands from shaking*."[23] [Emphasis added.]

In the 1990s, those manacles have taken the form of "political correctness."

SECTION FIVE

The Politically
Correct Victim

THIRTEEN

Sensitive Man

When *Newsweek* magazine reported on what it called the new "Thought Police" patrolling America's university campuses, it described academia's new fad—"political correctness"—as "strictly speaking, a totalitarian philosophy." Nothing escaped PC's attention; nothing was too trivial for its ministrations; no one was immune. From the reading lists peppered with ideologically approved Third World writers to a disciplinary apparatus poised to stamp out the slightest offense to the sensibilities of designated political and ethnic groups, campus opinion was smothered by a paternalism that would have been the envy of any college chaplain of the nineteenth century. Struggling to place all this repression in some sort of historical and philosophical context, *Newsweek* reported that PC "is Marxist in origin, in the broad sense of attempting to redistribute power from the privileged class (white males) to the oppressed masses."[1] But even as the magazine sought to trace PC's lineage, the inadequacy of citing any political philosophy as a likely parent was obvious. Despite the accompanying paraphernalia and rhetoric of left-wing politics, the peculiarly claustrophobic atmosphere of PC-ruled campus life often seems less like Big Brother than Big Nanny.

The focus of Big Nanny—excuse me, political correctness—is on "sensitivity," which is not a political term at all, nor one that is terribly helpful in sorting out the relationships of the various economic classes. Instead, "sensitivity" is a transplant from the world of culture and psychology, in which taste, feelings, and emotions are paramount. Political correctness turns out to be a subunit of the larger transformation of society reflected in the ascendancy of psychological over political terminology. What began as an attempt to politicize psychology (and psychologize politics) has led to the swallowing of each by the other and the emergence of synthesis: therapeutic politics. In the therapeutic culture, all of us are trembling on the verge of confusion, anxiety, and failed self-esteem. For the politics of victimization, the new ethos has been a real confidence builder.

Armed with the new political/therapeutic categories, and as the heirs to four decades of the endless elaboration of grievance and psychological fragility, victims have been transformed from capable citizens in need of fundamental legal rights into frail psychological chattels, easily cowed by the slightest gesture, facial expression, or word that they might find uncongenial. If the distinctive format of traditional liberal education was the patriarchal and phallocentric Socratic dialogue, the model for the new order is the therapeutic workshop and consciousness-raising session. Such approaches do not seek debate or a reasoned balancing of rights but an embracing of victims, often accompanied by the coached acknowledgment of guilt. The results, predictably, have been dramatic.

Once feelings are established as the barometer of acceptable behavior, speech (and, by extension, thought) becomes only as free as the most sensitive group will permit. One of the central dogmas of the new victimist politics is that only members of a victim group are able to understand their own suffering. Some postmodern political theorists, including Harvard's Judith Shklar, argue that traditional conceptions of justice are inadequate because they fail to take into account "the victim's version." Shklar argues that "the sense of injustice should assume a renewed importance" in political thinking, "for it is both unfair to ignore personal resentment and imprudent to overlook the political anger in which it finds its expression."[2] But at its extreme, this view turns injustice into a subjective experience and denies the validity of objective and shared understandings of equity and justice to which victim and nonvictim can appeal. Abolishing such norms makes contentious issues irresolvable, as each group is trapped within its own experience and sense of aggrievement. Not only does this accelerate the balkanization of ethnic groups, it also creates a protective barrier that hermetically seals off one group from another. Because only a victim can really understand his own plight, any criticism or questioning from nonvictims is rejected out of hand as an act of disrespect and insensitivity. One result of enforced correctness is what Bard College president Leon Botstein calls the "culture of forbidden questions."[3] The fear of hurt has trumped the search for truth.

This is not to suggest that all the concern over sensitivity is misplaced. Any student going to college in a strange town, facing unknown challenges, is prey to feelings of self-doubt, loneliness, fear, and confusion; minority students face even greater pressures. Many tend to suffer from feelings of exclusion or "competitive rejection" when they arrive on campus, and many experience considerable anxiety over the quality of their academic preparation. As colleges and universities have escalated affirmative-action programs, a central dilemma has been compounded. While denying that they are practicing favoritism, elite schools have in fact admitted nonwhite students with substantially lower test scores than their white counterparts. For many of those eagerly courted minority students—who have been repeatedly assured that their admittance is based strictly on their merits—the reality of academic life often comes as a cruel shock. Roughly two-thirds of African-American students who enter college drop out before graduating.

Because it is politically impossible for the institutions of higher learning to acknowledge their racial sleight of hand—and thus confront the educational inequities among their students honestly and openly—many have turned to the camouflage of symbolic politics. It is easier to "celebrate diversity" than to admit that one's school's academic standards have been bent; it is easier to blame "racism" than to reallocate scarce resources. Dinesh D'Souza describes the process: "Eager to prevent minority frustration and anger from directing itself at the president's or dean's office, the administration hotly denies the reality of preferential treatment and affirms minority students in their conviction that the real enemy is latent bigotry that everywhere conspires to thwart campus diversity. As the Harvard political scientist Harvey Mansfield puts it, 'White students must admit their guilt so that minority students do not have to admit their incapacity.'"[4]

MUM'S THE WORD

"Sympathy," remarked essayist Pico Iyer, "cannot be legislated any more than kindness can." Obviously, Iyer will never be a college president. Universities and colleges have rushed to create new bureaucracies to "protect" and shield victims from further victimization—whether the weapon of oppression is an Indian symbol at Dartmouth College, a student who sings "We Shall Overcome" in a "sarcastic" manner at Southern Methodist University,[5] or any expression of such proscribed attitudes as "ageism" ("oppression of the young and old by young adults and the middle-aged"), "ableism" ("oppression of the differently abled by the temporarily abled"), and "lookism" (the "construction of a standard of beauty/attractiveness") at Smith College.[6]

The University of Arizona takes a similarly expansive view of sensitivity. The University's "Diversity Action Plan" expresses concern over discrimination against students on the basis of "age, color, ethnicity, gender, physical and mental ability, race, religion, sexual orientation, Vietnam-era veteran status, socioeconomic background, *or individual style*." When John Leo, a columnist for *U.S. News & World Report*, tried to find out just what the university meant by "individual style," he was told by "diversity specialist" Connie Gajewski that the category "would include nerds and people who dress differently. 'We didn't want to leave anyone out,' she said."[7] Indeed.

Not to be outdone in their zeal, University of Wisconsin-Milwaukee officials handed out a list of forty-nine "Ways to Experience Diversity," which urged students to "Hold hands publicly with someone of a different race or someone of the same sex as you" and to "Go to a toy store and investigate the availability of racially diverse dolls."[8] The University of Connecticut has banned "inappropriately directed laughter"[9]; Duke University's president appointed a watchdog committee to search out "disrespectful facial expressions or body language aimed at black students"[10]; while Smith College's malediction upon "heterosexism" includes the crime of "not acknowledging their [gays'] existence."[11] Even that citadel of tradition, the College of William and Mary, has succumbed to the mood of the times. The alma mater of Thomas Jefferson and James Monroe has issued guidelines to nonsexist language, insisting that the term *kingpin* be changed to *key person*, and that *unwed mother* be replaced with the nonjudmental *mother*.

At Harvard, sensitive professors at a reeducation seminar joined in a chorus of therapeutic concern for the sensibilities of their students. One professor argued that faculty members should never "introduce any sort of thing that might hurt a group." He recognized the implications of his comments for a professor's freedom to teach. "The pain that racial insensitivity can create is more important," he insisted, "than a professor's academic freedom."[12] Or, he could have added, a student's.

At the University of Michigan, students faced discipline for suggesting that women were not as qualified as men in any given field; one student was actually brought up on charges of sexual harassment for suggesting that he could develop "a counseling plan for helping gays become straight."[13] Officials at New York University Law School bowed to pressure and canceled a moot-court hearing on the question of custody rights for lesbians after PC cadres complained, "Writing arguments [against the right of lesbians to win custody] is hurtful to a group of people and this is hurtful to all of us."[14]

At times, this new paternalism has gratuitously extended the status of victimhood to individuals who feel that they are doing quite all right without being liberated or otherwise protected. At the University of Minnesota, for example, cheerleaders have been banned from performing at sporting events on the grounds that their routines foster "sexual stereotypes" demeaning to the dancers. Said one of the cheerleaders: "We feel we're intelligent enough to know when we're considered objects." The sensitivity police did not agree; the cheerleaders were victims whether they recognized it or not.[15]

In part, this shift from substance to form can be traced to the civil rights movement's changeover in emphasis from combating discrimination to fighting racism. Although apparently a subtle shift in nomenclature, the new focus on racism abolished the distinction between private and public acts and between conduct and attitudes. It meant, according to Julius Lester, "that the opinions, feelings, and prejudices of private individuals were a legitimate target of political action. This was dangerous in the extreme, because such a formulation is merely a new statement of totalitarianism, the effort to control not only the behavior of citizens, but the thoughts and feelings of persons."[16]

But the shift in civil rights cannot fully account for the existence of a new politics of sensitivity and the metastasis of offended groups. To understand these, we need to look to a broader cultural shift.

EGO UBER ALLES

On one level, the push for sensitivity is little more than the age-old fight for human dignity, the demand that all individuals be treated with respect and sympathy. To oppose sensitivity is therefore to risk being seen as anti–good manners or hostile toward caring. The opposite of sensitivity, after all, is boorishness. The arguments in favor of sensitivity *do* have moral weight, and they deserve to be taken seriously. But it is the nature—and the tragedy—of victimism to take legitimate concerns and distort them for self-indulgent ends.

The victimist chancre marring sensitivity is the insistence that it is not enough to behave correctly—one must be *attuned* to the feelings of others and adapt oneself to the kaleidoscopic shades of grievance, injury, and ego that make up the subjective sensibilities of the "victim." The relationship between individuals and groups may no longer be mediated by mutual respect or principles of justice but must be recast solely in therapeutic terms: the avoidance of injury and offense, the need to sacrifice oneself for the self-esteem of the other. Superficially, latter-day sensitivity resembles Christian charity, but as a series of demands and mandatory obeisances it is something else altogether.

The essence of egotism is imposing one's likes, dislikes, subtle prejudices, and whining annoyances onto others. Society exists to keep the ego from making itself the center of the universe; maturity is (or, at any rate, was) defined as the child's gradual recognition that his emotions, demands, and sensitivities are no longer absolute.

"Sensitivity" (and please note the quotation marks here), however, transforms the self—especially the aggrieved self—into the imperial arbiter of behavior. Everyone must now accommodate themselves to the sensitivities of the self, whose power is based not on force or even shared ideology but on changeable and perhaps arbitrary and exaggerated "feelings." This is the historic (if not logical) culmination of the development of inner-directed man into anxiety-ridden, other-directed man and, later, into psychological man. David Riesman wrote that inner-directed man relied on an internal gyroscope and that other-directed man took his lead from emotional radar. But the mechanistic metaphors are now obsolete. Sensitive man is neither a gyroscope nor a radar. He is a raw nerve, frequently inflamed.

BIG NANNY IS WATCHING

Despite its psychological pedigree, "sensitivity" has proven to be a powerful political weapon. By redefining ideology in nonideological terms, it has provided a pretext for sweeping changes not only in American universities but also in the larger society.

In the late 1980s, a series of viciously crude racial incidents at leading universities shocked academia and focused attention on growing tensions on campus. One result was the rapid proliferation of speech and harassment codes, ostensibly aimed at banning the vilest of racial epithets. Some schools established hotlines for students to report racist incidents, while others established elaborate mechanisms to wipe out insensitivity in the classroom. But in many cases the incidents seemed to serve as a pretext for radical faculty and administrators to invoke politicized policies that might otherwise have met with opposition. Administrators vied with one another in demonstrating their zeal to don the sackcloth of newfound racial awareness. "I would plead guilty to both racism and sexism," declared Donna Shalala, chancellor of the University of Wisconsin-Madison. "The university is institutionally racist. American society is racist and sexist." And lest the message be lost, minority students received specific instruction in their status as soon as they arrived on campus. It should not, then, have come as a surprise when campus militants at the University of Wisconsin-Milwaukee who shouted down conservative speakers and pelted them with hard objects justified their assault on free speech by invoking their status as oppressed minorities. In one lengthy apologia, the vice president of the school's student association argued that the physical attack on the speakers by minority students "was a result of their systematic oppression by this university, this city and the nation."[17]

At Brown University, all minority students were assigned to the school's Third World Transition Program (a rather eccentric name for a program designed for black students from New Jersey). In a description of the program, journalist Pete Hamill noted, "It is race-driven; it assumed that non-whites are indeed different from other Americans, mere bundles of pathologies, permanent residents in the society of victims, and therefore require special help. 'They're made to feel separate from the first day they arrive,' one alumnus said. 'And they stay separate for the next four years.' "[18]

In that atmosphere, the scope of victim protections went far beyond simply punishing undergraduates who yelled "nigger" in the dormitory. Few schools so eagerly embraced the metaphysic of victimism and the therapeutic ethos of stamping out insensitivity as did Brown. To minister to the prejudices of its unenlightened undergraduates, Brown hired sensitivity "experts" and consultants, including Donald Kao, who openly acknowledged that his goal was to convince his audience that America is a racist society in which "privileged" whites have established arbitrary norms of acceptable behavior. Nor was Kao's goal merely to encourage tolerance; his "standard of gauging one's behavior" was far more demanding. "If you are feeling comfortable or normal," he insisted, "then you are probably oppressing someone, whether that person is a woman or a gay or whatever. We probably won't rid our society of racism until everyone strives to be abnormal."[19]

Having acculturated minorities to their oppressed status, Brown insisted on preternatural alertness to signs of racism—which, by definition, was everywhere. "It is both subtle and overt," a university publication announced. "Racism is encountered through our language, actions, non-verbal communications, institutions, access to privilege and educational processes." No one at Brown, it declared, was "immune." Like guilt, though, potential victimhood was seen as an equal-opportunity affair. Individuals were protected against slurs on the basis of such characteristics as "race, religion, gender, handicap, economic status, sexual orientation, ethnicity, national origin, or on the basis of position or function." (It is unclear whether the ban on ridicule "on the basis of position or function" would apply to jokes about dumb jocks or rich frat boys.)

Significantly, Brown's policy was not framed as a ban on improper activity; it was cast as a declaration of the right of victims "to live in an environment free from harassment." The distinction lay in the assertion that the right to be free of harassment could be enforced even in the absence of intent to harass or demean. Banned activities included "inappropriate verbal attention, name calling, using racial/ethnic epithets, vandalism and pranks." More explicitly, students were warned: "If the purpose of your behavior, language, or gesture is to harass, harm, *cause psychological stress or make someone the focus of your joke,* you are engaged in a harassing manner. *It may be intentional or unintentional and still constitute harassment.*"[20] [Emphasis added.] It is not, I think, an exercise in overscrupulous legalism to point out the inherent contradictions in that statement. In one sentence, harassment is described as the *purposeful* infliction of harm; the very next sentence renders that description meaningless by declaring that even "unintentional" acts may constitute harassment.

Brown's administrators had unintentionally but graphically revealed the slippery nature of the sensitivity issue and the near impossibility of grounding equitable policies on purely subjective judgments. This problem becomes even more obvious as the Brown policy goes on to describe the effects of harassment in purely therapeutic terms. In almost every case, the alleged damage is intangible—a matter of feelings and impressions—rather than a matter of actual or demonstrable harm. The listed effects include "loss of self-esteem," "a vague sense of danger" (rather than actual danger), "a feeling that one's personal security and dignity have been undermined," "feelings of impotence, anger and disenfranchisement," "withdrawal," "fear," "anxiety," "depression," and "a sense of embarassment from being ridiculed."[21]

Almost by definition, there is little or no defense to a charge of inflicting such ills. If a victim insists that he experienced "anxiety" or "embarrassment" because of something someone said, proof is beside the point. Lack of intention is no defense. Sensitivity demands *belief.*

This conviction that racism pervades higher education clearly affects the way black and white students regard one another. A survey of students at Stanford by John Bunzel found that white and black students have very different perceptions of racism.* While fewer than 30 percent of the black students said they had had firsthand experience of racism at Stanford, "most of them describe the racism they ran up against as 'subtle' and 'hard to explain' to non-blacks." While white students tended to discuss racism in terms of "negative views and comments," Bunzel reported, "most of the black students who said they had personally encountered racist behavior at the university were hard-pressed to describe what it was like or how it worked."[22]

Indeed, the comments from the Stanford students seem to illustrate

---

*The survey consisted of in-depth interviews with fifty-four undergraduates during the 1988–89 academic year. Twenty of the students were white, twenty-four were black.

the way that victimism tends to be self-verifying. Once convinced that he is trapped in a hostile, racially biased environment, the victim tends to see such hostility everywhere.

Bunzel noted:

> As many of [the black students] said, the racism they confronted, although it pervaded the whole campus, was subtle and could not be effectively explained to others. "I've felt like an outcast in classes," a black senior woman noted. "The class breaks up into study groups and people don't want you in theirs." A black freshman said, "There's nothing that's actually been done to me, but there are things that have been hurtful—like people who don't think black writers have anything to say." Others just talked of subtle changes in the behavior of whites in the presence of a black, and a certain tension they felt in social situations.

It is easy to sympathize with their reactions; and it is relatively easy for non-minorities to identify with them. Imagine for a moment going into a room of strangers. You have been told that they dislike you and that even their attempts at good manners and friendliness are ruses to conceal their malice toward you. Who would not feel uneasy? And who would not begin to interpret even the most innocent gestures as subtle confirmations of the strangers' bad faith?

But the challenge of racial sensitivity can be bewildering to white students, who are often accused of "subconscious racism." "It's hard to know how to react to charges of racism when there are no specific incidents or examples," Bunzel quotes one Stanford senior saying. "That's pretty damn subtle." Said a white freshman: "I've learned how easily comments that seem innocent to you can be misconstrued. But whether or not they are really intended to be racist—unfortunately, that seems irrelevant today."

Bunzel notes that a frequent issue on campus is "whether an individual can commit an act of racism without racist motives."

"Yes," a Stanford student insists, "if the person is subconsciously racist." Asks Bunzel: "But how can that be demonstrated, and by whom?" This is the business of the sensitivity police.

In the late 1980s, the University of Michigan adopted a sweeping "speech code" aimed at wiping out racist, sexist, homophobic, and ethnocentric slurs. Students were warned that they could be suspended or expelled for *any* act, "verbal or physical, that stigmatizes or victimizes an individual on the basis of race, ethnicity, religion, sex, sexual orientation, creed, national origin, ancestry, age, marital status, handicap, or Vietnam-era veteran status."

Because the policy was so broad—and vague—it raised the obvious question of how it would be enforced.* How would students know exactly what constituted stigmatizing someone on the basis of, say, his "Vietnam-era veteran status" or his "ancestry"? More important, what proof of offense would be needed? The university's answer was direct: None.

"Experience at the university," a UM publication explained, "has been *that people almost never make false complaints about discrimination.*"[23] [Emphasis added.] That generalization, as policy, included any alleged incident for which there were no witnesses, the school said. If it was one student's word against another's, the accused was presumed guilty.

Michigan's speech code did more than simply invert normal standards that require accusers to shoulder the burden of proof. It enshrined the doctrine that issues of victimism could and should be judged on radically new terms—further breaking down the distinction between fact and fabrication.

In March 1990, a black student at Emory University reported that she had been the object of a campaign of racial harassment. The nineteen-year-old freshman alleged that her room had been ransacked, that racial slurs had been written on her walls, and that she had received death threats. Her allegations received national media attention after she reportedly curled up in the fetal position and refused to speak.[24]

Emory's president—the episode clearly on his mind—penned an op-ed piece for *The New York Times* denouncing "renascent bigotry" and using the incident as a justification for his school's sweeping ban on any "conduct (oral, written, graphic or physical) directed against any person or group . . . that has the purpose or reasonably foreseeable effect of creating an offensive, demeaning, intimidating, or hostile environment."[25]

But the episode of "renascent bigotry" never happened.

After investigating the allegations, officials determined that the episode was an elaborate hoax on the student's part, designed to divert attention from her alleged cheating on a chemistry test. When

---

*It also raised questions of how it could be reconciled with the First Amendment. A federal judge later invalidated the policy.

asked for his reaction, the head of the Atlanta NAACP said, "It doesn't matter . . . whether she did it or not, because of all the pressure these black students are under at these predominantly white schools. If this will highlight it, if it will bring it to the attention of the public, I have no problem with that."[26]

At Emory, the metaphysic of victimization transcended the mundane world of reality and fact.

But if sensitivity to harassment often demands an excess of credulity it sometimes demands the absolute suspension of thought, depending on the race or gender of the harasser. Insensitivity, it seems, is not always insensitivity; only someone with a reliable and up-to-date scorecard can tell for sure.

Gayatri Spivak, a professor of English and Cultural Studies at the University of Pittsburgh, argued, for example, that it is unreasonable to expect minorities to practice the sort of tolerance demanded of white students. "Tolerance is a loaded virtue," he explained, "because you have to have a base of power to practice it. You cannot ask a certain people to 'tolerate' a culture that has historically ignored them at the same time their children are indoctrinated into it." His position was echoed by a group of professors at the University Michigan who declared, "Behavior which constitutes racist oppression when engaged in by whites does not have this character when undertaken by people of color."[27]

Similarly, one of the authors of Stanford University's speech code argued that a ban on offensive language would not apply to black students. By definition, they were incapable of "insensitivity." In the same way that the guilt of whites as universal racists was simply assumed, the innocence of blacks was axiomatic.

According to Professor Robert Rabin, whites do not need any protection from abusive language because they do not have a history of being discriminated against; only those who have been victims of oppression need to be shielded from offensive words. Rabin says, "Calling a white a 'honky' is not the same as calling a black a 'nigger.' "[28] This is essentially the same argument advanced by Stanford law professor Mari Matsuda in a 1989 article in which she argued for antiracist speech bans on the grounds that freedom of speech should be understood only as an instrument to help members of powerless groups. The emphasis on group rather than individual rights is crucial, because it locates constitutional protections not in one's citizenship but in one's status on the victim hierarchy. Under Matsuda's doctrine, critic David Rieff noted, "a rich woman would presumably be protected by the First Amendment but a poor white man (unless gay, or disabled, or otherwise 'disenfranchised') would not."[29]

As interpreted in the light of victimist politics, the Stanford policy embodied what Nat Hentoff called a "new sliding scale of permissible expression" that was completely dependent on comparative victimhood. Given their history of oppression, Hentoff wondered, shouldn't Native Americans get even more protection than blacks? Was a slur against an Italian American to be punished more harshly than an offense directed toward a Presbyterian? Given the history of anti-Semitism, Hentoff wondered whether Jews would "get special leniency when they insult members of other religions."[30] The question was not entirely frivolous. Once status is determined by the degree of one's victimhood, every nuance of oppression becomes crucial—one's rights now depend on the constantly shifting scorecard of aggrievement.

FOURTEEN

The Sexual Nightmare

The politics of victimization also overlay the increasingly delicate relations between the sexes. In particular, the early 1990s saw a boom in the marketing of the harassment and brutalization of women. By one estimate, half of the 250 made-for-television movies scheduled for 1991 depicted women undergoing "some form of physical or psychological mistreatment."[1] Reported *Newsweek*: "Eager to enhance TV's reputation for fairness and balance, the purveyors of jep [women in jeopardy] portray contemporary men as homicidal husbands . . . abusive lovers . . . alcoholic fathers . . . sadistic sons . . . psychotic doctors . . . sex-crazed hospital orderlies . . . even diabolical college professors. When the genre's males aren't oppressing women directly, they're messing up their children.

"Rape," *Newsweek* noted, "is a popular device."

This avalanche of fictive violence against women can, of course, be dismissed simply as a ploy by the major networks to increase their audience share, especially among women. But that begs the question. Obviously, there is a significant market for the portrayal of women as victims and an audience eager to share the travails of brutalized heroines. Steve Krantz, the executive producer of the one of the "jep" thrillers, concedes, "Though I hate the notion, it's prototypical of women's roles in society to see themselves as victims. So there's a high identification factor." But the relationship is more complex. As *Newsweek* noted in its account of the new trend—which it headlined "Whip Me, Beat Me . . . and Give Me Great Ratings"—several studies have found that people who are frequent viewers of such dramas tend to overestimate their chances of being victimized themselves. They begin to see menace everywhere, while their own sense of vulnerability is dramatically enhanced.[2]

The portrayal of women as victims thus creates its own market and its own constituency. Once enlightened, women can be forgiven if they begin to see more and more examples of hostility and discrimination and feel themselves besieged by sexism and harassment.

Such hypersensitivity is often extreme and occasionally assumes bizarre forms.

A former part-time English instructor at Joliet Junior College in Illinois, for instance, accused her department chairman of sexually harassing her when he refused to reschedule her classes because of what he called "space usage" constraints. She charged in a federal lawsuit that although she was not offended by the remark at the time, she later interpreted his comment as a veiled suggestion that she should open up her "personal space" to him and become "sexually compliant."*

The same month that *Newsweek* reported on the proliferation of "jep" dramas, five employees of the Stroh's brewery sued their employer, charging that "its television advertisements featuring women cavorting in bikinis had created a workplace tolerant of sexual harassment."[3] A week after the bikini suit, officials at Pennsylvania State University pulled a copy of Goya's *Naked Maja* from the wall of a lecture hall after a female professor declared that its presence was a form of sexual harassment.[4] The week after that, not to be outdone in either indignation or creativity, columnist Anna Quindlen declared herself the victim of what should probably be called "nameism." In a letter to the editor of *The New York Times*, Senator Alan Simpson had referred to Quindlen as "Anna."† Responding to this slight,

---

*The woman also alleged that the chairman told her that she could improve her low ratings from students if she would "change" her "approach." Later, when her summer-school class was canceled and she asked the chairman if there were any other openings, he replied, "I have my needs." As the federal judge later noted: "[The instructor] maintains that she was not offended by either of these statements at the time they were made, but later concluded that both statements were subtle attempts to let her know that her chances of employment would improve if she became sexually compliant." The judge rejected her claim. (*Tozzi v. Joliet Junior College et al.*, No. 88 C 10385, U.S. District Court, Northern District of Illinois, Eastern Division, August 10, 1989)

†"I find it so very ironic," Simpson wrote, "that while Anna crusades against female stereotypes, she wants to then wrap a male stereotype around me. . . ." In her response,

Quindlen approvingly quoted another correspondent who charged that the use of Quindlen's first name was a tactic that has "been used to belittle and demean women." An unidentified male friend assured Quindlen (she reported) that this flagrant use of her first name was "offensive to you, women in general as well as to truth." This was a bit ironic, since Quindlen acknowledged that she often used first names for (male) public figures she held in disdain, calling Vice President Dan Quayle "Dan" or "Dan-O," and she took note that males from George Bush to Mario Cuomo have to endure being referred to as "George" and "Mario." Even so, she ponderously concluded: "I suspect the Senator called me by my first name because I am female."[5]

Quindlen's brittle humorlessness was one-upped, however, by another article on the very same op-ed page of the *Times*, which called for "re-educating the guy who winks, blinks and smirks" in mandatory "sensitivity seminars." Although author Elinor Lipman ended by grimly reassuring male readers, "Right-thinking men have nothing to fear," her definition of harassing behavior was notably expansive. Men who say "hi" when they call women on the telephone rather than "Donna, this is Steve" are indicted for obnoxious sexism, as is any man who "wink[s] when you walk into his office and find him on the phone"; so is the man who blinks hard when an attractive woman leaves the room and even the guy who "studies her framed photos with a smirk."[6]

Lipman, of course, is not alone in her rolling redefinition of sexist insensitivity. She and Quindlen are riding the Zeitgeist for all it's worth.

Not all women, however, see the issue in quite the same way. Indeed, there are signs of a civil war among women themselves on this question. One dissident from the victimist mainstream, a doctoral candidate at Princeton, points out that the constant portrayal of women as helpless victims merely reinforces old images of feminine frailty. "Let's not chase the same stereotypes our mothers have spent so much energy running away from," Katie Roiphe writes. "Let's not reinforce the images that oppress us, that label us victims, and deny our own agency and intelligence, as strong and sensual, as autonomous, pleasure-seeking, sexual beings."[7]

Quindlen neglects to address the substance of Simpson's point and focuses her *entire* column on his use of the name "Anna."

THE SEARCH FOR "THE WOMEN'S STANDPOINT"

There is a paradox here: No group came close to the success that women achieved between the 1960s and the 1990s. The number of women elected to public office tripled; the number of women lawyers and judges multiplied more than twentyfold; the number of women engineers rose from 7,404 to 174,000. One-third of MBAs are earned by women (as are half of the nation's law degrees and a quarter of the medical degrees). Fully half of entry-level management jobs are now filled by women, as are half of the officer and manager spots in the country's fifty top banks.[8]*

This extraordinary record has, however, been paralleled by an increasingly insistent and shrill campaign to regard women as victims, a program that seems particularly urgent to those groups that claim to speak for women and that use the victimization of women as their raison d'être. For the feminist movement, one of the embarrassing facts of political life has been the refusal of most women to embrace either its rhetoric or its basic principles. Surviving this rejection requires some interesting intellectual calisthenics. Alison Jaggar notes that any theory of a special "women's standpoint" must be able to "explain why it is itself rejected by the vast majority of women." Jaggar declares that the "standpoint of women" cannot be discovered "through a series of women's existing beliefs and attitudes" under the current conditions of "male dominance" any more than "the standpoint of the proletariat [can be] discovered by surveying the beliefs and attitudes of the workers under capitalism."[9] In other words, the will of women, like the will of the people, cannot be determined through such bourgeois instruments as elections or surveys or any of the other usual means of determining opinion in a democratic society. Jaggar's conclusion: Women need their own vanguard elite who will speak for them and raise their consciousness.

Because they have become so much a part of our vocabulary, it is probably worth mentioning that the very terms *sexism* and *sexist*

---

*The Metaphysic of Victimization requires, of course, that such a record of success be dismissed. Perhaps the most creative gambit can be found in Naomi Wolf's *The Beauty Myth*. She cites the numbers above not as a sign of society's openness to women but as evidence of the white male patriarchy's motive for imposing a new arbitrary standard of good looks on women. Given the success of women, she insisted, "Someone had to come up with a third shift fast" to protect the status quo.

were once considered startling neologisms.* It is, of course, true that opportunities open to men were once routinely denied to women. And it is equally true that the West has a long and voluble tradition of denigrating women. But the coining of *sexism* made the audacious claim that the substatus of women was akin to the evils of racism. Equally radical was the notion that anyone who holds traditional views about the role of women is the equivalent of a racist. From a tactical point of view, the linguistic linkage was a bold and ambitious stroke. But the connection was by no means self-evident: Women were *not* being lynched, they were not being denied the right to vote, they did not tend to live in poverty. On the contrary, many Americans in the early 1960s saw women as occupying a uniquely *privileged* position compared to men.

The more extreme feminists recognized the need for an ideology that plausibly converted childbearing and child rearing into pseudo-slavery and the family into an instrument of oppression and exploitation. This transformation required the politicization of sexuality itself, the tearing down of barriers that separated the personal from the political. More fundamentally, it required redefining the "normal" itself as a mode of victimization. Emulating the metaphysic of racial victimology, the oppression of women had to be changed from *acts* of oppression to a state of *being*. The very nature of society—and of biology itself—had to be seen as an instrument of oppression. Radical feminists rose to the task without embarrassment.

Feminists, insisted Shulamith Firestone, must "question not just all of *Western* culture, but the organization of culture itself, and further *even the very organization of nature.*"[10] [Emphasis added.]

---

*Brigitte and Peter Berger assert, "Sexist language is an invention of the feminist movement" based upon misunderstandings about the nature of language. "Feminists, eager to wrap themselves in the mystique of the civil rights movement, like to compare so-called sexist language with the linguistic etiquette used to denigrate blacks. The comparison does not withstand close scrutiny. The language etiquette of race relations in America, especially in the South, was understood by everyone *at the time* as having the purpose of humiliating blacks. . . . Racist language, in other words, was *not* an invention of the civil rights movement, retrojected into the past prior to the advent of that movement." This is decidedly not the case with the use of words such as *he, man,* or *mankind.* The Bergers equate seeing such terms as sexist with regarding someone who says "drop dead" as homicidal or someone who uses the term *goddammit* as blasphemous. "Taken literally, this is a theory that elevates infantile misunderstandings to the level of hermeneutics. But it would be a mistake to take this literally. It matters little, in the final analysis, that here is a theory of language that rests on little or nothing beyond the emotions of the theorists. What matters a lot is that the theory legitimates a linguistic offensive that is part of a general political strategy." Brigitte Berger and Peter Berger, *The War over the Family*, 48.

Women were oppressed, radical feminist Anne Koedt insisted, by the emphasis on vaginal orgasm, which was merely an example of the way men defined sexuality "in terms of what pleases men." Typical of their bullying, men had made a big deal out of the penis and ignored the clitoris.

"An analogy is racism," declared Koedt, "where the white racist compensated for his feelings of unworthiness by creating an image of the black man (it is primarily a male struggle) as biologically inferior to him." Women who believed that they actually *enjoyed* vaginal intercourse were merely reflecting their victimized status, Koedt wrote; they were either confused, victims of male deception, or were "faking it."[11]

Ti-Grace Atkinson put the Revolution in medical terms—men were a "social disease." The male *need* for the "role of Oppressor," she wrote, was "the source and foundation of all human oppression." Men suffered from "a disease peculiar to mankind," which Atkinson called "metaphysical cannibalism."[12]

With remarkable unanimity, radical feminists insisted that Woman as Victim needed to transform every aspect of the social order, beginning with the family itself.

In *Sexual Politics*, her 1970 manifesto of feminist revolution, Kate Millett equated the condition of women with both feudalism and racism, declaring that all civilizations known to history had been patriarchies governed by an ideology of "male supremacy." Women had been conditioned to follow stereotyped sexual roles, which were enforced through "rape, attack, sequestration, beatings, murder." The instruments of male rule included "patriarchical religion, the proprietary family, marriage, 'The Home,' masculine-oriented culture, and a pervasive doctrine of male superiority."[13]

Not surprisingly, there were some curmudgeonly dissents. The narrator of Edward Abbey's novel *The Fool's Progress* confronts his feminist wife, who has discovered that men have conspired for twenty centuries to enslave and victimize women. "Women the victims, men the victors?" he asks.

> Tell it to the Marines. Tell it to those grunts, all boys, who sweated, fought, suffered and died in the green hell of Vietnam. . . . Tell it to the serfs of merrie olde England who plowed, sowed, reaped, and saw the fruits of their labor stolen from them by the lords—and ladies—who claimed ownership of the land . . . Tell it to . . . the slaves of the Deep South. . . .

Tell it those who died in the Coliseum, to Spartacus and the twenty thousand slaves, all men, who were crucified with him by the victorious Romans. Tell it to the slaves—men, women, and children—who built the Pyramids, the Great Wall of China, the Parthenon, the Appian viaducts, the walls of Toledo and Burgos, the Taj Mahal, the city of Machu Picchu, the cannibal temples of Mexico, the lost and forgotten horrors of imperial Africa. . . . Tell it to Aleksandr I. Solzhenitsyn and the surviving *zeks* of the Gulag and the KGB. . . ."[14]

But Abbey's self-described rant found few echoes, at least among those who shaped cultural attitudes. Within two decades of its invention, sexism was widely accepted—and legally declared—to be virtually on a par with racism as a social evil.

THE RAPE CULTURE

Rape is the central metaphor haunting the imaginations and writings of radical feminists, a symbol of the systematic violence of males against women. "It is nothing more or less than a conscious process of intimidation," Susan Brownmiller argued, "by which *all* men keep *all women* in a state of fear."[15] Rape is seen as the expression of Western civilization's fear and hostility toward women—a product of phallocentric political, economic, and social forces that demand the submission and humiliation of women. Sexual violence is not an aberration but the primal reality of universal oppression, cognate with the Holocaust, racism, colonialism, pornography, and phallocentric literature. "I was born in 1946, after Auschwitz, after the bomb," says a character in a novel by Andrea Dworkin; "I never wanted to kill, I had an abhorrence for killing but it was raped from me, raped from my brain; obliterated like freedom. I'm a veteran of Birkenau and Massada and deep throat, uncounted rapes, thousands of men, I'm twenty-seven, I don't sleep."[16]

However extreme, the outrage that gathers around the subject of rape is not without justification. Neither sexual harassment nor sexual assault are politicized fantasies. Rape is a horrific reality, and it is understandable that the campaign to combat it in all its forms—including date rape and acquaintance rape—has become so potent a cause. Few crimes inflict more suffering or long-term pain than rape, an act of dehumanizing viciousness that reduces a woman to the status of an object. First-person accounts from universities across the country indicate that female students have been mauled, grabbed, handled, and assaulted by males who either deny their crimes altogether or boast about their "scamming"* or fraternity gang rapes. There is nothing artificial about the pain or the sense of violation felt by rape victims. Their sense of degradation is often compounded by a feeling of isolation, a sense of shame, and the fear that their story will not be believed. Because of such fears, it is often difficult to reliably gauge the scope of violence against women.

But just as the genuine and unquestionable martyrdom of the early victims of racist violence in the civil rights movement was appropriated and trivialized for political ends, the genuine suffering of victims of sexual assault and harassment has proven eminently exploitable by those for whom rape is a convenient symbol of society's oppression of women. Typically, the result is confusion, as genuine concern is overlaid with shrill victimist indignation, and distinctions between truth and fiction are obscured.

"Sensational and anonymous accusation is a hallmark of the sexual abuse movement on campus," Phillip Weiss reports in *Harper's*. "Respect for students' civil rights does not seem to be a primary concern of the activists."[17] Nor does the veracity of the accusations. A *Time* magazine report on the subject quotes a female student arguing that rape is a subjective experience, defined not by physical assault or actual penetration but rather by the *feelings* of the victim. It is perfectly legitimate in some cases, she argues, to use accusations of rape as a means of calling attention to the general issue of the oppression of women. "If a woman did falsely accuse a man of rape," the student insists, "she may have had reasons to. Maybe she wasn't raped, but he clearly violated her in some way."[18] This politicized approach to accusation was echoed in the same article by an assistant dean of student life at Vassar, who explained to *Time* the value of a flexible use of the term *rape* and the acceptability of relativized standards of truth in leveling charges against male students. "To use the word carefully would be to be careful for the sake of the violator, and the survivors don't care a hoot about him," she contends. Since males must be sensitized to their status as potential rapists, she sees possible benefits even for those falsely accused: "They have a lot of pain, but

---

*"Scamming" is casual, often illicit sexual contact, ranging from what was once known as "copping a feel" to making out.

it is not a pain that I would necessarily have spared them. I think it ideally initiates a process of self-exploration. 'How do I see women?' 'If I didn't violate her, could I have?' 'Do I have the potential to do to her what they say I did?' Those are good questions."[19]

But they are good questions only if the goal is advancing a predetermined ideological agenda, not if the purpose is determining the truth or falsity of specific allegations. By showing contempt for normal standards of fairness and truth, such approaches seem likely to breed the sort of doubt and cynical skepticism that has exacerbated the suffering of victims of *actual* rapes.

But false accusations of rape play only a modest role in the sexual sensitivity campaigns. Far more important to its champions is the effort to redefine what constitutes sexual assault and to expand the zone of sexual oppression to cover the entire range of nuance, complexity, tentativeness, and confusion that surrounds the relations between men and women.

Some of the most highly publicized surveys on the subject of sexual assault have claimed that as many as half of all women in the United States have been raped or molested before their twenty-first birthday.[20] Researcher Mary Koss reported in *Ms.* magazine that of the 3,187 female college students in her survey, 862 reported incidents of rape or attempted rape in a single year. Diana Russell's study of 930 women led her to estimate that 46 percent of women will be the victims of rape or attempted rape in their lifetime; a poll of Stanford University students found that one-third of women there had suffered incidents of date rape. The coordinator of the University of California at Berkeley's Rape Prevention Education Program estimated that women students on her campus have a one-in-four chance of being raped.[21]

Taken at face value, these numbers indicate not only that we are experiencing an epidemic of sexual assault but that feminists are hardly exaggerating when they maintain that women are besieged by a wave of misogynistic violence. As researcher Neil Gilbert points out, however, the most widely accepted measurements of sexual violence do not support such claims. Indeed, while the number of rapes apparently rose sharply in the 1970s, the incidence of rape and attempted rape seems to have leveled off in the 1980s. Citing statistics from the National Crime Survey of the Bureau of Justice Statistics, which uses household surveys to measure previously unreported as well as reported cases of rape, Gilbert estimates that the actual number of rapes may be as much as 140 percent higher than the number of

rapes reported to police. In 1980, there were 150 reported and unreported cases of rape for every 100,000 women; by 1987, that number
had fallen to 113.[22] Even if those statistics were off by 100 percent—
if there were twice as many rapes as found by the BJS—assaults
would number about 300,000 annually. That would be a tragic number and, as Gilbert notes, would "represent an enormous amount of
human suffering." But he adds: "However, there is a staggering
difference between" one or two out of every thousand women being
raped and an " 'epidemic' of sexual assaults that harms one of every
two before they reach their mid-twenties."[23] Other recent studies
have put the number of rapes higher. A much-publicized survey by
the National Victim Center concluded that as many as 683,000 adult
women may have been raped in 1990—five times the number reported by the U.S. Justice Department for that year.

But several caveats are in order. The estimate of the number of
rapes was extrapolated from a federally funded survey of 4,008
women. In that survey 0.7 percent of the respondents reported a
forcible rape. That percentage was then multiplied by the approximately 96 million women in the United States to come up with the
projection of 683,000 rapes.

But 0.7 percent of the 4,008 women in the survey comes to only
28 women. So the headlines reporting "an epidemic of rape" (as *Time*
magazine put it) were based on the responses of *fewer than 30 women*.
Because the margin of error in a survey of this size is one and a half
percentage points—and the number of women reporting rape was
less than one percent—the results should be treated with extreme
caution. But *even if* these estimates are accurate, they would still
represent only a fraction of the rapes claimed by the activists.

The discrepancy, of course, can be traced to the way sexual assault
is defined.

Diana Russell claimed that 54 percent of women were victims of
incest or sexual abuse before age eighteen. But she included among
her measures of abuse "unwanted kisses and hugs." Notes Gilbert:
"If unwanted hugs and kisses are equated with the sexual abuse of
children, we have all been victims."[24]

Koss used penetration as the standard for rape in her survey, but
here too the definition of sexual abuse is notably broad and open-
ended. Questions in her survey included: "Have you had intercourse
when you didn't want to? Because you were overwhelmed by a
man's continual arguments and pressure? Because a man gave you
alcohol or drugs?"

Is emotional pressure really rape? Does *any* amount of alcohol make subsequent intercourse nonconsensual? And does having sex "when you didn't want to" mean actual resistance or simply not being in the mood? And does that include morning-after regret?

Gilbert notes how significantly this ambiguity changes the complex dance of romance and seduction. "The conventional script of nagging and pleading—'Everyone does it,' 'If you really loved me, you'd do it,' 'We did it last night,' 'You will like it'—is transformed into a version of sexual assault," he writes. "Under these definitions of rape and sexual coercion, the kaleidoscope of intimate discourse—passion, emotional turmoil, entreaties, flirtation, provocation, demureness—must give way to cool-headed contractual sex: 'Will you do it, yes or no? Please sign on the line below.'"

Gilbert also notes the uncertainty surrounding Koss's definition of attempted rape. He suggests this scene: A man and a woman who have been drinking embrace, the man with lust in his heart, the woman with more ambiguous intentions. As they kiss, the man, hoping to proceed to intercourse, touches the woman's genitals. The woman pushes the man's hand away and breaks free. Even though the man stops and apologizes and does not renew his advances, Gilbert notes, "he had already committed a sexual act that involved alcohol, force, intent to penetrate, and lack of consent. Many would say the young man misbehaved. As Koss would have it, this encounter qualifies as attempted rape."[25]

How, then, can men and women be sure of what constitutes sensitivity and right conduct, especially when hurt feelings, regrets, and a conviction of universal violation can figure so heavily into the spectrum of consent versus rape? As Philip Weiss notes, clarification is hard to come by, and when attempted often adds to the confusion. Ed Shanahan, a Dartmouth College dean, sought to explain what his school meant by its "No Means No" policy. Even by the exalted standards of academic vagueness, Shanahan's is a classic response:

A misreading of my "No means no" would be to put quotation marks around those words. When we say "No means no" and "The absence of a yes means no," that doesn't mean the absence of a verbalized yes means no. There is the courting, there is the initiation of an activity, and the response. It's the nature of the response that indicates the yes or the no. For example, if I am engaging in suggesting intimacies with somebody and touch that person, I don't need to get a yes, I don't need to ask permission.

That occurs within the context of what's happened just prior to it. What is the response that I get to that? Does that suggest that it is accepted or not?[26]

One suspects that a male Dartmouth student would be better off simply taking along a lawyer whenever he goes out on a date, so as to be able to resolve ambiguities on the spot.

I will leave it to others to comment on the irony of this feminist/puritan backlash against the Sexual Revolution. But the debate over the political etiquette of sexuality highlights the impoverishment of our modern moral vocabulary. Only those brave enough to weather accusations of prudery dare undertake a frontal assault on the sexual mores of the 1990s or suggest that the young man in Gilbert's scenario was guilty of more than merely bad sexual manners. But the suggestion that the feminist critique be combated simply by arguing that "boys will be boys" is obviously inadequate as well as starkly amoral.

As a society, we are committed to full candor about all things sexual, except, it seems, the morality of sexual self-restraint. Only a handful of critics (dismissed as reactionaries) warned that respect for women would be one of the first casualties of the culture of indulgence, unfettered appetite, and instinctual liberation. During the Sexual Revolution, the elaborate etiquette of restraint and respect seemed pointless, irrational, and oppressive. The usefulness of that morality in setting mutually understood limits and defining the parameters of acceptable conduct was forgotten in the rush for mutual gratification. Only afterward was its loss felt.

For many Americans today, the only way to voice concern over casual sexual indulgence is to invoke either the language of medicine (safe sex) or the language of victimization (lust as oppression). Victimist terminology has not usurped the role of traditional sexual ethics so much as it has filled the vacuum created by their disappearance. Increasingly, sexuality can be discussed only in terms of sound techniques for applying condoms, exchanging fluids, and avoiding microbes and babies. One often searches in vain for suggestions that sexual intimacy involves human beings whose obligations to one another might occasionally transcend the proper use of rubber dams.

In part, Dartmouth's "No Means No" campaign may be seen as an expression—however indirect—of the need to restore a sense of order to sexual relations and reestablish an etiquette (although its proponents would never call it that) governing the relations between the sexes. But although the yearning for the restoration of respect to

sexuality is given voice by the language of victimization, it is ultimately drowned out by the victimist ethos.

As the meaning of the word *harassment* is widened, the reality of
actual rape seems to recede into the background when it is not trivialized altogether. The Association of American Colleges' Project on
the Status of Women defined "peer harassment," in part, as any
comment or action that makes women "a negative reference group,"
and included in that definition men's domination of classroom discussions.[27] Feminist author Sandra Harding claims to detect "rape and
torture" metaphors in the early development of the scientific method
and has suggested that Newton's laws could more accurately be called
"Newton's Rape Manual."[28] Harvard has helpfully issued written
guidelines on "Sexism in the Classroom" that warn professors
against sending "alienating messages," including "calling only upon
women in a class on topics such as marriage and the family, imposing
the assumption that only women have a natural interest in this area."
This policy was issued only months after a visiting law professor was
denounced as a sexist for quoting from Byron's *Don Juan*: "A little she
strove, and much repented,/And whispering 'I will ne'er consent'—
consented." He was also arraigned for saying, "Sauce for the goose,
sauce for the gander—I don't know, is that sexist?" Thundered the
head of the Harvard Women's Law Association: "Sexist language is
not a joking matter. By using sexist language, you encourage sexist
thought and, in essence, promote hostility against women."[29] From
Byron to misogyny to campus rape seems the smallest of leaps.

At the University of Wisconsin, a group calling itself "Men Stop-
ping Rape" urged men to cross the street so as to avoid following
lone women and thus spare them the fear of imminent rape.[30]

At the Center for Advanced Studies at the University of Minnesota, Marilyn Frye has redefined heterosexuality as the primary me-
dium of women's "subordination and servitude to men." "The
primary sites of this reduction," she argues, "are the sites of heterosexual relation and encounter: courtship, sexual liaisons, f——ing,
marriage, prostitution, the normative family, incest, child sexual
assault. It is on this terrain of heterosexual connection that girls and
women are habituated to abuse, insult, and degradation, that girls
are reduced to women, to wives, to whores, to mistresses, to sex
slaves, to clerical workers, to the mothers of men's sons."[31]

Conflating clerical work with sexual slavery, motherhood with
prostitution, and courtship with the sexual assault of children, Frye
makes victims of virtually all women. But along the way, she loses

all capacity to distinguish real from projected oppression or actual suffering from "false consciousness." Instead of focusing outrage onto sexual violence, Frye reduces actual rape to merely one among many forms of oppression—nearly indistinguishable among the vast constellations of phallocentric domination.

A similar process is at work in the declaration by feminist guru Susan Estrich that women's oppression is so absolute that even "yes" cannot be taken seriously as a sign of sexual consent in relationships with men. "Many feminists would argue that so long as women are powerless relative to men," Estrich writes, "viewing 'yes' as a sign of true consent is misguided."[32]

"No" means no; but so, perhaps, does "yes."

What begins as a project to restore the dignity and respect of women—to empower them in their relations with men—ends with a doctrine that deprives them of their humanity by denying them any capacity for rational choice or free will. Woman as eternal victim cannot even decide whether and when to have sex with a man without becoming complicit in her oppression. It is a prison with no doors.

The debate over the definition of rape was mirrored, however imperfectly, in the disputes that flared in the wake of the 1991 Senate confirmation hearings of Supreme Court nominee Clarence Thomas, who was accused of sexually harassing a co-worker ten years earlier.

Feminist leaders and their spokespersons in the media portrayed Thomas's accuser, Professor Anita Hill—a Yale Law School graduate—as a frail, helpless, and powerless victim who could not have been expected either to resist or to report Thomas's alleged advances at the time they happened.

Many working-class women, however, loudly disputed such arguments, insisting that they were indeed capable of taking care of themselves. One thirty-three-year-old woman who worked at a shelter for battered women told *The New York Times*, "I was harassed and I nipped it in the bud; I stopped it right then and there. One guy said, 'I see you don't take any guff.' " And a fifty-two-year-old teacher mused, "Wouldn't you haul off and poke a guy in the mouth if he spoke in that manner?"[33]

Despite such demurrals, the terms of the debate and the definitions of harassment continue to be set by the ideological and cultural vanguards—especially in higher education.

SENSITIVE, SILENT, AND SULLEN

If the classroom was once the seat of learning and the forum for the vigorous exchange of ideas, it has in recent years become a testing ground for the politics of "sensitivity."

At prestigious Kenyon College, for example, the course known as Biology 14, "Biology of Female Sexuality," makes no secret of its radical feminist agenda, which is to expose the way that conventional medicine oppresses women. Its reading list includes *Witches Heal*, which combats phallocentric medicine by addressing itself to "wimmin." "As lesbians," the introduction declares, "we . . . must question male medical authority, dare to hear and follow the witches, uncover old wyves' tales, and heal ourselves." Given the current fashions in academia such a curriculum would not be particularly notable were it not for the explicit way the course's professor regards male students in her class. In essence, they are told to shut up. A handout distributed on the first day of class sets the ground rules: "For women, participation means making verbal contributions to discussion. . . . For men, participation means seriously listening more than contributing to discussion—attending to women's discussion and making contributions where you are strongly motivated by your knowledge of women in your experience or thought." Noted one student publication: "Given the conditions for male participation (an absurd concept itself), the rules effectively silence men."[34]

This mandated silence would, however, be questionable only if the goal of the class was to educate its male students; it makes perfect sense if the goal is to "sensitize" them.

The therapeutic/political classroom is a drama of challenge and conversion in which subtle factors of psychological and sexual dynamics are brought together as students "struggle with the realities of violence against women and the negotiation strategies women use to succeed and survive in a patriarchal society." Or at least that is the way Professor Magda Lewis of Queen's University in Ontario explains her mission and her tactics in combating "blatant and subtle forms of physical, social, emotional, and psychological violence against women" that are present *in her very classroom*.[35] These include, she explains, "forms of discourse, directions taken in discussion, [and] the subtleties of body language," in which "a dichotomy between desire and threat is reproduced and experienced inside the classroom itself."

She is quite serious about this link between body language and sexual violence, opening her discussion of the subject with ominous references to the murder of fourteen women at the University of Montreal in November 1989. "This was not the single act of a deranged mind," she insists darkly, "nor the outcome of peculiar conditions on that specific campus." Everyone is at risk, she writes, especially feminists. "Because of our identification with a politic that makes explicit our critique of women's subordination as a function of masculine privilege, my students' and my own safety were in question."

Thus, Magda Lewis approaches her classes in feminist theory as a warrior approaches a battlefield: issues of life, death, and gender equity hang in the balance. In an article in the *Harvard Educational Review*, Lewis describes two skirmishes in which she combated acts of victimization so subtle as to be undetectable by anyone not as finely attuned to oppression as she.

In the first case, Lewis devoted a class to a discussion of "the connections between patriarchy, violence, and political economy." As Lewis delivered her diatribe against men, a young woman raised her hand to say, "I was wondering and worrying about how the men in the room were feeling. What you said made sense to me, but I felt uncomfortable about how the men took it."

A novice at this sort of thing might imagine that this was an indication of sensitivity—a mark of empathy and concern on the part of the female student. Professor Lewis is quick to disabuse anyone of the notion that *this* is the sort of sensitivity she is aiming at. Rather, she explains, the young woman's concern was really a reflection of women's "historically produced nurturing capacity as a feature of our psychologically internalized role as caretakers."

To make matters worse, several other women had nodded their heads in agreement when the woman had expressed her concern. "Such a protective posture on the part of women on behalf of men is a common drama played out in many classrooms," Lewis reports. Much of this solicitousness takes the form "of hard-to-describe body language displayed as a barely perceptible 'moving forward'; a not-quite-visible extending of the hand; a protective stance accomplished through eye contact." In this instance, some of the men in Lewis's classroom seemed to feel that the young woman's comments had "vindicated" their own feelings and were emboldened to attempt to "redirect the discussion toward notions of violence as a *human* and not a gendered problem."

But this was something Lewis was not about to allow. The men, she explains, were attempting "to reappropriate a speaking space for themselves, which they saw to be threatened by my analysis. Even more troublesome for me was the pleasure some of the men seemed to take in encouraging women to take up the caretaking on their behalf and in how the women seemed to be brought up against one another in the debate that followed." Lewis suggests that this coalition of males and females who challenged her position was not demonstrating independent thought or the give and take of liberal education, but were evincing a recapitulation to male domination, with malevolent overtones. "We do not have language," she writes, "that can adequately express the social meaning of the practice of relaxing back in one's chair with a barely-there smile on one's face while eyes are fixed on the object of negation."

What was Professor Lewis to do?

Somehow the women in her class had got the idea that "sensitivity" meant treating their fellow students, regardless of gender, as human beings rather than as emanations or symbols of an oppressive patriarchal social structure. Lewis had to undo this, to make them "focus on social organizational practices rather than on the man sitting next to them in the classroom." In other words, she had to make the women sensitive not to other people but to their own status as victims.

Her response was somewhat anticlimactic. In answer to the young woman's expression of concern about the discomfort of the men in the class, Lewis asked her women students if any man had ever expressed concern for *their* discomfort "at the common public display of misogyny in such examples as billboards." And if not, why should the women care about the men's feelings? No, members of the class said, this had never happened. Lewis declared victory, although she does admit, "Whether or not men carry this new understanding into their public and private lives outside the classroom is unclear. If they do, they have not shared it with me."

Lewis's second confrontation with patriarchy was somewhat more straightforward. During a discussion of male violence against women, a frustrated male student asked why the class didn't consider "the other side of the story." Rather than seeing this as a request for a more evenhanded approach to the topic, Lewis declared that the student's interruption was "an attempt to redirect the discussion away from his own social identity as a male who, whether he acknowledges it or not, benefits from the culturally, legally, and politically encoded social relations of patriarchy." As far as Lewis was concerned, the male student's guilt as an oppressor/violator of women was not subject to discussion. Men, Lewis writes, "can no more deny the embodiment of their masculine privilege than any one us can deny the embodiment of our entitlement if we are White, economically advantaged, heterosexual, able-bodied, and carrying the valued assets of the privilege of Euro-American culture."

No summary can do justice to Lewis's breathless account:

> The power of teaching as dramatic performance cannot be discounted on this particular occasion. Following the question I allowed a few moments of silence. *In those few moments, as the question and the dynamics of the situation settled into our consciousness, the social history of the world was relived in the bodies of the women and men around the table.* [Emphasis added.] What is the "other side of the story" about violence against women? What could the women say? Faced with the demand to articulate their *reality in terms not of their own making*, the women visibly shrank into their chairs; their breathing became invisible. [Emphasis in original.] In contrast, whether I imagined it or not, it seemed to me that the men sat more upright and "leaned into" the response that began to formulate in my head. . . .
>
> The stage was set for dramatic performance. Reassuring the young man that indeed he was right, that "other sides" of issues need to be considered whenever possible, I wondered if *he* would perhaps be the one who could tell us about the "other side" of violence against women. *My memory of this moment again focuses on the breath: the men's as it escaped their bodies and the women's as it replenished them.* [Emphasis added.]

Again, anticlimax. The student failed to come up with a convincing answer and Lewis interpreted his silence as evidence of the triumph of her crushing retort. "Whether the young man experienced trans-formation or was simply intimidated into silence was something that required sorting out," Lewis concedes. But she was willing to chalk up another win—she had struck a blow for women as victims by showing a male what it felt like to be victimized. "If I had silenced him I could only hope that perhaps the experience would provide him a deeper understanding of an experience women encounter every day."

That is unlikely, inasmuch as injustice and unfairness are more apt to engender bitterness and fierce resentment than sympathy. More fundamentally, however, Lewis's carefully honed strategies are unlikely to win many converts for the simple reason that they do not treat students as ends, but rather as means. She views her male students not as independent thinkers—*that* would imply the need for a genuine exchange of ideas—but rather as embodiments of racial, cultural, and sexual privilege, as *opportunities* for her to strike a blow at what she believes they represent. She confesses as much. She admits she does not know what they are thinking, what their reactions might be, or even why they ask the questions they do. They are opaque to her; their experience is cut off from hers as radically as she believes the experience of women is cut off from men's. Lewis can imagine no way to transcend those barriers or meet on any sort of common ground except as fellow victims, as shared sufferers, and as angry outsiders.

What is the ideal consciousness of the suffering victims? How should they react to the world and to others? How best to wage war on oppression? Again, Lewis is obliging.

With considerable pride, she cites a letter from one of her female students, who seems to represent the goal to which all Lewis's pedagogy is tending. The student wrote that the readings in one of Lewis's courses "have plunged me into the next phase of my feminist awareness, which is characterized by anger and a pervading sense of injustice. . . ."

What follows is less a statement of feminist principle than a riff of victimist outrage:

> The "feminist" anger that I feel is self-perpetuating. I get angry at the discrimination and the stereotyping I run up against so I blame the patriarchal society I live in in particular, and men in general. Then I think about women who feel that feminism is unnecessary or obsolete and I get angry at that subset of women. Then I think about the good guys like Mike and Cam and I get angry because the patriarchal society biases the way I think about these men, simply because they're members of a particular gender (sex class?) Then I think about men who stereotype and discriminate against women and criticize us for being "overly sensitive" when we get uptight or even just point out or suggest humanistic egalitarian changes that are good and smart and I get REALLY angry because I realize that they're all a bunch of (expletives deleted) [*sic*]. . . . One of the most

difficult aspects of this anger is that I become frustrated and impatient with people who can't see the problems or don't see the urgent need for solutions. [I am writing] a lot during this time because I often can't communicate orally with people who don't at least respect my feminist views.

This, Lewis writes with evident satisfaction, is an example of "how one woman took up these struggles in her private life." But the dominant impression here is not that of a raised consciousness or a constructive zeal that might be mobilized to fight injustice. Cut off from others by her ideological hysteria, angered by everything in her life, the writer expresses impotence and frustration as evident as her unhappiness. She is the eternal victim.

FIFTEEN

Presumed Victimized

Nowhere is the institutionalization of victim status more obvious than in the way we deal with race. Here the assumption of victimization is so pervasive that victimization is often simply taken for granted—and expanded upon at will.

In New York, for instance, a training manual for the State Insurance Fund declared:

> All White individuals in our society are racist. Even if a White is totally free of all conscious racial prejudice, he remains a racist, for he received benefits distributed by a White racist society through its institutions.[1]

If *all* whites are guilty of racism, it follows that *all* blacks are victims of racism. History is thus transformed into a relentless saga of repression, degradation, intimidation, and denial of rights. Every individual and institution is complicit in the brutalization of minorities and continues—to this day—to perpetuate their suffering. In this vision, the "cumulative disadvantages from past racism" have permanently disadvantaged contemporary minorities in terms of education and job skills.

Given the pervasiveness of victimization, according to this scheme, lack of education, unwillingness to work, even a criminal record cannot and must not be held against the victim. Victimhood is *prior* to personality, certainly prior to conduct.

Thus, the argument goes, employers who require certain job skills—the ability to read or write at a certain level, for instance—may not be intentionally discriminating against blacks, but they are still part of a pattern "of racial exclusion and inequality."[2] The same principle can be applied to criminal behavior. A rule that bars hiring convicted felons, for example, is color-blind on its face. But because it disproportionately affects black applicants, such a restriction can be denounced as "discriminatory." At one point, a federal court ruled that a New York City policy denying employment to methadone users was illegal because it tended to discriminate against blacks and Hispanics. (A higher court later reversed the ruling.) A federal court ruled that a trucking company could not require prior over-the-road experience (even though such experience is the best known predictor of driver safety) because such a rule would have a disparate impact on women.[3] So too, if a company or a police department has a test that is on the surface fair and unbiased, but which is flunked by 80 percent of black applicants, it is *assumed* that the cause of this disparity is racism, therefore indicating a pattern of discriminatory behavior. In New York, minorities who failed the test for police sergeant, for example, did not have to prove that the test was biased at all, only that the skills required were somehow "irrelevant" to actual job performance. As a result, many blacks and Hispanics who failed the exam were promoted, while white applicants who passed it were not. Such a process descended into cruel farce in New York when half a dozen ostensibly white officers who had been denied promotion suddenly declared that they were, in fact, minorities because of their mother's surname or the race of one or the other of their parents. Writes Jim Sleeper: "They were duly promoted—a blunt demonstration that individual merit and performance, as measured by the department's admittedly flawed examination, had become irrelevant to advancement in at least one highly visible sector in American society."[4]

The insistence that minorities be given all the benefits they would have had, had they not been the victims of racism drove the civil rights movement to shift its focus from equality of *opportunity* to equality of *results*. This translated into policies of redress in which race alone was regarded as an entitlement. Since the victimization of blacks had been total, no distinction could be made between middle-class and poor blacks, or between educated and uneducated blacks.

Similarly, no distinction could be drawn between blacks who had successfully pulled themselves out of poverty and those who had adopted criminal life-styles. The only entitlement that mattered was one's race. All blacks must be *assumed* to be victims of racism.

Civil rights historian Herman Belz draws a distinction between social programs that seek to eliminate barriers to opportunity (and thus are "future-oriented") and those programs that are designed to somehow compensate individuals or groups for past injustices (and thus are "backward-looking").[5]

The moral rationale of affirmative action is to redress past wrongs. All such programs of preferential treatment, with their "goals" and "timetables," take as their starting point the persistent and systematic denial of equal opportunity to minorities *in the past*. Thus, they tend to be backward-looking both in conception and execution. "You guys have been practicing discrimination for years," declared Justice Thurgood Marshall with refreshing candor. "Now it's our turn."[6]

If this seems an extreme formulation of civil rights law, consider the way it has been implemented by the courts.

COLOR BY THE NUMBERS

The belief in universal victimization was effectively institutionalized in federal law as a result of a series of Supreme Court cases that radically changed the original meaning of the Civil Rights Act of 1964. Title VII of that act was quite explicit in banning *intentional* discrimination in employment against *individuals* because of race, color, religion, sex, or national origin. There was no hint in the original act that it could ever be interpreted as conferring *group* rights, or that it could be used to mandate "goals," "timetables," or "quotas." Indeed, Hubert Humphrey insisted that the bill did not "require an employer to achieve any kind of racial balance in his work force by giving any kind of preferential treatment to any individual or group."[7]

But that changed, first through interpretations by a politicized EEOC, and ultimately by the high court in *Griggs v. Duke Power Co.* The decision in *Griggs* was a turning point for civil rights because it adopted the principle that any act that had a "disparate impact" on minorities could be considered discriminatory, *even if no discrimination was intended*. Moreover, the *Griggs* court ruled that employers had the burden of showing that "any given requirement must have a manifest relationship to the employment in question." In 1986, the Supreme Court ruled explicitly that preferential treatment for previously victimized groups was permitted "even when those who benefit have not themselves suffered from discrimination in the past and when those who are hurt have not themselves been responsible for past discrimination." The next year, the court extended such treatment specifically to women.[8] Essentially, the court had transferred the victimist idea of "institutionalized racism" directly into federal law.

"The theory" adopted by the Supreme Court, explains Herman Belz in his study of civil rights law, "holds that discrimination is not an individual act or injury or denial of rights caused by racial prejudice (as it had traditionally been conceived of in civil rights law), but is rather the sum of the unequal effects of employment procedures and business practices on racial groups."[9] Thus, any policy or job qualification that results in a disproportionate racial mix in a company's work force is prima facie evidence of racial discrimination. In time, courts ruled that alleged victims of discrimination no longer had even to specify *what* policy was discriminatory. The mere numerical imbalance in hiring was deemed evidence of discrimination—the burden of proof was shifted to the employer to prove somehow that he had *not* discriminated. Because that is an almost impossible burden in many cases, Belz notes, the whole notion of "disparate impact" became "a powerful incentive to engage in hiring quotas in order to avoid liability and costly litigation."[10] This issue was at the heart of the debate over the Civil Rights Act of 1991.

The effect of *Griggs* was somewhat moderated by the Supreme Court in 1989 when it ruled in *Wards Cove Packing v. Atonio* that statistical imbalances could be used as a basis for an "initial" inquiry, but that the pool of "qualified applicants" in the labor pool should be the relevant standard. Furthermore, the *Wards Cove* court ruled that plaintiffs would henceforth have to specify specific employment practices that were discriminatory. Upset by this decision and other similar limitations imposed by the court, civil rights advocates sought to restore the full flower of *Griggs* through legislation. With the acquiescence of President Bush, they succeeded in codifying the *Griggs* decision in the Civil Rights Act of 1991. In the end, both major political parties accepted the victimist assumptions underlying "disparate impact" standards.

What is noteworthy here is the way the definition of *discrimination* had been radically transformed from intentional and specific acts to a global explanation of group differences. By continuing to use the term *discrimination*, with all of its moral weight and historic associations, leaders of the civil rights movement managed partially to obscure the magnitude of the shift. They were able, Belz notes, to exploit the "moral opprobrium associated with traditional discrimination in support of socially redistributive policies" that would otherwise have provoked powerful opposition.[11]

Ironically, the chief beneficiaries of such policies are often members of the black middle class—arguably, a group that is least in need of preferential treatment.

William Raspberry, a black columnist for *The Washington Post*, derides what he calls the "hocus-pocus" of using the plight of poor blacks to advance the interests of well-to-do blacks by pushing for promotions in colleges, corporations, and government jobs. "The result is that some blacks—most likely those that have been least crippled by racism—get special-admission college seats and affirmative action promotions," he writes. "My children—and the children of my middle-class colleagues, who already enjoy important advantages—no longer need to compete with their white counterparts. They compete instead with the children of Anacostia, Watts, Hough, Cabrini Green and Overtown. . . ." This, Raspberry notes wryly, is "a competition they are likely to win."

By emphasizing race as an entitlement, the rewards have tended to go to the already rewarded. "Black executives who already hold good jobs get promoted to better ones," writes Raspberry; "blacks who already sit on important corporate boards get another directorship. *And the people who provide the statistical base get nothing.*"[12] [Emphasis added.]

Such policies also send a very direct message to the rest of the black community.

"The most devastating form of racism is the feeling that blacks are inferior so let's help them," said Clarence Thomas when he headed the EEOC. "What we had in Georgia under Jim Crow is not as bad as this. This racism is based on sympathy that says that because of your race, we will give you excuses for not preparing yourself and not being as good as you can be."[13]

Jim Sleeper echoes this sentiment. As a result of the new politics of resentment and entitlement, he writes, too many blacks "have stopped following Martin Luther King's admonition to 'burn the midnight oil' in order to compete with their white counterparts, demanding instead a formulaic inclusion on the grounds that stipulated qualifications are not only irrelevant to job performance but intentionally racist as well."[14]

The replacement of merit and character with formulas was an inevitable product of the civil rights establishment's insistence that statistical models rather than individual cases of provable discrimination should be the focus of the movement. The decision to adhere to such models was based on the belief that all ethnic groups should naturally be represented in all job categories in more or less equal proportions to their numbers in the general population. Any indication of statistical "underrepresentation" was deemed to be the result of systematic and invidious discrimination.

THE FALLACY OF
INFERRED DISCRIMINATION

The assumption that all ethnic groups would randomly find themselves represented in population-proportionate numbers in all job categories, sociologist William R. Beer notes, defies virtually every known finding of modern sociology, ignoring long-recognized differences in cultural and educational backgrounds. Surprisingly, the related assumption that any numerical gaps in representation are the result of racial prejudice (what Beer calls the "fallacy of inferred discrimination") has gone largely uninvestigated. Beer adds that the fallacy is based on "a patently false reading of American ethnic history."[15] Is the shortage of Jews, for example, in the forestry profession and the National Basketball Association a sign of systematic anti-Jewish discrimination? Or are other factors possibly at work?

Beer argues that discrimination alone cannot account for the social mobility of various ethnic groups. Although Jews, Japanese Americans, and Chinese Americans have all suffered from widespread discrimination, all now exceed the median income of white Americans. Irish Protestants had little trouble being assimilated into mainstream society but now lag behind Irish Catholics in income, even though the Catholics were subjected to more discrimination. Nor does the discrimination model account for the success of black West Indians, who are theoretically subject to the same discrimination as other black Americans. The notable success of the West Indians, Beer notes, "raises doubts about racial discrimination as an explanatory variable." He could easily have cited the more recent examples of Cambodian and Vietnamese refugees, who have arguably been the victims of some of the century's most brutal acts of violence and repression.

None of this is to argue that racial discrimination does not play a role in employment decisions. It would be unpardonably naïve to believe that racial bias does not affect employment and promotion decisions. But evidence suggests that such instances of outright bias have become increasingly infrequent; it is far from clear that overt racial bias is the dominant or determining factor in employment disparities. According to one study reported in *Public Opinion*, a majority of black Americans reported that they had never themselves been discriminated against on the basis of their race.[16]

Despite the heated political debates that affirmative action and its various modifications have inspired, there has been remarkably little research into how it works or as to its consequences. Despite the obviously high stakes, Beer reveals, "social scientists have been almost entirely mute. . . . There has been no systematic inquiry into the effects of affirmative action on American society, neither its costs to the nation's economy nor its impact on our country's morale." This is especially noteworthy when one considers the explosion of social-science research in recent decades. Most social programs, Beer insists, "are studied almost to death. . . ." In contrast, social scientists have adopted a posture of "resolute ignorance" on the issue of racial hiring policies.

"It is as if affirmative action has assumed the status of a religious article of faith," Beer wrote in 1987, concluding that affirmative action had become a "sacred cow of American liberalism." Questioning it was tantamount to "heresy."

Sociologist Frederick R. Lynch came to a similar conclusion when he examined media coverage—or, rather, noncoverage—of the issue of racial preference in the early years when affirmative-action policies were being put in place. Lynch calls the subject a "look-away" issue, "a topic that people have preferred to look away from or ignore, a sort of semiconscious mass self-censorship." Perhaps the most dramatic manifestation of the look-away syndrome was the hands-off attitude of whites toward the question of the black family after the release of the Moynihan report. Only when accepted black spokesmen raised the issue was it permissible for anyone to examine it again.[17]

This cult of silence on racial matters can be traced to the fallout from the politics of victimization, in which the moral authority of victims themselves and the stigma attached to their opponents effectively chilled dissent. People tend to keep silent when they perceive themselves to be in a minority on any issue. But since the vast majority of Americans have always opposed preferential treatment of minorities, why has there been a reticence to speak out? Lynch concludes that the lack of public debate (until recent years) can be attributed to the fact that "most Americans were not aware of the issue, much less majority opinion on the topic." This was largely due to a lack of media attention, but was also attributable to other factors, including the "enormous guilt" felt by would-be critics of programs designed for the benefit of the less fortunate. Beyond a sense of collective guilt, dissenters from the policy of preferential treatment also had to "calculate the chances of being labeled a racist." This helps explain the acquiescence of conservative businesses in the new racial ethos. As late as 1991, business opposition to quota plans— especially among large companies—was muted at best.

The paucity of solid empirical research on the subject may, however, be beside the point, given the status of racial victimization as a *belief* rather than provable fact. Absent reliable research, and given the silence that has for so long surrounded racial issues, it is perhaps not surprising that race has become the one issue which Americans find nearly impossible to discuss openly or honestly. Wrapped in the rhetoric of benevolence, guarded by taboos, hedged by conventional (and untested) wisdom, the subject of race has, not surprisingly, degenerated into a series of assumed postures, mandatory fictions, and manufactured indignations.

PIOUS FRAUDS

By refusing to probe too deeply into the gap between their intentions and the consequences of their policies, the practitioners of the politics of victimization are forced to maintain a precarious psychic balancing act of attitudes and ideas that often flatly contradict one another. This is only a polite way of saying that they engage in doublethink and rely upon the political equivalent of pious fraud. How else can one describe the insistence that victims not be held responsible for their personal behavior conjoined with the belief that all members of so-called oppressor groups are responsible for crimes they themselves did not commit?

At the heart of this doublethink is an irresolvable tension between the mutually exclusive beliefs that the victim is simultaneously disabled and fully qualified. By making deficiency into an entitlement, victimism both asserts the victim's inability and denies it. Thus, affirmative action demands special privileges for members of minority groups (regardless of personal history) but turns with ferocity on any suggestion that they are beneficiaries of favoritism.

Because not everyone can succeed in holding such contradictory ideas in perfect equilibrium, it is essential in doublethink to regulate the gap between what people believe and what it is permissible for them to actually *say*. The recent redoubling of efforts to stamp out even the slightest hint of incorrect political thought by invoking the standards of "sensitivity" reflects this tension between belief and speech. Given the logical stresses and strains in the victimist position, the reliance on "feelings" rather than reason is, perhaps, understandable.

Pious fraud is also necessary in the support of victim politics because even its most avid proponents must deal with the nagging doubt that its policies stigmatize all successful minority individuals. Despite the array of entitlements held out to victims as a group, the process has proven to be profoundly demoralizing for individuals. Shelby Steele has argued that shifting responsibility from the individual to society encourages passivity and resignation. The decline of racism and the failure of black Americans to fully take advantage of an atmosphere of tolerance has therefore posed a terrible dilemma. To admit any personal responsibility, Steele notes, is to risk losing "the innocence we derive from victimization. And we would jeopardize the entitlement we've always had to challenge society." As a result, "We are in the odd and self-defeating position in which taking responsibility for bettering ourselves feels like a surrender to white power."[18] One result is the phenomenon Steele calls "race-holding," which he describes as a response to the shock of integration and opportunity, the shock of "being suddenly accountable on strictly personal terms. . . . Instead of admitting that racism has declined, we argue all the harder that it is still alive and more insidious than ever. *We hold race up to shield us from what we do not want to see in ourselves.*"[19] [Emphasis added.] Steele writes:

The race-holder whines, or complains indiscriminately, not because he seeks redress, but because he seeks the status of victim, a status that excuses him from what he fears. A victim is not responsible for his condition, and by claiming a victim's status, the race-holder gives up the sense of personal responsibility he needs to better his condition. . . . The price he pays for the false comfort of his victim's status is a kind of impotence.[20]

Unfortunately, the underlying dynamic is always an upward spiral, what Steele has described as "race fatigue" among beneficiaries of affirmative action who must constantly defend their vested interest in their status as victims by extending and elaborating the definition of racism. The victim's rhetoric becomes increasingly bitter and denunciatory as his position becomes more tenuous and the evidence to support it more ambiguous.

THE NEW RACISM

By almost any measure, the civil rights movement succeeded in changing racial attitudes dramatically. By the end of the 1960s, only 15 percent of white Americans believed that blacks were less intelligent than whites, and only 8 percent favored racially segregated schools.[21] Studies indicated that individuals did not rely on lingering racial stereotypes when dealing with specific decisions.[22] Nor was there much evidence to support the belief that a "white backlash" had undone progress in race relations. The National Research Council recounted what it called a "remarkable 'liberal leap' forward" between 1970 and 1972, followed by steady positive change between 1972 and 1976.*[23]

By the end of the 1970s, there were strong indications that racial discrimination had declined substantially over the previous thirty

---

*"In sum, from the early 1940s to the late 1970s there were important shifts in white attitudes, from widespread belief that blacks were born less intelligent than whites to the belief that the races were of equal intelligence and from majority support for segregation of public places, schools, and housing to majority support for equal treatment. Even assuming that social pressures for 'correct' answers affected responses and that attitudes were only tenuously connected to behavior, the change had been impressive." National Research Council, *A Common Destiny* (Washington, D.C.: National Academy Press, 1989), 120.

years. Most striking of all: By 1979, the average black woman earned 8 percent *more* than a white woman with identical characteristics.[24]

This raises questions about the weight that should be accorded to racism in the analysis of social, educational, economic, and political trends. But the investment in racism was apparently too great for it to slip quietly into obscurity.

Rather than acknowledging the historic shift in attitudes, a cottage industry arose whose primary product was the elaboration of new and expansive definitions of racism that minimized or denied altogether the progress in race relations. Enter the social psychologists and the idea of "symbolic racism."

To be a symbolic racist did not require that one hold any of the bigoted views traditionally attached to ideologies of racial superiority. Two psychologists wrote in the mid-1970s that symbolic racism could be rather genteel, because it was a set of "abstract moral assertions about blacks' behavior as a group, concerning what blacks deserve, how they ought to act, whether or not they are treated equitably, and so forth."

Specifically, these psychologists argued that anyone was a "symbolic racist" by definition if he voted against black candidates for office, opposed racial quotas in hiring or college admission, and opposed school busing to achieve integration. Other indicators of the new racism included believing that "Streets aren't safe these days without a policeman around," that "Negroes have it better than they ever had it before,"[25] or that "Irish, Italian, Jewish and many other minorities overcame prejudice and worked their way up. Blacks should do the same."[26]

Theoreticians of symbolic racism stressed that the new prejudice was not the result of personal experience or animus but was based on the traditional American values of personal responsibility, obedience, and discipline. The much-maligned bourgeois ethos again proved its serviceability as an all-purpose scapegoat. Where Theodor Adorno had found that ethos to be fascistic and authoritarian, his successors now found that it was really racism in disguise.

In 1985, University of Illinois professor James Kluegel linked "modern racism" and the "dominant ideology theory" that emphasized "hard work, individualism, delayed gratification, and so on."

It appears that for many whites, attributing the race difference in economic standing to a lack of motivation or similar factors offers a means of expressing their disapproval of what they

perceive to be the values and behavior of at least certain
segments of the black population without seeming to themselves
to be prejudiced.*[27]

"The sheer presumption of this is mind-boggling," psychology
professor Byron Roth declared, "and reveals more, of course, about
the biases of social psychologists than it does about those of the
Americans they study."[28] But Kluegel was simply elaborating on
the basic point of William Ryan's *Blaming the Victim* by arguing
that belief in personal responsibility could now be redefined and
stigmatized as racism.

It is interesting to note that Gunnar Myrdal had suggested in 1944
that traditional American values were the greatest foes of racism
because they emphasized equality and liberty—values inherently in
contradiction to policies of segregation and exclusion. Now, however, American values were made the centerpiece of the new racism.

Not surprisingly, the new standards created by the authors of
symbolic racism made it possible to argue that a majority of whites
could still be considered racists. A study of attitudes in Los Angeles
conducted in 1969 and 1973, for example, asked whether respondents
agreed that "It is wrong to set up quotas to admit black students to
college who don't meet the usual standards." Seventy-three percent
of the respondents agreed, thus indicating their predilection for symbolic racism. The scores were even more one-sided for busing, which
was opposed by 86 percent of the respondents.[29]

The researchers sought to correlate these attitudes with voting
patterns in two Los Angeles mayoral elections that pitted black liberal
Tom Bradley against white conservative Sam Yorty. Researchers
John B. McConahay and Joseph C. Hough, Jr., noted that support
for Yorty was not correlated with "belief in black intellectual inferiority" or other measures of old-fashioned racism. They went so far as to
admit that "Yorty supporters were not simply alienated, dissatisfied
powerless bigots." A vote for Yorty did, nonetheless, place one into
the category of symbolic racist.[30] As one critic later noted:

In other words, people who opposed busing and hiring quotas
(though not necessarily affirmative action—at the time the two

---

*Kluegel was not alone in his assertions, nor did he initiate this line of argument. Researchers
Donald Kinder and David Sears wrote as early as 1971 that symbolic racism was "based on
moral feeling that blacks violate such traditional American values as individualism, the worth
ethic, obedience and discipline."

were still understood as distinct) were characterized as racist because they voted for a conservative candidate who seemed more representative of their own views.[31]

As Paul Sniderman of Stanford University and Philip Tetlock of the University of California at Berkeley have observed, these theorists of symbolic racism presented no evidence whatsoever that opposition to busing or to quotas was per se an indication of racism rather than of a nonracist political viewpoint.* And even if such opposition were explained as arising from economic individualism or antipathy to government programs, the expounders of symbolic racism would likely argue that those stances were signs of racist attitudes. In that sense, it was impossible to disprove the theory: *Any* motivation for taking the condemned political positions would be taken as evidence of symbolic racism. As Sniderman and Tetlock point out, the argument becomes tautological: "Racists, according to this approach, are by definition conservatives; and conservatives, again by definition, are racists."[32] The researchers conclude: "In short, as currently formulated, symbolic racism theory fails the fundamental test expected of any scientific theory—falsifiability. It is unclear what evidence it would take to convince symbolic racism researchers they were wrong."[33]

Even the suggestion of proving or disproving the concept of symbolic racism assumes that we are dealing in the area of social science rather than metaphysics. As psychology professor Byron Roth points out, the issue has become one of "belief." "The belief in deep-seated racial intolerance and the harm it causes," he writes, "has become an article of faith for most social scientists which must be defended at almost any cost."[34] Beyond the bogus science that underlay the new theory, however, the rise of symbolic racism had a profound and chilling impact on the climate of debate on racial issues. It was now possible to make sweeping accusations of racism and to wield the term against opponents in nakedly ad hominem attacks. Sniderman and Tetlock note the irony of the situation. They wonder, for example, how the social-science community would react to research that sought to "second-guess" the motives and psychology of political

---

*Of the connection between traditional values and symbolic racism, Sniderman and Tetlock wrote: "One must . . . ask what justification exists for [the connection]. Scarcely any, it turns out. Symbolic racism researchers have not yet analyzed the relation between prejudice and values; indeed they have not yet measured the traditional values that are supposedly an integral part of symbolic racism."

groups on the left. If opposition to busing is really racism, what would they make of a study that identified "people as symbolic Marxists by virtue of their support for the civil liberties of American communists? Or that they should be labeled as Marxists if they oppose aid to extreme right-wing governments resisting left-wing insurgencies?" Obviously, Sniderman and Tetlock write, symbolic racism and symbolic Marxism are not quite parallel. "But we should be astonished if social scientists did not look with distaste on the branding of people, on such tenuous grounds, as Marxists. Why, then, should it be less objectionable to brand people, on similarly tenuous grounds, as racists?"[35]

The answer lies in the dynamics of the politics of victimization.

Having established the immanence of racism, it is easy to make a plausible case for "institutionalized racism." Again, it is not necessary to show instances of individual bias or discrimination. The idea of institutionalized racism substantially improves on the notion of mere symbolic racism because it eliminates the need to make any judgment on individuals whatsoever. Racism is no longer conduct *or* psychological attitude; it is *everything*.

An aroused sense of injustice and an indignant defiance of segregation, poverty, and discrimination inspired the original civil rights movement. But the moral fervor of the movement has been increasingly manipulated by crass opportunists who see in victimism the powerful trump card of political and economic advantage. Inevitably, this is a breeding ground for cynicism.

SIXTEEN

The Racial
Nightmare

In the last two decades, charges of racism have become so routine
that eyebrows are hardly raised when black college students attend
demonstrations clad in chains (to dramatize their status as the descen-
dants of slaves) or form groups with names like SUFR (Students
United for Respect) to emphasize their suffering at and oppression
by prestigious universities.[1] Nor is it especially noteworthy when
heavyweight boxer Mike Tyson and promoter Don King—multi-
millionaires both—don the cloak of martyrdom. "Everything's
against us," Tyson complained in an HBO video produced by Spike
Lee. "We're two black guys from the ghetto and we hustle and they
don't like what we're saying." King, the self-proclaimed master of
"trickeration," piously complained that "they always change the
rules when black folks come into success."[2]

Racism has been automatically invoked by dozens of black officials
accused of misconduct in office. In some cases, there may have been
merit to this defense; in others, race was merely a cynical card played
in an elaborate game of moral avoidance and political advantage.
Shortly after Washington, D.C., Mayor Marion Barry was video-
taped puffing on a pipe filled with crack cocaine and subsequently
arrested, he attended a convention of the National Conference of
Black Mayors in New Orleans. Although much of the convention's
focus was on the question of drug policy, Barry's appearance was
met with a standing ovation, and by one account, he was "mobbed by

well-wishers and autograph-seekers." Reported *The New Republic*: "With unintended aptness, the mayor remarked that it was 'frightening that people have been so supportive.' "[3]

Barry practiced the politics of victimization with considerable skill, first by exploiting the "recovery" movement (after his arrest, he checked himself in for "treatment") and then by waving the bloody shirt of racism. That gambit won shrill support from much of Washington's black press, from talk-show hosts, and even from NAACP director Benjamin Hooks, who suggested that there was a concerted campaign to target black elected officials.

Barry's grab for martyr status descended into near farce as he aligned himself with the notoriously anti-Semitic Louis Farrakhan and appeared onstage at one rally with Tawana Brawley (who had fabricated a story about being assaulted by hooded white men), Congressman Gus Savage (who had been accused of sexual misconduct), and George Stallings (a former Catholic priest who has been accused of molesting children). Embracing Barry, Farrakhan cried, "I don't care *what* comes out. Just remember that our accuser is guilty of the worst crimes of humanity."[4]

Barry's linkup with fellow victim Tawana Brawley was a calculated and revealing maneuver. Under the tutelage of handlers Al Sharpton and Alton Maddox, Brawley had become perhaps the first Victim Celebrity, a status to which she clung tenaciously even after her story of attack and rape was discredited. For many sympathizers, she was a symbol of centuries of white sexual abuse of black women. Even if her charges were false, they reasoned, she was a rallying point for black men who could finally stand up for their abused women. The larger obscenity went largely unnoticed. "The use of a confused fifteen-year-old as a prop in a pathetic fantasy of historic redemption is, of course, an abuse of her," Jim Sleeper notes. "Forced miscegenation is transmuted into misogyny."[5]

None of this mattered to the flamboyant Sharpton, who found himself once again at the center of controversy, where he held the media mesmerized with his "venomous one-liners, pithy catchphrases, and inflammatory charges delivered with delicious bombast."[6] Sharpton instinctively understood the appeal of victim politics for the news media and the irresistibility of the theater of outrage. But he also understood something else about the media: They *needed* him. "It was easier to reach Sharpton than to seek out diverse views among blacks," the six *New York Times* reporters who covered the Brawley case later concluded; "reporters didn't waste time wondering whom he spoke for. And the various civil rights groups, in turn, needed him for his access to the media. For nobody knew better what buttons to push to get on the six o'clock news, to get on Oprah and Phil and Downey and Koppel."[7]

The *Times* reporters' analysis of the media culture applies as equally to Marion Barry's case as to Brawley's and goes a long way toward explaining the disproportionate influence of victimist ideology in discussions of racial issues. The six reporters admitted that the press in general was "ill-prepared" to cover racial conflicts.

> In such matters, civil rights activists were comparable to the public relations functionaries that politicians and corporations, police departments, and other government agencies hired to polish their images and smooth over their miscues. And because reporters who covered race-related news for the *Times* had come to regard civil rights organizations and black political leaders as their main sources, those institutional and political voices—not the less articulate ones of ordinary people—were the ones that most often came through to readers. *As a result, rhetoric about "justice" or the lack thereof often relegated the "facts" of controversial cases to a side issue.*[8] [Emphasis added.]

The Barry case, of course, reflected the peculiar dynamics of politics in the nation's capital and specifically the racial divisions in a city that is overwhelmingly black but governed by a white-dominated Congress. Even so, it demonstrated the resonance of what can only be described as the politics of paranoia, which is scarcely confined to Washington, D.C. In late 1990, a *New York Times*/CBS poll of 1,047 New Yorkers found that 77 percent of the blacks surveyed said that it was true or "might possibly be true" that the government deliberately singled out black officials "in order to discredit them in a way it doesn't do with white officials."[9]

Far more troubling, however, was the belief of 60 percent of the blacks in the survey that it was true or might be true that the "government deliberately makes sure that drugs are easily available in poor black neighborhoods in order to harm black people." Fully a quarter of the black New Yorkers said flatly that the government was engaged in such a conspiracy. Twenty-nine percent of the blacks endorsed the theory that it was true or possibly true that "the virus which causes AIDS was deliberately created in a laboratory in order to infect black people." One man told the *Times*, "Because of who's being devastated the most, and growing up in the U.S. and knowing the history of slavery and racism in this country, you can't be black and not feel that AIDS is some kind of experiment, some kind of plot to hit undesirable minority populations."[10]

The charge that blacks have been targeted by "The Plan" has become a staple of some black radio call-in shows and black newspapers. One black Los Angeles newspaper trumpeted the headline: "Blacks Intentionally Infected." The AIDS-conspiracy theory has also been embraced by the chairman of the black-studies department at City College of New York, Professor Leonard Jeffries. "AIDS coming out of a laboratory and finding itself localized certainly has to be looked at as part of a conspiratorial process," Jeffries insists. The *Times* interviewed a number of the students in Jeffries's class: *All* accepted the idea that both crack and AIDS were part of a white conspiracy.[11]

Believing that society is intent on the destruction of blacks amounts to what author James Traub calls a "counter-reality, a counter-mythos with alternative facts and alternative motives." Traub reports in *Harper's* that a popular black radio show in New York City has become a forum for a racialist mythology in which Jewish doctors inject AIDS into black babies, in which elaborate conspiracies are invoked to account for the Tawana Brawley rape hoax, where George Bush's "New World Order" is a code for white supremacy, where Christopher Columbus is charged with importing "institutionalized genocide and enslavement," and which insists that a black Cabbage Patch doll costs ten dollars more than a white one.[12]

But counter-reality is not the same as fantasy; it is the belief that *whatever the facts of any specific case, they do not matter, because the reality of victimization is the larger Truth.* "The stories were true," writes Traub, "because they were True—because they corroborated a big truth. Conspiracy theories require the soil of such an overwhelming truth in order to take root." In championing the Emory student who'd fabricated a story of racial harassment, the head of Atlanta's NAACP did not care whether the student had really been harassed; for him, the incident—real or not—was symbolic of the larger and more pervasive victimization of blacks. This attitude was echoed by radical lawyer William Kunstler, who similarly dismissed the importance of whether Tawana Brawley had really been attacked at all. "It makes no difference whether the attack on Tawana really happened," he said. "It doesn't disguise the fact that a lot of black women are treated the way she said she was treated." What mattered for Kunstler was that her allies now "have an issue with which they can grab the headlines and launch a vigorous attack on the criminal justice system."[13]

What Traub calls a counter-reality is the metaphysic of victimization; a worldview that peoples the universe with invisible demons who infiltrate every corner of reality and menace their victims with stealth, cunning, and relentless malice. But such paranoia leads inevitably to paralysis. What compromise is possible with a white society so thoroughly malevolent? What sort of communication can take place in atmosphere of such fear and mistrust? However small its beginnings, the politics of paranoia redivides and grows until it blots out all sense of possibility, hope, or accommodation.* "It spreads the poisonous notion that white racism is so overwhelming," Joe Klein wrote in *New York* magazine, "that success is impossible for blacks, that hard work in school is pointless, that violence may be an occasionally 'laudable' reaction to racial outrages."[14]

CLEOPATRA WAS BLACK—
SO WAS BEETHOVEN

The appeal of victimist counter-reality has proven so potent that it has made significant inroads into academia. Under the all-purpose banner of "diversity," Afrocentric scholars have established significant beachheads from which to launch their attacks on white Euro-centric history and culture.

There is really nothing new about the practice of what Arthur M. Schlesinger, Jr., calls "compensatory history," in which downtrodden groups invent and reinvent their pasts so as to provide themselves with a sense of dignity. At one time, the Irish American community was flooded with pamphlets insisting that three-quarters of the sol-

---

*Among the tragic fruits of the culture of victimization is the notion among some inner-city black youngsters that academic achievement is a form of "acting white." Writing in *Time* magazine, Sophronia Scott Gregory reported: "The phrase 'acting white' has often been the insult of choice used by blacks against those who moved forward. Once it was supposed to invoke the image of an African American who had turned his back on his people and community. But the phrase has taken an ominous turn. Today it rejects all the iconography of white middle-class life: a good job, a nice home, conservative clothes and a college degree." Thus, she reports, students who try to excel in school face accusations that they are "turning white." ("The Hidden Hurdle," *Time*, March 16, 1992.)

diers in George Washington's army had been Irish, and that the first
president had gotten many of his ideas from Irish Catholic priests.[15]
Even Plato suggested that there was a legitimate role for the "noble
lie" to sustain the sort of utopian society he envisioned.

But few movements have been as aggressive in creating and ex-
pounding a counter-reality, or so dogmatic in insisting on its absolute
truthfulness, as Afrocentrism.

Afrocentric guru Asa Hilliard insists that Egyptian civilization was
"black" and the "mother of Western civilization." In Hilliard's
world, blacks invented birth control, carbon steel, medicine, science,
and the arts, and they discovered America long before Columbus
even thought of it. (The original name of the Atlantic Ocean, Hilliard
asserts, was "the Ethiopian Ocean.") Moreover, such Western lumi-
naries as Beethoven and poet Robert Browning turn out to have been
"Afro-European."[16] Other Afrocentrists insist that Cleopatra and
Socrates were also black, a fact we would all know were it not for
the cunning and duplicity of racist white Europeans.

Most of the other figures of the classical world (in the Afrocentric
version) were either cads or crooks. Aristotle runs into some particularly bad press at the hands of the Afrocentrists. It seems, according
to G. M. James's 1954 book, *Stolen Legacy*, that Aristotle used money
from his pupil Alexander the Great to purchase African books from
the library at Alexandria.[17] In *Africa, Mother of Western Civilization*,
Yosef ben-Jochanan goes even further, flatly declaring that Aristotle
literally stole his ideas from the Africans, having "sacked the temples
and lodges of the African Mysteries in Egypt upon his arrival in 332
B.C.E. with Alexander the Great."[18]

Nonsense. Arthur Schlesinger is blunt on the point: "Cultural
pluralism is not the issue. . . . The issue is the teaching of *bad* history."[19] Socrates, an Athenian citizen, could not have been African;
Cleopatra was likely of Macedonian stock.[20] Frank Yurco, a noted
Egyptologist at Chicago's Field Museum of Natural History, describes one of the popular Afrocentric texts as "a melange of misinfor-
mation, inconsistence, outright fallacious information, half-truths,
and outdated information . . . virtually useless as scholarship."[21]

Mary Lefkowitz, the Andrew W. Mellon Professor of the Humani-
ties at Wellesley College, writes of the Afrocentric claims:

> Not a single one of these assertions about cultural expropriation
> and scholarly dishonesty can be directly substantiated from
> ancient sources. . . . There is no reason to believe that Aristotle

had much contact with Alexander after he ceased to be his tutor, before 338 B.C. It is simply untrue, to the best of my knowledge, to claim that Greek philosophy was stolen from Egyptian sources. There is no evidence whatsoever for [G.M.] James's claim that Alexander took books from the library at Alexandria—*which was founded long after his death*—to give to Aristotle, or for ben-Jochanan's assertion that Aristotle came to Egypt with him and sacked the temples of ideas and books.*[22] [Emphasis added.]

But evaluating Afrocentrism from a scholarly perspective may miss the point. Temple University's Molefi Kete Asante, for instance, has a view of Africanness that is closer to mysticism than social science. Asante insists that there is a single "African Cultural System" that embraces all African peoples. "We respond to the same rhythms of the universe, the same cosmological sensibilities. . . . Our Africanity is our ultimate reality."[23]

But is there indeed one African culture? As black columnist William Raspberry notes, "While some Africans were establishing a university at Timbuktu, others were engaged in slavery or tribal warfare or cannibalism. Some Africans were monotheists, while others were animists. As with their European counterparts, some were promoting brilliant philosophies, while others were savages."

All of this diversity is, however, subsumed in Asante's counterreality.

Holding Afrocentrism to a scholarly standard misses the point of its practitioners. Increasingly, this history functions less as an academic discipline than as a form of therapy. The goal of therapeutic history is not to *study* the past but to *transform* it—to raise the self-esteem of minority youngsters by creating a version of the past most congenial to their psyches and their self-image. But, as Schlesinger notes, "History is not likely to succeed where psychiatry fails."[24]

Nonetheless, Asa Hilliard's "African-American Baseline Essays," which present much of the Afrocentric Truth as unquestioned

---

*Howard University professor Frank Snowden, whose book *Blacks and Antiquity* documented the actual extent of black influence on classical society, is similarly skeptical of Afrocentric claims. As Dinesh D'Souza notes, "Snowden's study, combining archeological, historical, and literary evidence, shows the extent of African (primarily Ethiopian) influence on classical civilization, from Homer to the early Christians. The influence was real, Snowden argues, and yet quite limited. Egyptian influence was considerable, but Egypt is a Middle Eastern, not an African culture." Dinesh D'Souza, *Illiberal Education* (New York: Free Press, 1991), 115.

dogma, were made part of the curriculum of the Portland, Oregon, public schools in 1987 and have been the inspiration for Afrocentric curricula in at least ten other major cities.

These new curricula are notable both for what they say and for what they leave out. Needless to say, none of these curricula have much to say about the hidden skeletons of the celebrated African civilizations: "the tyrannous authority" exercised by African societies, "the ferocity of their wars, the tribal massacres, the squalid lot of the common people, the captives sold into slavery, the complicity with the Atlantic slave trade, the persistence of slavery in Africa after it was abolished in the West."[25]

Nor are these curricula content with merely enhancing the self-esteem of minorities. In the new alternative reality of Afrocentrism, whites are generally reduced to thieves, interlopers, and oppressors, practitioners of what Professor Leonard Jeffries calls the three *D*s: "domination, destruction, and death."

Afrocentrists see the world through the fixed lens of race—in which pigmentation is the decisive fact of humanity. So it is perhaps understandable that they make little mention of the influence of European writers on such figures as Frederick Douglass (who was inspired by a volume of orations by Edmund Burke, Richard Sheridan, William Pitt, and Charles Fox), or W.E.B. Du Bois, who wrote that "across the color line I move arm in arm with Balzac and Dumas. . . I summon Aristotle and Aurelius and what soul I will, and they come all graciously with no scorn nor condescension." Nor do they give much credit to the views of Ralph Ellison, who read Marx, Freud, T. S. Eliot, Ezra Pound, Gertrude Stein, and Hemingway. Their books, "which seldom, if ever, mentioned Negroes," Ellison wrote, "were to release me from whatever 'segregated' idea I might have had of human possibilities." He concluded: "It requires real poverty of the imagination to think that this can come to a Negro only through the example of other Negroes."

But this impoverished segregationist view is precisely the doctrine often embraced by educationists anxious to celebrate "diversity," "multiculturalism," and cultural sensitivity. Perhaps because of his own history as a supporter of civil rights, Arthur Schlesinger is particularly eloquent in his critique of counter-reality Afrocentric education and its effect on young blacks. Will it really increase the self-esteem of minority youngsters, he asks, who will "grow up and learn that many of the things the Afrocentrists taught them were not true?"[26] And how many will find the counter-reality of racial pride to be a dead end whose only payoff is despair and self-loathing?

> Indeed, it is hard to imagine any form of education more likely than Afrocentrism to have a "terribly damaging effect on the psyche." The best way to keep a people down is to deny them the means of improvement and achievement and cut them off from the opportunities of national life. *If some Kleagle of the Ku Klux Klan wanted to devise an educational curriculum for the specific purpose of handicapping and disabling black Americans, he would not be likely to come up with anything more diabolically effective than Afrocentrism.*[27] [Emphasis added.]

Ironically, the result of the politics and scholarship of paranoia is neither empathy nor solidarity with fellow victims but a retreat into a prickly tribal loyalty that is defended with bitter and uncompromising xenophobic shrillness.

This perhaps explains the genuine nastiness of intervictim politics. When identity is bound up in one's status as a victim, the politics of comparative victimology becomes the decisive battleground— whether the issue is the vicious rape of a young white woman by black teenagers in Central Park, a black-organized boycott of grocery stores owned by Asian American immigrants, attacks on Korean-owned stores in Los Angeles, tensions between blacks and Hispanics, or the burgeoning black anti-Semitism that culminated in shouts of "Heil Hitler" aimed at Hasidic Jews in New York's Crown Heights area.

THE MISOGYNISTIC VICTIM

One of the bitterest fruits of victimist politics has been the grotesque marriage of misogyny and black activism in cities like New York. In the case of the Central Park jogger, a young woman was attacked by a gang of youths who raped her, smashed her head with rocks, bricks, and a twelve-inch pipe, fracturing her skull, and left her for dead. She lost 80 percent of her blood before she was found. But in the context of growing racial tension—the deaths of black youths at the hands of whites in Howard Beach and Bensonhurst, and lingering suspicions about the Brawley case—the jogger's tragedy became embroiled in victimist metaphysics. Callers to black radio stations in New York claimed that it was impossible for the woman to have been raped because there were no signs of trauma on her body. *The New American*, a black weekly, reported "the truth" about the case (referring to the victim by what *The New York Times* called a "sexual epithet") and charged that the woman had really been attacked by her white boyfriend. The activists who had played key roles in the Tawana Brawley case organized protests on behalf of the accused attackers and declared that the real hoax was the story of the white woman's rape. Finally, Tawana Brawley herself made an appearance at the trial, cordially shaking hands with the alleged rapists.[28]

All of this drew a stinging denunciation from black columnist Sheryl McCarthy, who wrote in *Newsday*:

> After the crimes against the jogger were committed there was only denial—by the teens, their parents, and their supporters—who saw racism in the mere fact that the jogger was white and that black teenagers were charged with the crime. . . . Because of all the denial and the frenzy whipped up by the trial, I suspect the teens view themselves as the wronged ones. Though there is a young woman with a scarred face and body . . . these young men see themselves as victims.[29]

Although the outrageous claims of activists like Al Sharpton did not by any means reflect the views of the black community as a whole, there were few black voices raised in protest against the viciousness of the slurs against the victimized woman. And among the white left, apologists went to extraordinary lengths to account for the bizarre claim that the youths had been framed—ultimately blaming that too on white racism. "Such extreme defensiveness," Erika Munk offered in *The Village Voice*, "is only comprehensible as the result of a long history of police bias, combined with a reaction against the white media's treatment of the crime."[30]

WHOSE BURDEN?

A similar pall of silence and apologia fell over the black boycott of Korean-owned grocery stores in New York. Although the boycott began as a result of the alleged mistreatment of a Haitian woman by the owner of *one* store (assault charges were later dropped against the store owner), the wider campaign embraced wider concerns. The success of the Asian stores in the inner city had bred distrust and resentment; their prosperity contrasted provocatively with the general deprivation in their neighborhoods. In Spike Lee's movie *Do The Right Thing*, which fictionally addresses the issue, the subject of Asian success is raised: "I bet you they haven't been off the boat a year before they open up their own place," says the black character Coconut. "They already have got a place in *our* neighborhood—a good business occupying a building that had been boarded for longer than I care to remember." Either the Koreans are geniuses, he offers, or blacks are dumb. "It's got to be because we are black," answers another black. Annoyed, a third character says: "Tired of hearing that old excuse."

As it actually unfolded, the boycott of the Korean stores became a sort of Rorschach test of victimist ideology. No stranger himself to playing the victim card on occasion, Spike Lee rejected victimist explanations of Korean prosperity. The success of the Koreans, he told *The New York Times*, occurred because "they came in as families. That family is very intact. We should use the Koreans as models."[31] But other black activists, including boycott leader Sonny Carson, saw in the Korean successes only another aspect of "The Plan," in which he implicated Jews as well as Asians. "The Jews, when they left, they made sure they turned those stores over to people who would continue the trickery," he told the audience of New York's black-owned WLIB radio. A veteran of racial politics, Carson made no secret of the basis of the anti-Korean boycott. One leaflet he distributed urged blacks not to shop "with people who don't look like us."[32] In the counter-reality of WLIB, callers charged that a raid on one grocery store had found a freezer crammed with "skinned rats and cats, with onions on the other side," while Carson himself charged that "the fish that's fried in Korean stores is fish that's ready to go bad."[33]

Not even tales of skinned rats, however, could distract attention from the nagging questions posed by the failure of black entrepreneurs to match the success of the Korean immigrants in their own communities. Even those who rejected the boycott were quick to provide excuses. In one extraordinary episode, New York Governor Mario Cuomo descended on Asian merchants to lecture them on the special "historical burden borne by blacks" and the legacy of slavery.

Although some of the Asian American merchants had themselves endured attempted genocide (in Cambodia), survived harrowing escapes in leaky boats on rough seas (from Vietnam), overcome life in refugee camps (in Thailand), and had, in some cases, arrived in this country penniless, Cuomo—seemingly impervious to the irony of the situation—instructed them on the unique sufferings of blacks who, he said, required "special efforts" from government. "We are cognizant of the fact that for a long period of time we deprived them not just of their civil rights, we deprived them of their human rights. And so in a kind of weak attempt to in some way compensate for that, we constructed special programs called affirmative action programs."

With a mixture of paternalism and condescension, Cuomo continued: "I don't understand people who resent it. Because they [blacks] are different. Because the Italian Americans were not locked in chains and dragged here from Naples and then tied to machines and made to haul them like beasts of burden. It's a different experience and you have to recognize that."[34]

A *New York Times* account of Cuomo's visit notes that none of the Asian merchants appeared to take offense at Cuomo's lecture. They were presumably too busy running their businesses to argue Cuomo's point that some people were "different."

VICTIM vs VICTIM

A cartoon published after an outbreak of Jewish-black violence in New York reflected the dynamics of the politics of difference. A black man and a Hasidic Jew are shown walking alongside each other.

The Jewish man says: "I am a minority in this neighborhood."

Responds the black man: "I am a minority in this neighborhood. And I am a Victim."

"I am a Victim," echoes the Jewish man, ". . . and because of my religion I am viewed differently."

"Because of my race," answers the black man, "I am viewed differently. . . ." But then he continues: "And you don't know what it's like to be me."

Answers the Jewish man: "You don't know what it's like to be me. . . . So you have nothing in common with me."

"And you have nothing in common with me," responds the black, "which is why I hate you."

"And," the Jew retorts, "I hate you."[35]

In August 1991, a car driven by a Hasidic man killed one black child and seriously injured another in New York's Crown Heights neighborhood. Within hours, a group of black teenagers stabbed a young Hasidic student to death in retaliation. Remarked *The New York Times*: "For both groups, the circumstances surrounding the accident became a metaphor for victimization."[36]

Although they shared the same Brooklyn streets, the same challenges of urban life, and similar barriers to full participation in society, the Jews and blacks found themselves locked into a confrontation of mutual distrust, misunderstanding, and hatred.

Unconscious of the historical tragedy they were reliving, black youths reportedly shouted "Heil Hitler" at Jews, who saw the blacks' anger as a replay of the Holocaust and European pogroms. In turn, blacks complained of the insularity of the Hasids and bitterly attacked what they perceived as the special privileges of their fellow minority. "Do we live in America?" one Crown Heights resident asked plaintively. "This is Lebanon."[37]

Black anti-Semitism can explain only part of the phenomenon. The Lebanonization of urban American life grows not merely out of the hatred between Jews and blacks, but also from the divisions that pit blacks against Koreans; inner-city activists versus women; and blacks against Hispanics.

The tensions between blacks and Hispanics in Washington, D.C., erupted into violence in 1991 after a Hispanic man was shot by a black police officer. The complaints of Hispanics about the black establishment in the nation's capital were eerily reminiscent of black rhetoric about the white power structure—but with the added tension of challenging the black monopoly on permanent victimhood. Black–Hispanic animosity has continued to rise as the numbers, prosperity, and clout of Hispanics have continued to grow. In some American cities, it is the Hispanics, not the blacks, who have become the dominant minority. Inevitably, the two groups' interests clash as redistricting fights, the allocation of social and educational resources, and employment policies pit the demands of blacks against those of Hispanics.

This division poses a critical dilemma for the politics of victimization because it destroys the symmetry of oppressed and oppressor, of victimizer and victim. When the lines were simply drawn, it was easy to equate innocence with entitlements and privileges. Emphasizing "difference" merely sharpened the dichotomy, isolating the oppressed from the history, morals, and customs of the oppressor. The rise of the politics of "otherness" was a direct attack on the ideology of assimilation represented by the belief that America could be a "melting pot." In the service of that vision, various groups had set aside many of their differences and merged their aspirations into a distinctively egalitarian and democratic polity. Whatever their origins or original group loyalties, individuals submitted themselves to common norms and a shared system of justice. The politics of difference, however, revolted against such a melding. Aligned closely with the politics of victimization, groups repudiated the notions of shared history and culture. On college campuses, students resegregated themselves into African, Asian, Hispanic, Jewish, and foreign houses. Each group demanded its own history, literature, and culture, and insisted that its own sufferings endowed it with an ineffable and untranslatable set of claims on the world.

But the multiplication of victims complicated the geometry of victimism. By emphasizing each group's "otherness," the politics of victimization had turned difference into an existential chasm, which cannot be bridged by shared notions of justice or principles of equity. No common language existed for resolving intergroup disputes except the rhetoric of demand and accusation. In a politics based on aggrievement, where the norm is "You've got yours, now I want mine," disputes will turn largely on the question: Who is the greater victim? What began as righteous indignation directed at racist oppression becomes a rage turned against competitors for the honor of most downtrodden.

ANTHEMS OF HATE

At this point it is worthwhile to inquire which is the more deadly: the paralyzing rage of the victim or the smooth ratification and excuse making of the victim's compassionate defenders? The insistence that blacks are "different" because they are indelibly scarred with slavery and are the target of vast, coordinated conspiracies breeds a festering rage that first cuts blacks off from others, and ends by devouring them whole, as "difference" turns inward into self-loathing. But no matter how self-destructive victimism becomes, there are always "helpers" on hand to *explain* and justify.

Perhaps the purest voice of victimism is found in the anthems of hatred produced by rap groups such as N.W.A., whose oeuvre includes such lines as "So what about the bitch that got shot/ Fuck her/ You think I give a damn about a bitch?/I ain't a sucker," or 2 Live Crew, whose lyrics celebrate the brutalization and rape of women, who are described as "whores" and "dogs." Their anthems ooze with contempt for women in general—and black women in particular. Women are ordered to "suck my dick, bitch, and make it puke," while one rap intones: "Evil 'E' was out coolin' with a freak one night/Fucked the bitch with a flashlight/Pulled it out and left the batteries in/So he could get a charge when he begin."

When they are not celebrating the domination and humiliation of women, the lyrics of groups like 2 Live Crew are often an endless recapitulation of pornographic fantasies. What they lack in originality, they make up for in catholicity. In finding 2 Live Crew's lyrics to be obscene, a federal judge described them as "replete with references to female and male genitalia, human sexual excretion, oral-anal contact, fellatio, group sex, specific sexual positions, sado-masochism, the turgid state of the male sexual organ, masturbation, cunnilingus, sexual intercourse, and the sounds of moaning."[38]

The obscenity itself would not, of course, shock any of the cultural cognoscenti, who pride themselves on their unshockability and broad-mindedness on issues of sexuality. But the constant refrain about slapping black "bitches" who won't put out should have been another matter altogether. It wasn't.

In his glossary of political correctness, Lewis Lapham writes: "VICTIMS: Always and forever innocent. Embrace them."[39]

So rather than denouncing as slanders on black culture the ugly vileness that such groups were peddling, columnist Tom Wicker rushed forward to defend 2 Live Crew's work as containing "quintessentially black lyrics."[40]

Eager to place rap in its rightful place in the pantheon of avant-garde culture, Jon Pareles, a music critic for *The New York Times*, opines, "Put simply, rap is an affirmation of self . . . rappers live by their wit—their ability to rhyme, the speed of their articulation—and by their ability to create outsized persona through words alone." Pareles manages to find an assistant professor of anthropology willing to insist, "The skills you need to be a good rapper are the same skills you need to get ahead in mainstream society. . . . Rap is about making something of yourself—it's the American dream."[41]

Most ambitious of all is Harvard's Henry Louis Gates, Jr., a leading guru of multiculturalism. Drawing on all his erudition as an au courant culture critic, Gates insists in an op-ed piece in *The New York Times* that 2 Live Crew was really "engaged in sexual carnivalesque." Far from celebrating vicious and barbaric misogyny, Gates writes that "2 Live Crew is engaged in heavy-handed parody, turning the stereotypes of black and white American culture on their heads.

"For centuries," he writes, "African-Americans have been forced to develop coded ways of communicating to protect them from danger." So their "exuberant use of hyperbole" is merely a legacy of this allegoric style. While he dismisses the "so-called obscenity," not even Gates can pass over "the group's overt sexism." But in a twist that must be described as Orwellian, Gates turns the sheer nastiness of the group's sexual violence into a denial that they are really sexist. In a paragraph that only a tenured professor of English could write, Gates presents this tortured apologia:

> Their sexism is so flagrant, however, that it almost cancels itself out in a hyperbolic war between the sexes. In this, it recalls the inter-sexual jousting in Zora Neale Hurston's novels.

Having slurred Hurston's memory, Gates proceeds to turn the rappers into martyrs of racism. With his own heavy-handedness, Gates warns, "Censorship is to art what lynching is to justice."[42]

While the efforts to censor 2 Live Crew were perhaps misguided, Gates's defense is rank sophistry. No one would dare suggest that an Italian involved in child porn was engaging in "sexual carnivalesque" that grew out of the Italian American immigrant experience. No one has come forward to defend the vile so-called humor of comedian Andrew Dice Clay—who also specializes in attacks on women—as "quintessentially Jewish."

Nor is it plausible to argue that there is anything at all carnivallike about the brutality of these anthems. In a bizarre intersection of art and reality, the young men involved in the "wilding" attack on the Central Park jogger chanted the lyrics to "Wild Thing" after their arrest.

One black woman—a professor at the University of Rochester—wonders whether apologists like Tom Wicker really believe "that his black colleagues sit at their desks harboring secret desires to break into chants and slap black 'bitches' who don't gratify their sexual desires. Does he think that his black female colleagues are pleased at being presented, as they are in 2 Live Crew's lyrics, as subhuman creatures who exist solely to gratify the violent sexual fantasies of men?"

More pointedly, she asks: "Are the black people who do not sanction the sentiments expressed in 2 Live Crew songs inauthentic, not genuinely black?"[43] Other black critics have been even more scathing. *The Village Voice*'s Stanley Crouch calls 2 Live Crew "spiritual cretins," "slime," and "vulgar street-corner-type clowns." Warns Crouch: "We do not have to celebrate the lowest elements in our society. . . . We cannot make a powerful Afro-American culture if we're going to base it on what hustlers and pimps think about the world."[44]

But the apologias for 2 Live Crew's misogyny were not without precedent. In the 1960s, when Eldridge Cleaver romanticized rape as a political act, many liberals accustomed to the unconditional embrace of victimism were either silent or joined in rhapsodizing about ghetto street life. "By romanticizing these irresponsible activities—criminality, sexual 'freedom,' drug use, and general lack of ambition," Joe Klein notes, "whites were lending support to a subtle system of oppression that had existed since slavery times."[45]

This is the irony of victimism, this intersection of condescension, self-loathing, and bigotry. Only the most virulent of rednecks would argue that violence, criminality, drug abuse, and illegitimacy are "quintessentially black"; only a bigot would insist that blacks are "different" and cannot be expected to compete on a level playing field with whites; only a racist would object to demands for literacy among black children. At the extremes, however, racism becomes indistinguishable from the compassionate embrace of victimism. Finally, both—by different routes—arrive at the same point; both deny the essential humanity of the victim. They associate him with his degraded condition and declare it inevitable and immutable.

By changing "victimhood from accident to essence," author Herbert Schlossberg argues, the individual is deprived of his humanity and given instead "the ontological status of victim." The victim is relieved of responsibility, but at the price of being reduced to a creature with no control over his nature or his destiny. "He was born out of circumstance, molded by circumstance, determined by circumstance. That hard taskmaster will never release its hold on him, will always keep him in the thrall of ontological victimhood."[46]

What passes for moral restraint, or a ponderous respect for the diversity of cultural forms, often translates into nihilism as members of "victim" groups are assured by a chorus of caring and articulate voices that they cannot be held to a socially-agreed-upon standard of morality. The burden of this victimist compassion inevitably falls heaviest on those groups who are told that they are more likely to be incarcerated, unemployed, uneducated, addicted to drugs, or die violently solely because of white racism. It is not, however, the culturally privileged who pay the price for raising up cretinous role models as symbols of authenticity and genuine "blackness."

"When aggrievement was proclaimed the central psychic factor of black life," Joe Klein writes in *New York* magazine, "the most aggrieved and alienated—the most amoral, the criminals—became the defenders of 'true' blackness in the media and also in the streets."[47] In Milwaukee, a city alderman has formed a Black Panther militia that he says will begin terrorist attacks on whites if his demands are not met by 1995. His pledge won him coverage on "60 Minutes" and praise from a startling array of black community leaders, including members of the Wisconsin legislature. This terrorist-in-waiting insists: "No black man in America should be held physically or morally responsible for anything that he does in the United States. . . . I can see why a black man cracks at one of those malls and just goes in there and starts killing people. When you've got all these people conspiring against you, man, it's war."[48]

This call for open warfare is grimly ironic. Far more young black men have been murdered in America's cities than in the entire Vietnam War. More than four out of five of the killers are black.

The defense of 2 Live Crew was merely a new verse in a very old song.

SECTION SIX

The Dead Hand
of Victimism

SEVENTEEN

Wrong Questions, Wrong Answers

Social myths can have tragic consequences. Being wrong about the source of society's problems is only the start.

In the mid-1980s, sociologist Eva Etzione-Halevy broke ranks to challenge the most cherished orthodoxies of her colleagues in the social sciences. If the Knowledge Elite—and by this she meant not merely social scientists, but Western intellectuals in general—really understood so much about social change and human nature, she asked, why were they so often wrong? Why was it that despite the explosion in studies, research papers, books, and symposia in recent years, none of this work had led to better policy decisions? And why had it contributed so little to the moral, economic, psychological, or social betterment of society? "On the contrary," she suggested, "although no causality can be shown, it is nevertheless worth noting that the years in which the influence of the social scientists on policy has been growing have also been the years in which policy failures have been rife and in which a variety of formidable social problems have been multiplying."[1]

Her conclusion was that the West's Knowledge Elite were "prophets who have failed," not because their advice had been ignored but rather that when "their ideas have been put to the test of actual practice and the necessary ensuing compromises, they have frequently proved disappointing." Their advice, she wrote, "has itself created problems for society."[2] What struck Etzione-Halevy was the refusal of the elite to recognize the consequences of its failure. Despite being wrong so often, she noted, "intellectuals . . . continue to act as if nothing has happened. They continue to be more adamant than ever in their belief in the fruitfulness of their knowledge, in the soundness of the advice emanating from that knowledge and in the salutary effects of policy emanating from that advice."[3] Because they must continue to justify their grants, privileges, and their right to nag and cajole society, they must never under any circumstances admit their "stunned helplessness" in the face of crises they neither foresaw nor understand. Thus the failure of their predictions, Etzione-Halevy noted, "has frequently been followed by an even firmer conviction of their truthfulness. The failures have been rationalized away, new evidence has been looked for and existing evidence has been reinterpreted."[4] Even so, reality has proven recalcitrant, resisting attempts to mold it into conformity with the elaborate scientific models of the would-be soothsayers.

Among this pantheon of notable failures, the continuing dilemmas posed by race and poverty must be accorded a place of special honor. Integration, civil rights legislation, and affirmative action have not led to racial amity or even parity. Antipoverty programs have not raised up the impoverished, nor have attempts to eliminate inequalities in education snuffed out ignorance. On the contrary, poverty has proven far more intractable than either liberal or conservative savants would have predicted; the failures of inner-city schools have bred resignation and despair; race relations seem poisoned by chronic misunderstanding.

Blessed with the best of intentions, many of the social programs designed to ameliorate the worst evils have had the unintended consequence of creating whole new categories of social pathology. Even so, despite widespread disillusionment with much of the social engineering of the 1960s and 1970s—a disillusionment that seems to cross ideological lines—the focus of debate often continues to turn on the nature of proposed solutions rather than on the original diagnosis itself.

One reason is the dominance of the politics of victimization, which has provided a durable explanation for an extraordinary range of social, economic, and personal problems. This is not, of course, to suggest that there are no genuine victims. There are real injustices; racism remains a reality; life is frequently unfair. But it is increasingly obvious that victimization has become the too plausible, too pat explanation for all that ails us. Tragically, its evocation has the effect of distracting attention from actual causes and from legitimate policy responses to those problems. The science of victimization is the quackery of our times.

But that dismissal trivializes its consequences. A diagnosis that insists that a man ravaged by cancer is really the victim of witchcraft is not merely ignorant, it is deadly as well.

Victimism's power to set the social agenda is based on its ability to be both prescriptive and proscriptive. Victimist ideology determines not only the shape of remedies but sets rigid limits to the sort of questions that can be asked, lest we engage in the primal sin of "blaming the victim." It creates an elaborate protocol of taboos while simultaneously offering a theory whose potency derives from its remarkable ability to *explain*. Once begun, the explanatory power of victimism is endless. Any act can be explained as the fruit of racism, sexism, capitalism, mental disorder, addiction, codependency, or what have you. The victim explanation provides a dramatic key to the inner workings of society, the model into which any experience can be fitted. In that sense, it is a successor to the ideologies described by Karl Popper, which could accommodate any reality and thus could never be proved wrong. But as Popper noted, this seeming strength is also a basic weakness. Only pseudoscience behaves in such a way. Genuine science always subjects itself to rigorous challenges that seek to falsify its premises. True believers find in the world only *confirmation*, never doubt. Having embraced the politics of victimization, social science substituted *faith* for empirical science.

Take, for example, the case of school discipline:

Many urban schools have become free-fire zones where learning has been subordinated to survival and teaching is held hostage to never-ending attempts to maintain a semblance of order. But when two experts on school discipline—Irwin Hyman and John D'Alessandro—listed fourteen causes of student misbehavior, their list was notable for what *it did not say*. They listed the causes as: "(1) inadequate parenting, (2) ineffective teacher training, (3) poor school organization, (4) inadequate administrative leadership, (5) inappropriate curricula, (6) the overuse of suspensions and other punishments, (7) inborn traits of individual students (such as neurological impairments) that may interact with certain environments to cause severe behavioral or learning disorders, (8) poor self-esteem and frustration with learning, (9) overexposure to violence through television and the other mass media, (10) racism, (11) lack of employment opportunities, (12) peer pressures, (13) overcrowding, and (14) specific social and bureaucratic factors that ignore the needs of the young."*[5]

What is most striking about this list is the complete absence of any suggestion that student misbehavior might be the fault of *the student* rather than of society or school officials; not one of the fourteen factors relates to personal responsibility.

Hyman and D'Alessandro's analyses reflect the dominance of therapeutic and victimist thinking. Not surprisingly, so do their solutions, none of which deals with the development of character, self-restraint, or personal responsibility. Instead, the familiar armory of psychoanalysis is wheeled out. The pair's seven proposals include: "(1) providing feedback to students about their behaviors, feelings, and ideas; (2) using diagnostic strategies to better understand students and student/teacher interactions; (3) modifying the classroom climate; (4) applying techniques of behavior modification; (5) using democratic procedures for solving classroom problems; (6) expressing emotions appropriately; and (7) using therapeutic approaches to behavioral problems."[6]

Cutting through the jargon and setting aside the vagueness of the prescriptions (what exactly does it mean to modify a classroom climate?), Hyman and D'Alessandro's analysis regards the misbehaving student as a victim not of his own conduct but of a malignant society. It rejects a moral analysis of the problem as well as sanctions designed to stigmatize bad behavior.

This bent reflects the phenomenon known as the "depersonalization of blame." Education researcher Daniel Duke described the process:

> Finding someone or something to blame for social problems has
> emerged as a full-time occupation for a host of social scientists.
> The recent history of research in the social sciences has
> witnessed the unrelenting depersonalization of blame. No longer
> do scholars hold an individual responsible for his triumphs or
> his transgressions. . . . The blame for school discipline problems

*Hyman was the director of the National Center for the Study of Corporal Punishment and Alternatives in the Schools and a professor of school psychology at Temple University; D'Alessandro was a doctoral student in school psychology.

has been shifted from individual students to other factors. Once upon a time in American education, individual students were apparently held accountable for their behavior in school. The net result of [recent research] has usually been to minimize the responsibility of the individual student for his inappropriate behavior at school. This process is not always in the best interest of the student, the school, or the society, though in the short run it may be politically expedient.[7]

But there is another notable ellipsis in such research. While Hyman and D'Alessandro list the family as among the "causes" of misbehavior, it is not even mentioned among the possible solutions. Blamed for the problem, it is given no role whatsoever in dealing with it.

This is especially curious given the growing recognition of the family as an important social and economic institution. Harvard professors James Q. Wilson and Richard Herrnstein, the authors of perhaps the definitive study on the causes of crime, charge that a subtle bias against the family pervades much of the literature and research of social science—especially those schools of thought that continue to attribute all social breakdowns to social and economic factors. The two scholars write that "contemporary advocates of the supremacy of social factors in causing crime are reluctant to think through the implications of" evidence suggesting a central role for the family in developing social controls.

> We suspect there are at least two reasons for this caution. One is
> that families occupy a privileged position in a free society. . . .
> The other is that the family is the locus and nursery of
> traditional values, and some students of crime may worry that
> any proposal (difficult as it may be to conceive) that might
> strengthen the family for the purpose of reducing crime will at
> the same time strengthen those traditional values of which these
> students are personally somewhat skeptical. To help the family
> is to foster middle-class life and middle-class thought, an
> unhappy prospect for those who think that the evils of our
> society stem from its excessively middle-class nature.[8]

This omission in the study of social behavior is all the more remarkable when recent history is considered.

During the 1970s, when affirmative-action programs began to kick into high gear, economic conditions in the black community began to diverge radically. In earnings, black women (as mentioned earlier) actually topped white women with similar backgrounds; black men with some college education significantly closed the earnings gap with white men. Intact black families continued to rise into the middle class. In 1970, 15.7 percent of black families earned more than thirty-five thousand dollars; adjusted for inflation, their number grew to 21.2 percent by 1986.[9]

But at the other end of the spectrum a social nightmare was unfolding, as more and more young blacks dropped out of school and out of the labor force altogether. One of the decisive developments of the years since the 1960s has been the proliferation of female-headed households. Although in the 1970s William Ryan led a chorus of critics who denied that the breakdown of black families was a central cause of poverty, the years since have provided eloquent refutation of this position. In 1989, the National Research Council, in its comprehensive study of race relations, *A Common Destiny: Blacks and American Society*, declared: "While some female-headed families are middle class just as some two-parent families are poor, *it is not an exaggeration to say that the two most numerically important components of the black class structure have become a lower class dominated by female-headed families and a middle class largely composed of families headed by a husband and wife.*"[10] [Emphasis added.]

The evidence is thus compelling that the roots of inequality may be, at least in part, *behavioral* rather than strictly racial. Sound education, intact families, and a reliable work ethic still provide the clearest path to prosperity. Dropping out of school, illegitimacy, crime, and dependency remain the formulas for poverty. The gap between white and black is being closed even as the gap between blacks who embrace middle-class values and those who do not has deepened into an abyss. According to the National Research Council, intact black families have nearly three times the median income of female-headed black families. But the implications extend far beyond economics. "Although the findings are not definitive," the report concluded, "they strongly suggest that as compared with children of two-parent families, children from one-parent families have lower scores on standardized tests of IQ and educational achievement, lower educational attainment, lower occupational status and income, and higher rates of early marriage, births to unmarried women and marital dissolution."[11]

All this suggests the need to rethink traditional categories of class and race. "The West as a whole," notes poverty expert Lawrence

Mead, "seems destined for a politics of conduct rather than class."[12] If Mead is right, then much of what passes for political and social analysis will turn out to be irrelevant, while faintly archaic notions such as character may return to the vocabulary of sociology and economics.

On the question of poverty, both conservatives and liberals would have to rethink their respective positions: Conservatives might have to modify their view that the ranks of the poor are overflowing with potential entrepreneurs who can be motivated simply by tinkering with economic incentives; liberals would have to discard the security of attributing economic inequities to racism or the lack of opportunity.

Mead argues that the poverty of the present-day underclass differs fundamentally from the poverty of the past because it stems less from "the absence of opportunity than from the inability or reluctance to take advantage of opportunity." This new poverty has proven intractable precisely because of its sufferers' passivity. While conservatives have long argued that welfare creates financial disincentives to work, Mead argues that such disincentives cannot fully account for the failure of such large numbers of people to either get or hold jobs. Nor does inequality of opportunity explain chronic unemployment. Disincentives and inequality explain differences in income levels, but "they usually do not explain the failure of nonworkers to work steadily *at all*."

Traditional progressive political analyses of the problems of unemployment and poverty were based on a willing work force whose demands were based on strength rather than weakness. To address the new culture of dependency—and the politics it has generated—Mead argues, requires addressing a new style of politics that bases its claims not on its strengths but on its weaknesses, and that relies on individual inadequacies and disabilities as its primary asset in securing government support.

The analyses of the past do not apply to modern realities.

A QUESTION OF CONDUCT

Ruling out questions of conduct and ignoring the role of personal values grossly distorts our view of complex social realities. The argument, for example, that middle-class values are the basis of "symbolic racism" or the "authoritarian personality" tends to stigmatize attitudes without, however, enhancing our understanding of the role they may play in society.

For example: To what extent can social tensions be attributed to differing standards of behavior rather than race? Is it possible that the primary and apparently intractable divisions in society are not predominately racial but rather primarily value based? Is resentment against the politics of dependency a sign of racism or a commitment to individualism?

The theoreticians of symbolic racism try to obscure any such distinction simply by redefining individualism and a belief in self-reliance as a form of racism. But this shuts off a critical line of inquiry.

Do white parents who object to sending their children to predominately black schools, for instance, make their decision out of racial prejudice? Or because those schools are often educationally deficient and dangerous?

Despite the claim that value-based decisions are the result of symbolic racism, the distinction between opinion and prejudice is of immense importance. If anti-integration attitudes, for instance, are the result of racism, they can be changed as society's attitudes evolve toward tolerance. But if such attitudes are conduct based, the issue is rather different. Attempts to further discredit middle-class values will probably be met by further escalations of distrust and hostility. More fundamentally, is it in society's interests to wage war against middle-class norms, including individual initiative and the work ethic, under the guise of combating "symbolic racism"?

Evidence suggests that racial tensions decrease sharply when whites and blacks who share similar values live in proximity with one another. Attempts to mix white middle-class children with lower- or under-class black children continue to be met with resistance. But there seems to be far less resistance to residential or educational integration *among groups of similar social class, regardless of race*. People with shared ideas about work, education, and family life seem to mix more easily than those with radically divergent ideas—even if those who share values are of different races and those with differing attitudes share a common ancestry.

No small part of the tragedy of victimist politics is the way that these dilemmas have been obscured or denied by the simple process of extending the definition of victimization. By defining the central dynamic of black-white relations as "racism," the role of personal values and conduct is diminished and often ignored altogether—with grave consequences both for minority groups and for interracial understanding.

EIGHTEEN

A Moratorium
on Blame

What, then, are the prospects for a society that has emphasized rights over responsibilities, refused to hold individuals accountable for their own behavior, and made a national industry out of the manufacture and elaboration of grievance?

There is a shortage of easy answers.

The culture of victimization is deeply entrenched. Powerful groups continue to have a vested economic, social, and political stake in extending the boundaries of the society of victims. And the impulse to blame others seems to have become an integral part of the American personality, almost as a reflexive response to adversity. So dominant is the therapeutic/victimist ethos that its overthrow may require an entirely new vocabulary—or, perhaps, a very old one.

TOWARD A CULTURE
OF CHARACTER

We can start with the notion of "character." At the bottom of every social scheme, every design of economic competitiveness, every blueprint of educational reform, and every plan for self-improvement lies the question of personal conduct. This has not always been evident, especially since the notion of "character" has fallen into obsolescence along with the rest of bourgeois culture. But there are signs that it is making at least a modest comeback.

In 1985, political scientist James Q. Wilson wrote an essay entitled "The Rediscovery of Character: Private Virtue and Public Policy."[1] Over the previous two decades, he noted, there had been a deepening concern for the development of character in the citizenry, and even more important, "a growing awareness that a variety of public problems can only be understood—and perhaps addressed—if they are seen as arising out of defects in character formation."

In welfare policy, it is clear that financial incentives do indeed change behaviors. But social norms and attitudes have also changed. In 1967, less than two-thirds of those eligible for Aid to Families with Dependent Children were actually on the welfare rolls; just three years later, 91 percent had signed up. "In short," Wilson concluded, "the character of a significant number of persons changed."[2]

In public finance, the tradition of moral restraint that had prevented our society's willfully beggaring its children by incurring massive debt has similarly been eroded. The loss of this tradition constitutes a virtual moral revolution.[3] In the law, the proliferation of causes of action has created a society whose leitmotif is the cry "Don't Blame Me!"

Wilson makes his case for character by historical analogy. In his study of the causes and history of crime, conducted with Richard Herrnstein, Wilson noted the importance of social mores in determining whether or not individuals would commit criminal acts.

The decline of crime during the Depression, for example, seems to have been the result of "tightened, rather than loosened, social controls on crime," by the acceleration of "the movement of young males into adult responsibilities."

During the nineteenth century, a similar emphasis on self-control was responsible for dramatic decreases in drinking and crime throughout the latter half of the century. Although Victorian morality is often derided for its philistinism and crabbed morality, the era witnessed an extraordinarily successful effort to contain the negative excesses of rapid urban growth and social change. The emphasis was not on ethnicity, gender, or class—but *conduct*. The early decades of the nineteenth century saw an influx of young men into the cities, where they were often bereft of adult supervision. Free of traditional social restraints, this early youth culture ran riot; the increase in drinking paralleled the new urban youth movement. In 1790, Americans drank only about 2.5 gallons of liquor per capita; in thirty years that number quadrupled. By 1820, Americans were drinking at the prodigious rate of 10 gallons of liquor a year for every man, woman, and child in the country. Violence and disorder, not surprisingly, rose alarmingly.

Society's response was not—as it is often caricatured—to rely merely on repression or external controls, but as Wilson and Herrnstein write, to create "internalized inhibitions, reinforced by social sanctions."[4] The means were primarily religious: revivals, temperance movements, Sunday-school instruction, YMCAs, public education, and the foster-home movement, all of which "had in common a desire to instill 'decision of character,' by which was meant a 'strenuous will' aimed at 'inner control' and 'self-restraint.' "

As a social movement, the emphasis on "character" was unprecedented in its success. By 1829, 40 percent of New York's children between the ages of four and fourteen attended Sunday school; by 1860, almost half of all Protestant males in New York City were members of some sort of religious voluntary organization.[5] For whatever reason, it all seemed to work. Between 1829 and 1850 alcohol consumption fell from 10 gallons per person a year to a more moderate 2.1 gallons.[6] The decline in crime rates was similarly dramatic.

The modern era has taken more or less the opposite tack. "In the nineteenth century," note Wilson and Herrnstein, "scarcely anyone dissented from the view that character formation required people to restrain self-indulgent impulses."[7] But in the therapeutic culture of the twentieth century, self-restraint came to be looked upon as the scourge—if not *the* original sin—of modern life.

By the 1960s, America had embraced the "youth culture," with its celebration of self-assertion and self-expression. During the prolonged period of prosperity following World War II, social controls were weakened, questions of character and responsibility were deemphasized, and social sanctions on criminal behavior were loosened. Rather than being cut short, childhood was prolonged indefinitely. Crime rates soared.

All this reflected a dramatic change in public policy toward human nature. Where the movement of "moral uplift," led by many of the most admired and brilliant young men of the era, had been widely popular in the nineteenth century, the elites of the latter half of the twentieth century have little interest in religion in any form.

An emphasis on character, of course, challenges the dearest notions of victimism and defies many of the fashionable assumptions of modern society. It is certainly at variance with public education's current fascination with "self-esteem" rather than achievement. It challenges the ethos that puts feelings ahead of actual learning, an ethos that has turned out a generation or more of quasi illiterates, unable to write a coherent letter but convinced of their absolute entitlement to fashionable jeans, astronomical salaries, and full self-actualization.

Critics, inevitably, will snipe that the advocacy of character is a simplistic way to approach complex social problems. But the complexity of these problems may be one of the strongest arguments *for* a politics of personal responsibility.

At the end of their monumental study of crime, Wilson and Herrnstein acknowledge all the factors that may contribute to criminal behavior. "We know that crime, like all human behavior, has causes, and that science has made progress—and will make progress—in identifying them," they write. But ultimately, "the very process by which we learn to avoid crime requires that the courts act *as if crime were wholly the result of free choice.*"[8] [Emphasis added.]

The key words here are *as if.* Wilson and Herrnstein do not reject out of hand social, economic, or medical explanations of behavior. Rather, they recognize the "complexity and mystery of human behavior" and argue that the important consequences of social policy may not be the direct effects they have but rather the example they set for society as a whole. By treating people "as if" they are personally responsible, society is "reaffirming the moral order of society and reminding people of what constitutes right conduct, in hopes that this reaffirmation and reminder will help people, especially in families, teach each other about virtue."[9]

This principle extends to the way society allocates economic benefits, the way judges and juries dispose of legal claims, as well as to employment practices and educational policies. In each instance the question that must be asked is: "Do we appear to be rewarding the acceptance or the rejection of personal responsibility?"[10] That seems to be emerging as one of the central cultural and political issues of our time.

CITIZENS, NOT CLIENTS

An increasing array of proposals to link empowerment with responsibility have found their way onto the public agenda. Several states are experimenting with programs that give poor inner-city parents the power to choose their children's schools. Jack Kemp, the Secretary of Housing and Urban Development, has been a vocal advocate of tenant management of public housing units and, further, the sale of those units to their tenants.

The principle behind such programs is relatively simple: Society should treat its members as *citizens* rather than as *clients*. This is not a trivial distinction; there is a vast difference between basing rights upon respect and linking rights to personal inadequacy. There are tentative signs that the difference is being recognized.

In criminal law, the pendulum has swung away from therapeutic rehabilitation and toward punishment as "just deserts." Perhaps most important, some juvenile courts have begun to recognize their role in instilling a sense of the consequences of criminal behavior in young delinquents. This is especially notable given the decades-long aversion to punishment that weakened juvenile justice—a there-are-no-bad-boys policy that turned the system into the nation's longest running bad joke.

Proposals to link welfare payments to responsible conduct have also become popular. In Wisconsin, the governor has proposed a welfare initiative aimed at encouraging parental responsibility. His plan would provide incentives for women on welfare to marry the father of their children. Under current law, women risk the loss of their benefits if they marry. It would also provide both job training and courses on parenting for families on welfare. At the same time, the proposal would cap benefits by no longer providing automatic increases for every additional child. Under its existing Learnfare program, Wisconsin already requires the high school children of welfare mothers—and teen mothers themselves—to attend school regularly in order to continue to receive welfare benefits. New Jersey has already adopted similar proposals. In Connecticut, one reform proposal would deny benefits to any welfare recipients who abused drugs and refused treatment, while a Maryland proposal would require welfare mothers not only to make sure their children were in school, but also to provide them with regular health care and pay the rent on time—or risk a 30 percent cut in their checks. In each case, the proposals marry responsibility with benefits.

One of the most successful reform efforts may involve a private company called "America Works," which provides job training and placement to welfare recipients. The company, according to *The Wall Street Journal*, "aspires to be the Federal Express of the welfare system," by taking over a job the government does poorly and providing better and more efficient service. According to a 1990 report, the company had helped more than a thousand recipients to get off welfare by finding productive jobs. Its modus operandi is the opposite of an entitlement program. Skeptical employers have four months to evaluate prospective workers before hiring them permanently. America Works gets paid (five thousand dollars by New York State) only after the former welfare recipient has been on the job for seven months.[11]

Partly as a result of the spread of AIDS, the notion of sexual responsibility has shaken off its puritanical image and is increasingly urged as an antidote for both disease and illegitimacy. "If we are to reverse the trend toward fatherless families," U.S. Health and Human Services Secretary Louis W. Sullivan wrote in 1992, "we must reinvigorate a 'culture of character' in our nation. . . . We must re-evaluate our cultural values and the messages we send our children about marriage, family, and sexual relations." The barriers to such a cultural shift remain formidable: In a typical year, Sullivan noted, "the three major networks will depict more than 10,000 sexual incidents, 93 percent of them outside of marriage."[12] Still, *any* serious discussion of sexual restraint would have been inconceivable two decades ago. While society is unlikely to return to a pre-Freudian view of sexuality, it is equally unlikely to adhere to the notion that sexual repression is the root of all unhappiness.

Perhaps most radical of all, holding people responsible for their behavior means restoring social stigmas that shrink the zone of acceptable conduct. In the 1960s, removing the disrepute associated with dependency, illegitimacy, and family breakup amounted to what Christopher Jencks called tearing up the moral contract. Censoriousness had once held intact the worn seams of minority communities; their restoration is a precondition for restoring social stability. Recreating the moral contract—with its power to dish out opprobrium—gives back to the poor an essential weapon in the struggle against despair and decline.

Indeed, this may already be happening in the area of homelessness. Many cities initially rushed to provide free, guaranteed shelters for the homeless, only to discover that their largess had unintended consequences. Not only did the offer of free shelter prove to be a magnet for the homeless, but it also provided an excuse for families who might have made a place (however cramped) for poor relatives to toss them out. Overwhelmed by what has come to seem an epidemic of homelessness, big-city mayors including New York's David Dinkins, Philadelphia's Wilson Goode, and Washington, D.C.'s, Sharon Pratt Kelly have called for a fundamental rethinking of their cities' approach to the problem.

In Philadelphia, officials have adopted new regulations that replace the open-door shelter policy with tough requirements stressing self-sufficiency rather than entitlement. To stay in a shelter, residents are required to set aside 60 percent of their income (from whatever source, including welfare) for a general housing fund, pay another 15 percent to the city as rent, and obtain treatment, if warranted, for drug or alcohol problems. Shelter residents must also make sure that their children attend school regularly. Breaking the rules means eviction. In the first two years of the program, about 800 of the approximately 5,600 residents of the shelters were tossed out.[13] After three years of the new regulations, the number of homeless in the shelters has been cut by 50 percent.

An account in *U.S. News & World Report* describes how this new approach changed the life of one shelter resident:

Sharon Johnson, a ninth-grade dropout, was among those saved by the new regulations. The unwed mother was just 17 in 1986, when she started regularly smoking crack with her older sister and mother at a Philadelphia shelter as her infant son played on the floor. Before long, she was using her entire welfare check to buy crack. On a couple of occasions, she even prostituted herself to get a little extra money. But under the new shelter protocols, officials threatened to put her, her sister and mother into the street for failing to pay rent or save money for a security deposit.

Right away, Johnson and her family tried to wiggle around the regulations. In a teary meeting with [shelter official] LaVon Bracy . . . the three women lied, saying they had missed their rent payments only to cover debts for their grandmother's funeral. Bracy consented to give them $20 (which they used to buy more crack). A streetwise administrator, Bracy was stunned by the women's neglect of their children. "The smell was horrible," she says. "The diapers of the children hadn't been changed for four or five days, their little girl's hair hadn't been combed in six weeks. I had to put Pine-Sol in the room afterwards to get rid of the stench—it made *me* feel filthy."

Finally, after the three women missed another rent payment,

Bracy warned them they would be evicted from the shelter. That brought the trio around. With Bracy's help, all three entered drug rehabilitation, and the two sisters spent more than a year in a rigorous on-site rehab program run by Gaudenzia Inc. Sharon now earns $15,000 a year as a bookkeeper at Gaudenzia, rents a subsidized three-bedroom house and has earned her GED. Her mother and sister are living independently and drug-free, too. "I guess," says Sharon, "that the fact I'm even here is a miracle."[14]

Critics might argue that it was unfair to put so much pressure on Sharon Johnson and her family, that it is unreasonable to expect anyone so downtrodden, disadvantaged, and victimized to adhere to such inflexible guidelines of conduct. But Sharon Johnson's story demonstrates the latent power of invoking personal responsibility. Had society shown her more "compassion," it is quite possible that Sharon Johnson would be dead.

REINING IN THE LITIGATORS

An emphasis on personal responsibility should not be limited to the poor and homeless. The same principle should also be applied to the well off—especially to lawyers.

America's obsession with litigation has proven an onerous burden on the nation's enterprise; the proliferation of lawyers and causes of action threatens to strangle the economy while further fraying our already tattered social fabric. A substantial reform of tort liability could begin to roll back the tide of briefs, injunctions, and writs that has flooded the culture of victimization. This might include limiting the attractiveness of questionable suits by capping awards and requiring anyone who brings a frivolous lawsuit to pay the cost of the defense as well as his own bills. It should be harder to sue and harder to win. Litigation should once again become a weapon of *last* rather than *first* resort.

We must also sharply limit the definitions of victimization in the law itself—civil rights legislation and protections of the handicapped included. Civil rights are not necessarily best protected by endlessly extending our definitions of oppression and discovering new classes of victims. The way back to sanity is clear enough: The weight of the law should be brought to bear against individual acts of discrimination rather than used to create blanket group entitlements. So, too, our attention should be directed toward helping the genuinely handicapped rather than expanding the categories of disability. And lawmakers, judges, and juries should remain especially skeptical of any creative attempts to further redefine aberrant conduct as psychological infirmity.

But ultimately, the culture of character cannot be conceived of as a series of programs or proposals at all. It is far beyond the capacity of government—even the most benign and enlightened state that ever existed—to create the moral and social climate a new culture requires. No social policy by itself can recreate a sense of *civitas* in the body politic.

CIVITAS

Daniel Bell defined *civitas* as "the spontaneous willingness to make sacrifices for some public good. . . ."[15] *Civitas* regards individuals as integral parts of the community, sharing its norms and its virtues, bound to it by ties of obligation and mutual respect. It is the antithesis of the culture of hyperindividualism and self-ishness, which denies the self's obligations not only to the community but also to the family and the church. Nothing could be more alien to a society of grievants incessantly searching for someone else to blame for their problems.

Concern for the loss of *civitas* in American society cuts across ideological lines. In 1989, the liberal People for the American Way organization released a survey of young Americans that documented the decline of the concept of civic obligation.

> Young people have learned only half of America's story. Consistent with the priority they place on personal happiness, young people reveal notions of America's unique character that emphasize freedom and license almost to the complete exclusion of service or participation. Although they clearly appreciate the democratic freedoms that, in their view, make theirs the "best country in the world to live in," they fail to perceive a need to reciprocate by exercising the duties and responsibilities of good citizenship.[16]

However troubling, the group's findings are hardly surprising: Young people are unlikely to grow beyond themselves when their parents are embarked upon a search for their own "inner children." But the barriers to the re-creation of a sense of *civitas* are more formidable than simple self-obsession. Wasted by compassion fatigue, Americans have grown increasingly skeptical of and impatient with the demands of caring. Too many Americans feel disconnected from their fellow citizens, and the rush to balkanize society along racial, ethnic, class, and gender lines has merely accelerated divisive forces.

The traditional American ideal sought to meld together disparate races and creeds under a shared commitment to the values of freedom, justice, and equality. In practice, that ideal has never been fully realized, and has often excluded significant portions of the population. Nevertheless, it provides what is perhaps the best hope for a genuinely multicultural society, balancing unity with diversity. In contrast, the politics of difference emphasizes not what we have in common but rather what divides us.

Arthur M. Schlesinger, Jr., is quite right when he says that the debate over multiculturalism and Afrocentrism in the academic curriculum is not primarily a pedagogical fight over reading lists, teaching styles, or even educational goals. "The debate about the curriculum," he observes, "is a debate about what it means to be an American."[17]

CARITAS

Ultimately, societies are not held together simply by geography or mutual economic interests—they must be bound by what Emile Durkheim called the shared sentiments and affective ties that are provided by a common religious faith. Faith is inextricably enmeshed with the ties that bind man to man. The decline of religion in our time is not simply a loss of faith in God or a sign that the sense of the sacred is decaying, Daniel Bell points out, but an indication that "the shared sentiments and affective ties between men have become diffuse and weak. . . . To say, then, that 'God is Dead' is, in effect, to say that the social bonds have snapped and that society is dead."[18]

It is, therefore, too facile to simply call for the restoration of "community." Robert Nisbet has described the dead ends into which the search for community has already led our century. Communities founded on ideology, race, class, gender, or therapeutic subspecialty have generally proven unsatisfactory when they have not become actual nightmares.

They are merely shadows of the genuine community of free individuals joined in a *moral* society shaped by transcendent values—values that provide the glue that modern society so obviously lacks. Listing the "three things that last," Saint Paul enumerated "faith, hope, and *caritas*; and the greatest of these is *caritas*."[19] The word is usually translated as "love," occasionally as "charity." But the word also originally connoted respect and esteem; *caritas* was not a self-indulgent love, but a sober and respectful affection.

Caritas should not be confused with the politicized and self-involved posturing that uses "compassion" as a form of self-therapy. Nor does it have anything in common with the servile deference of browbeaten guilt. Because it is concerned with others rather than the self, *caritas* does not aim at self-realization, amour propre, the glow of moral superiority, or the pleasure of striking the correct moral pose. It is thus radically different from the various brands of "sensitivity" that infantilize the objects of their concern.

The politics of victimization demands that we judge policies on the basis of the benign intentions and "conspicuous benevolence" of their proponents. But *caritas* does not confuse sentiment with consequences; rather, it insists that programs be judged on their results—on whether they improve the lives of people rather than on whether they enhance the self-esteem of their authors.

The best model for *caritas* is the functioning family, which blends instruction, affection, and reproof. Just as the family is the crucible of character, it is also the indispensable institution for transmitting values. Only in the family do we see that freedom and responsibility are not necessarily exclusive or contradictory. Society can offer support and assistance to the family in its mission; it can never take its place.

EXAMPLES OF VIRTUE

How then does society go about creating a culture of character? It is perhaps the oldest question in the Western tradition. Aristotle's answer was simple: Men do not become virtuous simply by precept, but by "nature, habit, rational principle." "We become just," he wrote, "by the practice of just actions, self-controlled by exercising self-control."

Put simply, character is formed by placing examples of virtue in front of young people. Ironically, the recent resurgence of interest in teaching values and ethics has too often ignored this basic principle. Reflecting on the modern world's replacement of the notion of personal sin with the idea of collective guilt, Christina Hoff Sommers notes that many educational programs purporting to deal with moral issues concern themselves almost exclusively with social policy, "with little or no attention being paid to private morality."[20]

Too often, Sommers notes, "students taking college ethics are debating abortion, euthanasia, capital punishment, DNA research, and the ethics of transplant surgery while they learn almost nothing about private decency, honesty, personal responsibility, or honor. Topics such as hypocrisy, self-deception, cruelty or selfishness rarely come up."

Despite this apparent allergy to questions of personal virtue, Sommers notes, "The best moral teaching inspires students by making them keenly aware that their own character is at stake."*[21]

Sommers recognizes that the reestablishment of a moral community requires the reaffirmation of a moral vocabulary declaring that it is wrong to be cruel, to steal, to lie, to abuse children, to father children you do not support; that it is morally objectionable to gamble (or eat, or drink, or snort) away a family's resources; that it is immoral to refuse to take responsibilities for one's obligations; that if you commit these offenses, there is no one to blame but yourself. Ultimately, this approach restores dignity along with responsibility—something that young people can instinctively recognize.

*She offers three recommendations for moral education that are notable for their simplicity and directness:

(1) Schools should have behavior codes that emphasize civility, kindness, and honesty.
(2) Teachers should not be accused of brainwashing children when they insist on basic civility, decency, honesty and fairness.
(3) Children should be told stories that reinforce goodness. In high school and college, students should be reading, studying and discussing the moral classics.

Christina Hoff Sommers, "Teaching the Virtues," *Imprimis* 20, no. 11 (November 1991).

Perhaps the most important moral battle will be against the impulse to reduce human choices to drives, instincts, and newly hatched maladies. "Reductionism," writes Viktor E. Frankl, "is the nihilism of today." While previous brands of nihilism had taught "nothing-ness," Frankl writes, "reductionism now is preaching nothing-but-ness"—that we are nothing but the product of our upbringing, nothing but the victim of our circumstances.

The antidote, fortunately, is easily found. It is the reassertion of the basic principles of humanity. "A human being," Frankl reminds us, "is not one thing among other things. Things determine each other. Man, however, determines himself. Rather, he decides whether or not he lets himself be determined, be it by drives and instincts that push him, or the reasons and meanings that pull him."[22] Ultimately, he says, quoting humanist Magda Arnold, "All choices are caused but they are caused by the chooser."[23]

A MORATORIUM ON BLAME

Recognizing our own responsibility and the need to stop blaming others is the first step toward dismantling the culture of victimization. This does not mean suspending the search for justice, but it does mean we should strive for a moratorium on the politics of blame.

A recent conference on urban poverty highlighted the paralysis to which victimism leads. Representatives of local business blamed the schools for the quality of employees; the schools blamed parents; parents blamed the schools; both blamed institutionalized racism; social workers blamed the businessmen and the culture of poverty; clergymen blamed MTV. They agreed on only one thing. *They could not be expected to do anything to improve the lives of their neighbors, unless the others first fixed their own problems.* One official confessed that in good conscience he could no longer urge young people in his neighborhood to work hard and stay in school. Because they lived in a climate of "hopelessness," he argued, it was cruel and deceptive to ask them to try to improve themselves.

It seemed never to have occurred to him that such attitudes had become self-fulfilling prophecies. Blame has become the all-purpose excuse to do nothing.

It is time to drop the crutch. While no one person or group has the ability to solve social problems by themselves, they *do* have the capacity to enact remedies. Parents cannot change American education overnight, but they can improve the environment in which their children learn at home. Schools cannot change the home environment of their students, but they can raise the standards of their instruction. Neighborhoods cannot cure the social ills of poverty and joblessness, but they can clean up their streets and they can make them safer. Counselors cannot abolish joblessness or race discrimination, but they can urge youngsters to stay in school, acquire valuable skills, and develop a work ethic that employers will find attractive. These are not solutions. But they *are* remedies, and they represent a powerful alternative to the endless search for others to blame.*

A moratorium on blame is not Panglossian; it does not deny the complexity of society's problems. But it does question how *useful* it is to focus our efforts on self-exculpation and victimist posturing. And it suggests that we can do more if we focus on our own responsibility and refuse to be overwhelmed by notions of oppression and victimization.

COMMON SENSE

It is always a mistake to underestimate the reservoirs of good sense that have survived the various attacks of political, cultural, and therapeutic elites. Simple native good sense has already experienced a modest comeback on college campuses, where the more lugubrious and heavy-handed aspects of political correctness have foundered on their own absurdity.

Common sense can certainly go a long way toward making distinctions between a bungled pass and an act of rape, between greed and "compulsive shopping syndrome," between victims of racial discrimination and victims of "motorism" or "sizeism," between the genuinely handicapped and the "chronically late," and between bad luck and acts of social victimization.

In short, Americans need to *lighten up*.

The politicized culture of victimization often confuses difference with inequity and oppression, while common sense reminds us that

---

*This distinction between "solutions" and "remedies" is Irving Kristol's, and I am indebted to him for the concept.

difference is often, well, just being different. Most of us can discern between making a mistake and being victimized; between excelling and oppressing someone. All of us experience unfairness and injustice, but that does not mean we need to turn them into all-purpose alibis.

Most important, our common sense, and the human tradition it reflects, reminds us that we are all fallible, all beset with human foibles and limitations. Any movement that fails to take those into account, or that overlays our frailties and our humanity with ideology, misunderstands what our lives are all about—and diminishes us as human beings. Ultimately, common sense is the stumbling block that victimism may not be able to overcome. At some level of our being, we all know that something is required of us, however much we may try to shake it off. Instinctively and rationally, we know our responsibilities; we know that we are not sick when we are merely weak; we know that others are not to blame when we have erred; we know that the world does not exist to make us happy.

At the end of Saul Bellow's novel *Mr. Sammler's Planet*, Arthur Sammler, a survivor of the Nazi concentration camps and an eternal witness to the follies of his fellow man, sums up the life of a dead friend by declaring that, in the end, "he did meet the terms of his contract. The terms which, in his inmost heart, each man knows. As I know mine. As all know. For that is the truth of it—that we all know, God, that we know, we know, we know."[24]

NOTES

PROLOGUE

1. *Rezza v. United States Department of Justice et al.*, No. 87-6732, 12 May 1988, U.S. District Court, Eastern District of Pennsylvania.

2. *School District of Philadelphia v. Friedman*, No. 2073 C.D., 7 April 1986, Pennsylvania Commonwealth Court.

3. Jesse Birnbaum, "Crybabies: Eternal Victims," *Time*, August 12, 1991.

4. Mike Royko, "Wisconsin Puzzle Solved in a Flash," *Chicago Tribune*, 7 April 1988.

5. Craig W. Allin, "Drivers Intolerant of Bicyclists Are the Bigots of the Highway," *Chicago Tribune*, 2 September 1991.

6. Daniel Farber, "Sexism Rides a Bicycle Built for Two" (letter to the editor), *New York Times*, 2 October 1991.

7. Naomi Wolf, *The Beauty Myth* (New York: William Morrow, 1991), 16.

8. Ibid., 26.

9. Leslie Carbone, "Re-education in the Name of Tolerance," *Campus Report*, October 1990.

10. "Overdo the Right Thing?" *Harper's*, September 1990.

11. Walter Goodman, "Decreasing Our Word Power: The New Newspeak," *New York Times Book Review*, 27 January 1991.

12. "Fact Sheet on Bias-Free Communication," Division of Women's Program/ Department of Human Relations, Michigan State University.

13. Mike Royko, "A Discrimination Charge Hits Bottom," *Chicago Tribune*, 22 May 1991.

14. "Only in America (Cont'd.)," *Fortune*, 5 November 1990.

15. "Fat Prejudice," transcript, "The Oprah Winfrey Show," 28 August 1990.

16. Ibid.

17. "Fat Group Faults Shows," *Milwaukee Journal*, 23 September 1990.

18. Susie Orbach, *Fat Is a Feminist Issue* (New York: Berkeley Books, 1979), 5–6.

19. Daniel Goleman, "Reining In a Compulsion to Spend," *New York Times*, 17 July 1991.

20. Melinda Blair, "Recovery Fever," *New York*, 9 September 1991.

21. Jon Pareles, "9 Hours Worth of Rock and Alienated Rage," *New York Times*, 13 August 1991.

A SOCIETY OF VICTIMS

1. David Lehmann, *Signs of the Times* (New York: Poseidon Press, 1991), 103.

2. Just kidding. Actually, these are topics suggested by *Time* in "Running Off at the Mouth," 14 October 1991.

3. Barbara Amiel, "The Noise of Women's Turmoil," *McLean's*, 28 October 1991.

4. Lawrence M. Mead, "The New Politics of the New Poverty," *The Public Interest*, no. 103, Spring 1991.

5. Cited in Paul Johnson, "Menacing Manipulators," *Insight*, 23 September 1991.

6. Henry Allen, "Give Us This Day Our Daily Dread," *Washington Post National Weekly Edition*, 17–23 December 1990.

7. John Taylor, "Don't Blame Me!" *New York*, 3 June 1991; Lance Morrow and Jesse Birnbaum, "Busybodies & Crybabies," *Time*, 12 August 1991; Pete Hamill, "A Confederacy of Complainers," *Esquire*, July 1991; David Rieff, "Victims All," *Harper's*, September 1991.

8. David Allen Larson, "Mental Impairments and the Rehabilitation Act of 1973," *Louisiana Law Review* 48 (1988).

9. Martin E. P. Seligman, "Boomer Blues," *Psychology Today*, October 1988.

10. Stanton Peele, *The Diseasing of America* (Lexington, Mass.: Lexington Books, 1989), 25.

11. Ibid., 139–40.

12. Dr. Stan J. Katz and Aimee Liu, *The Codependency Conspiracy* (New York: Warner Books, 1991), 3.

13. David Margolick, "Address by Quayle on Justice Proposals Irks Bar Association," *New York Times*, 12 August 1991.

14. "From Here to Intolerance," *The Economist*, 20 July 1991.

15. Joseph Amato, *Victims and Values* (New York: Praeger Publishers, 1990), xxii.

16. James Coleman, "Self-Suppression of Academic Freedom" (Address to the National Association of Scholars, New York, 19 June 1990.)

17. Frederick Lynch, "Tales from an Oppressed Class," *Wall Street Journal*, 11 November 1991.

18. See Allan Bloom, *Giants and Dwarfs* (New York: Simon & Schuster, 1990), 196.

19. Robert Grudin, *The Grace of Great Things* (New York: Ticknor & Fields, 1990), 87.

20. Saul Bellow, *Mr. Sammler's Planet* (New York: Penguin Books, 1972), 33–34.

21. Seligman, "Boomer Blues."

22. Bernie Zilbergeld, *The Shrinking of America: Myths of Psychological Change* (Boston: Little, Brown and Company, 1983), 83.

23. Shelby Steele, *The Content of Our Character* (New York: St. Martin's Press, 1990), 14.

THE PURSUIT OF HAPPINESS

1. "Nobody Is Mad with Nobody," *Life*, 4 July 1955.

2. Landon Y. Jones, *Great Expectations: America and the Baby Boom Generation* (New York: Ballantine Books, 1980), 51.

3. Jeffrey Hart, *When the Going Was Good!: American Life in the Fifties* (New York: Crown Publishers, 1982), 27.

4. Quoted in Jones, *Great Expectations*, 53.

5. Zilbergeld, *The Shrinking of America*, 38.

6. C. Wright Mills, *White Collar: The American Middle Classes* (New York: Oxford University Press, 1951), xvi.

7. Robert Nisbet, *The Quest for Community: A Study in the Ethics and Order of Freedom* (San Francisco: Institute for Contemporary Studies, 1990), 6.

8. Ibid., 10.

9. Ibid.

10. Ibid., 9.

11. Alexis de Tocqueville, *Democracy in America*, Vol. 2, 105–6.

12. Ibid., 144.

THE THERAPEUTIC CULTURE

1. Loren Feldman, "Strikeouts and Psych-outs," *New York Times Magazine*, 7 July 1991.

2. James Deese, *American Freedom and the Social Sciences* (New York: Columbia University Press, 1985), 31.

3. Cited in Zilbergeld, *The Shrinking of America*, 33.

4. George Beard, *American Nervousness: Its Causes and Consequences* (New York: G. P. Putnam's Sons, 1881). See also Tom Lutz, *American Nervousness 1903* (Ithaca, N.Y.: Cornell University Press, 1991), 4*ff.*

5. Thomas Szasz, *The Myth of Psychotherapy* (Syracuse, N.Y.: Syracuse University Press, 1988), 9.

6. Zilbergeld, *The Shrinking of America*, 32.

7. Martin Gross, *The Psychological Society* (New York: Random House, 1978), 6–7.

8. Brigitte Berger and Peter Berger, *The War over the Family: Capturing the Middle Ground* (New York: Anchor Books, 1984), 117.

9. Ibid. See also 110–11.

10. David Riesman, *The Lonely Crowd* (New Haven: Yale University Press, 1961), 18, 25.

11. Ibid., 137–38.

12. Ibid., 19.

13. Ibid., 24.

14. Ibid., 25.

15. Zilbergeld, *The Shrinking of America*, 195–96.

16. Ibid., 89.

17. Cited in Gross, *The Psychological Society*, 5.

18. Cited in Zilbergeld, *The Shrinking of America*, 17.

19. Gross, *The Psychological Society*, 6.

20. Zilbergeld, *The Shrinking of America*, 18.

21. Ibid., 19.

22. Ibid.

23. Ibid., 201.

24. See Szasz, *The Myth of Psychotherapy*, 196–203. See also Zilbergeld, *The Shrinking of America*, 110.

25. Szasz, *The Myth of Psychotherapy*, xv–xvi.

26. Seligman, "Boomer Blues."

27. Cited in Zilbergeld, *The Shrinking of America*, 85.

28. Wayne W. Dyer, *Your Erroneous Zones* (New York: Funk & Wagnalls, 1976).

29. Alasdair McIntyre, *After Virtue* (Notre Dame, Ind.: University of Notre Dame Press, 1984), 149.

30. Max Scheler, *Ressentiment*, ed. Lewis Coser and trans. William Holdheim (Glencoe, Ill.: Free Press, 1961), 52. For an excellent discussion of *ressentiment*, see Herbert Schlossberg, *Idols for Destruction* (Nashville: Thomas Nelson, 1983), 51–61*ff*.

31. Quoted in Jane Ciabattari, "Will the '90s Be the Age of Envy?" *Psychology Today*, December 1989.

32. Garth Wood, *The Myth of Neurosis* (New York: Harper & Row, 1986), 15.

33. Zilbergeld, *The Shrinking of America*, 22.

34. Berger and Berger, *The War over the Family*, 12, 122.

35. Riesman, *The Lonely Crowd*, 49.

36. See Szasz, *The Myth of Psychotherapy*, 25*ff*.

37. Franz Kafka, *Wedding Preparations in the Country, and Other Posthumous Prose Writings*, trans. E. Kaiser and E. Wilkins (London: Secker and Warburg, 1954), 330.

38. Philip Rieff, *The Triumph of the Therapeutic: The Uses of Faith After Freud* (Chicago: University of Chicago Press, 1987), x, xii.

39. Ibid., 3–4.

40. Ibid., 15.

41. Christopher Lasch, "The Illusion of Disillusionment," *Harper's*, July 1991, 22.

42. W. Haller, *The Rise of Puritanism* (Philadelphia: University of Pennsylvania Press, 1976), 153.

43. Berger and Berger, *The War over the Family*, 112.

44. Daniel Bell, *The Cultural Contradictions of Capitalism* (New York: Basic Books, 1976), 22.

45. Irving Howe, *The Decline of the New* (New York: Harcourt, Brace & World, 1970), 5.

46. Nisbet, *The Quest for Community*, 44–45.

47. Peter Laslett, *The World We Have Lost: England Before the Industrial Age*, 2d ed. (New York: Scribner's, 1971), 22.

48. Rieff, *The Triumph of the Therapeutic*, 13.

49. Szasz, *The Myth of Psychotherapy*, 140.

50. John T. McNeill, *A History of the Cure of Souls* (New York: Harper & Row, 1951), 320.

51 Szasz, *The Myth of Psychotherapy*, 28.

52. Cited in Szasz, *The Myth of Psychotherapy*, 112.

53. Berger and Berger, *The War over the Family*, 121.

PSYCHOLOGICALLY CORRECT

1. T. W. Adorno et al., *The Authoritarian Personality* (New York: Harper & Brothers, 1950).

2. Szasz, *The Myth of Psychotherapy*, xiii.

3. Adorno et al., *The Authoritarian Personality*, 229.

4. Ibid., 231.

5. Ibid., 249.

6. Ibid., 235.

7. Ibid., 255.

8. Ibid.

9. Ibid., 233.

10. Ibid., 235.

11. Ibid., 256.

12. Ibid., 254.

13. Ibid., 781.

14. Ibid., 783.

15. Ibid.

16. Ibid.

17. Christopher Lasch, *The True and Only Heaven* (New York: W. W. Norton & Co., 1991), 452.

18. Adorno et al., *The Authoritarian Personality*, 975.

19. Lasch, *The True and Only Heaven*, 451.

20. Ibid., 453.

21. Ibid., 453–54.

22. Kenneth Keniston, *Youth and Dissent* (New York: Harcourt, Brace, Jovanovich, 1971), 7–9.

23. Ibid., 10.

24. Richard Weaver, *Ideas Have Consequences* (Chicago: University of Chicago Press, 1984), 81.

"I HAVE A DREAM . . ."

1. Lionel Trilling, *Beyond Culture* (New York: Viking, 1965), xii–xiii.

2. Ibid., 4.

3. Bell, *The Cultural Contradictions of Capitalism*, 41.

4. Ibid.

5. Trilling, *Beyond Culture*, 26.

6. Daniel Bell, *The End of Ideology* (Glencoe, Ill.: Free Press, 1960), 373.

7. Norman Podhoretz, *Breaking Ranks* (New York: Harper & Row, 1979), 81.

8. Rieff, Philip, *The Triumph of the Therapeutic*, 63n.

9. David J. Garrow, *Bearing the Cross* (New York: Vintage Books, 1988), 105.

10. Lasch, *The True and Only Heaven*, 399.

11. Garrow, *Bearing the Cross*, 43.

12. Reinhold Niebuhr, *Moral Man and Immoral Society* (New York: Scribner, 1960), 252.

13. Ibid., 249. Niebuhr is here quoting from E. A. Ross.

14. Ibid., 246.

15. Ibid., 248.

16. Ibid., 249.

17. Ibid., 252.

18. Ibid., 255.

19. Garrow, *Bearing the Cross*, 71.

20. Allen J. Matusow, *The Unraveling of America* (New York: Harper & Row, 1984), 185.

21. Lasch, *The True and Only Heaven*, 400.

22. Matusow, *The Unraveling of America*, 375.

THE RISE OF THE VICTIM

1. Amato, *Victims and Values*, 105.

2. Bloom, *Giants and Dwarfs*, 211.

3. Ibid., 196.

4. Ibid.

5. Amato, *Victims and Values*, 113.

6. Ibid., 106–7.

7. Julius Lester, "Whatever Happened to the Civil Rights Movement?" (Paper delivered to the "Second Thoughts About Race in America" conference, Washington, D.C., May 3, 1990.)

8. Quoted in Stanley Crouch, *Notes of a Hanging Judge* (New York: Oxford University Press, 1990), 202.

9. Ibid.

10. Albert Memmi, *Dominated Man* (Boston: Beacon Press, 1968), 19.

11. Ibid., 74.

12. Ibid., 16.

13. Ibid., 196, 198.

14. Ibid., 23.

15. Ibid., 11.

16. Ibid., 13.

17. Ibid., 15.

18. Ibid., 24.

19. Frantz Fanon, *The Wretched of the Earth* (New York: Grove Press, 1968), 37.

20. Ibid., 38.

21. Ibid., 43.

22. Ibid., 47.

23. Ibid., 44.

24. Memmi, *Dominated Man*, 10.

25. Schlossberg, *Idols for Destruction*, 69.

THE REVOLT OF THE KIDS

1. Abraham H. Maslow, "A Theory of Metamotivation," *Journal of Humanistic Psychology* (Fall 1967).

2. Kenneth Keniston, "The Sources of Student Dissent," *The Journal of Social Issues* 23 (1967): 108–37.

3. Bell, *The Cultural Contradictions of Capitalism*, 41.

4. Charles Reich, *The Greening of America* (New York: Bantam Books, 1971), 13.

5. Ibid., 14.

6. Ibid., 15.

7. Randall Jarrell, *Pictures from an Institution* (New York: Alfred A. Knopf, 1954), 104.

8. John Updike, *Self-Consciousness* (New York: Ballantine Books, 1989), 125.

9. Keniston, "The Sources of Student Dissent."

10. Bell, *The Cultural Contradictions of Capitalism*, 45.

11. Ibid.

12. Ibid., 51.

13. James Q. Wilson, "Liberalism versus Liberal Education," *Commentary*, June 1972.

14. Sidney Hook, *Academic Freedom and Academic Anarchy* (New York: Cowles Publications, 1970), 177.

15. Wilson, "Liberalism versus Liberal Education."

16. Ibid.

VICTIM CHIC, VICTIM THERAPY

1. Tom Wolfe, *Radical Chic & Mau-Mauing the Flak Catchers* (New York: Farrar, Straus and Giroux, 1970), 3–31.

2. Nat Hentoff, "Them and Us: Are Peace Protests Self-Therapy?" *Evergreen Review* 2, no. 48.

3. Ronald Radosh, "From Civil Rights to Black Power: The Breakup of the Civil Rights Coalition" (Paper delivered to the "Second Thoughts About Race in America" conference, Washington, D.C., May 3, 1990.)

4. Ibid.

5. See cover of Reich, *The Greening of America*.

6. Ibid., 255.

7. Ibid., 280.

8. Ibid., 241.

9. Ibid., 148.

10. Ibid., 242–43.

11. Ibid., 247.

12. Ibid., 276.

BLAMING THE VICTIM

1. Richard John Neuhaus, "All Too Human," *National Review*, 2 December 1991.

2 Daniel Moynihan, *The Negro Family: The Case for National Action* (Washington, D.C.: U.S. Department of Labor, U.S. Government Printing Office, 1965).

3. Statistics from *To Establish Justice, to Insure Domestic Tranquility, The Final Report*

of the National Commission on the Causes and Prevention of Violence (New York: Praeger Publishers, 1970).

4. James Q. Wilson and Richard Herrnstein, *Crime and Human Nature* (New York: Simon & Schuster, 1985), 438.

5. Moynihan, *The Negro Family*, 5.

6. Matusow, *The Unraveling of America*, 197.

7. See James Farmer, "The Controversial Moynihan Report"; Frank Riessman, "In Defense of the Negro Family;" and William Ryan, "Savage Discovery: The Moynihan Report"; all reprinted in Lee Rainwater and William Yancey, editors, *The Moynihan Report and the Politics of Controversy* (Cambridge: MIT Press, 1967).

8. William Ryan, *Blaming the Victim* (New York: Vintage Books, 1971).

9. Ibid., 7.

10. Ibid., 27.

11. Ibid., 11.

12. Ibid., 25.

13. Ibid., 29.

14. Ibid., 120.

15. Ibid., 122.

16. Ibid., 34.

17. Ibid., 37.

18. Ibid., 42.

19. James Coleman, *Equality of Educational Opportunity* (Washington, D.C.: U.S. Office of Education, 1966), 192, 320.

20. Ryan, *Blaming the Victim*, 53.

21. Ibid., 61.

22. Ibid., 114.

23. Ibid., 72.

24. Ibid., 78.

25. Ibid., 77.

26. Ibid., 196–97.

27. Ibid., 192–218*ff.*

28. Ibid., 226.

29. Ibid., 239.

30. Ibid., 228.

31. Ibid., 237.

32. Ibid., 242.

33. *Report of the National Advisory Commission on Civil Disorders* (New York: Bantam Books, 1968).

34. William Ryan, *Blaming the Victim*, revised edition (New York: Vintage Books, 1976), xiii.

35. Midge Decter, "Looting and Racism," *Commentary*, September 1977.

36. Ryan, *Blaming the Victim* (first edition), 285.

37. Jim Sleeper, *The Closest of Strangers* (New York: W. W. Norton & Company, 1990), 33.

38. Kate Millett, "Sexual Politics: A Manifesto for Revolution," in *Notes from the Second Year* (New York: Radical Feminism, 1970), 111–12.

39. Berger and Berger, *The War over the Family*, 18.

40. Ibid., 63.

41. Charles Sykes, "Fuller's Chance," *WI: Wisconsin Interest* 1, no. 1 (Winter/Spring 1992).

42. Quoted in Chester E. Finn, *We Must Take Charge* (New York: Free Press, 1991), 108.

43. Ibid., 106.

44. Ibid., 109–10.

45. Ibid., 109.

46. Ibid., 32.

47. Ibid., 33.

48. Sleeper, *The Closest of Strangers*, 83.

49. Douglas Glasgow, *The Black Underclass* (New York: Vintage Books, 1981), 25.

50. Nathan Glazer, *The Limits of Social Policy* (Cambridge, Mass.: Harvard University Press, 1988), 15.

51. Christopher Jencks, "Deadly Neighborhoods," *The New Republic*, 13 June 1988.

52. Glazer, *The Limits of Social Policy*, 4–5.

53. Robert Nisbet, *The Present Age* (New York: Harper & Row, 1988), 122.

54. Steele, *The Content of Our Character*, 118.

THE RIGHTS REVOLUTION: *E PLURIBUS VICTIM*

1. Berger and Berger, *The War over the Family*, 25.

2. Shulamith Firestone, *The Dialectic of Sex* (New York: William Morrow & Co., 1970), 1.

3. Quoted in Sleeper, *The Closest of Strangers*, 165.

4. Ibid., 159–60.

5. Tom Bethell, "Anti-Discrimination Run Amuck," *Newsweek*, 17 January 1977.

6. Mary Ann Glendon, *Rights Talk* (New York: Free Press, 1991), 14.

7. Ibid., 5.

8. Ibid., 16.

9. Lawrence M. Friedman, *Total Justice* (New York: Russell Sage Foundation, 1985), 71.

10. Ibid., 51.

11. Ibid., 8.

12. John Taylor, "Don't Blame Me!" *New York*, 3 June 1991.

13. Mike Royko, "Everybody's a Victim These Days," *Milwaukee Journal*, 8 June 1990.

14. Walter Olson, *The Litigation Explosion* (New York: Dutton, 1991), 9.

15. Taylor, "Don't Blame Me!"

16. "Can't Win for Losing," *Insight*, 20 May 1991.

17. Editorial Research Report, *The Rights Revolution* (Washington, D.C.: Congressional Quarterly, 1978), 4.

18. Olson, *The Litigation Explosion*, 170.

19. Ibid., 152–53.

20. "Trouble Brewing," *BNA's Employee Relations Weekly*, 26 November 1990.

21. "Only in America (Cont'd.)," *Fortune*, 9 September 1991.

22. Larson, "Mental Impairments."

23. Ibid.

24. Ibid.

25. This and subsequent accounts based upon Larson, "Mental Impairments."

26. "Only in America (Cont'd.)," *Fortune*, 12 March 1990.

27. *School District of Philadelphia v. Friedman*, No. 2073, C.D. 7 April 1986, Pennsylvania Commonwealth Court.

28. *Lucas v. Saint Mary's Medical Center*, Ruling on Motion to Dismiss and Order, ERD Case Number 9051034, State of Wisconsin Department of Industry, Labor and Human Relations, Equal Rights Division, 12 July 1991.

29. *Chambers v. Illinois Fair Employment Practices Commission and Ford Motor Company*, Illinois Appellate Court, First District, First Division, No. 80-594, 26 May 1981.

30. *Blackwell v. Department of Treasury*, U.S. District Court, District of Columbia, No. 85-2097, 27 May 1986.

31. *Panzavides v. Virginia Board of Education*, CA 4, No. 91-2313, 10/10/91; see also

"Court Revives Rehabilitation Act Claim," *BNA's Employee Relations Weekly*, 4 November 1991.

32. *Adams v. GSA*, U.S. District Court, District of Columbia, No. 87-3449, 15 June 1989.

33. *Fields v. Lyng*, U.S. District Court, District of Maryland, No. JFM-88-1772, 29 September 1988.

34. P. J. O'Rourke, *A Parliament of Whores* (New York: Atlantic Monthly Press, 1991), 72.

35. Interview with author, 2 September 1991.

ARE WE ALL SICK?

1. "Notes & Asides," *National Review*, 15 April 1991.

2. Herbert Fingarette, "Alcoholism: The Mythical Disease," *The Public Interest*, no. 91 (Spring 1988).

3. Katz and Liu, *The Codependency Conspiracy*, 4.

4. Peele, *The Diseasing of America*, 117.

5. Ibid.

6. Ibid., 143.

7. Ibid., 28.

8. Ibid., 118.

9. Ibid., 136.

10. Aristotle, *Rhetorica*, in *The Basic Works of Aristotle*, ed. Richard McKeon (New York: Random House, 1941), 1360.

11. Peele, *The Diseasing of America*, 148.

12. Katz and Liu, *The Codependency Conspiracy*, 9–10.

13. "Helping Themselves," *Newsweek* (special issue: "How Kids Grow"), Summer 1991.

14. Melody Beattie, *Codependent No More* (San Francisco: Harper/Hazelden, 1987), 46.

15. Ibid., 6.

16. Cited in Katz and Liu, *The Codependency Conspiracy*, 17.

17. Beattie, *Codependent No More*, 37.

18. Elizabeth Kristol, "Declarations of Codependence," *American Spectator*, June 1990.

19. Katz and Liu, *The Codependency Conspiracy*, 43.

20. Kristol, "Declarations of Codependence."

21. Ibid.

22. Susan Forward, *Toxic Parents* (New York: Bantam Books, 1990).

23. Ibid., 8–9.

24. Ibid., 11.

25. Cited in Zilbergeld, *The Shrinking of America*, 206–7.

26. Cited in Katz and Liu, *The Codependency Conspiracy*, 16.

27. "A Psychiatrist Discusses Creative Writers and Alcohol," *Philadelphia Inquirer*, 2 January 1989.

28. Kenneth J. Gergen, *The Saturated Self* (New York: Basic Books, 1991), 244–45.

29. Ibid.

30. Wood, *The Myth of Neurosis*, 29.

31. Ibid., 2.

32. Cited in Zilbergeld, *The Shrinking of America*, 13.

33. Wood, *The Myth of Neurosis*, 41–42.

34. Ibid., 9.

35. Ibid., 42–43.

36. Peele, *The Diseasing of America*, 218.

37. "Criticism of Clemency May Affect Efforts to Help Battered Women," *New York Times*, 2 April 1991.

38. Ibid.

39. For a full discussion of the case, see Willard Gaylin, *The Killing of Bonnie Garland* (New York: Penguin Books, 1983).

40. Peele, *The Diseasing of America*, 219–20.

41. "Defense Lawyer May Blame Trauma of Central City Life," *Milwaukee Journal*, 7 November 1991.

42. Peele, *The Diseasing of America*, 221.

43. "Earlier Prosecutor Urged Prison for Dahmer," *Milwaukee Sentinel*, 26 July 1991.

PICK A DISORDER, ANY DISORDER

1. *Diagnostic and Statistical Manual of Mental Disorders, Third Edition*, American Psychiatric Association; all subsequent references will be to *DSM-III-R*.

2. Ibid., xxvi.

3. Ibid.

4. Ibid.

5. Ibid., 89–90.

6. Ibid., 349.

7. Ibid., 353.

8. Ibid., 56.

9. Ibid., 329–30.

10. Ibid., 331.

11. Ibid., 354.

12. Peele, *The Diseasing of America*, 137.

13. Advertisement in *Isthmus Manual*, Madison, Wisconsin, 1991–92.

14. C. Potera, "Stress Epidemics," *Psychology Today*, November 1988.

15. "Environmental Illness May Be Mental," *New York Times*, 26 December 1990.

16. Muriel Dobbin, "Is the Daily Grind Wearing You Down?" *U.S. News & World Report*, 24 March 1986.

17. Ronni Sandroff, "Is Your Job Driving You Crazy?" *Psychology Today*, July/August 1989.

18. Joseph Berger, "Costly Special Classes Service Many with Minimal Needs," *New York Times*, 30 April 1991.

19. Ibid.

20. Ibid.

21. Ibid.

22. Nisbet, *The Quest for Community*, 13.

23. John Buchan, *Pilgrim's Way* (Cambridge, Mass.: Houghton Mifflin, 1940), 276.

SENSITIVE MAN

1. "Taking Offense," *Newsweek*, 24 December 1990.

2. Judith N. Shklar, *The Faces of Injustice* (New Haven: Yale University Press, 1990), 14.

3. "Upside Down in the Groves of Academe," *Time*, 1 April 1991.

4. Dinesh D'Souza, "Racism 101," *WI: Wisconsin Interest* 1, no. 1 (Winter/Spring 1992).

5. "3 Incidents of Bias Provide Lessons for a Class on Race," *New York Times*, 7 May 1990.

6. Fred Siegel, "The Cult of Multiculturalism," *The New Republic*, 18 February 1991.

7. John Leo, "PC Follies: The Year in Review," *U.S. News & World Report*, 27 January 1992.

8. Department of Residence Life, University of Wisconsin-Milwaukee, "Ways to Experience Diversity."

9. University of Connecticut *Student Handbook*, 1990, 62.

10. Siegel, "The Cult of Multiculturalism."

11. Thomas L. Jipping, "Shedding Rights on the American Campus," *The World & I*, March 1991.

12. Robert Detlefsen, "White Like Me," *The New Republic*, 10 April 1989.

13. Carnegie Foundation for the Advancement of Teaching, *Campus Life: In Search of Community*, 1990, 19.

14. "Taking Offense."

15. "Female Dancers Banned at Games of Men's Teams," *New York Times*, 2 July 1990.

16. Lester, "Whatever Happened to the Civil Rights Movement?"

17. Article by Tammy Johnson, *UWM Post*, 31 October 1991.

18. Pete Hamill, *Esquire*, April 1990.

19. Stephen Goode, "Selling Diversity: Harmony Gurus on Campus," *Insight*, 25 November 1991.

20. "Racism at Brown" (Brown University policy).

21. Ibid.

22. John H. Bunzel, "Black and White at Stanford," *The Public Interest*, no. 105 (Fall 1991).

23. Office of the President, University of Michigan, "Discrimination and Discriminatory Harassment by Students in the University Environment."

24. "Hoax Suspected over Allegation of Racial Crime," *New York Times*, 1 June 1990.

25. James T. Laney, "Why Tolerate Campus Bigots?" *New York Times*, 6 April 1990.

26. "Hoax Suspected."

27. D'Souza, "Racism 101."

28. Nat Hentoff, "Stanford and the Speech Police," *Washington Post*, 21 July 1990.

29. David Rieff, "The Case Against Sensitivity," *Esquire*, November 1990.

30. Hentoff, "Stanford and the Speech Police."

THE SEXUAL NIGHTMARE

1. Harry F. Waters, "Whip Me, Beat Me and Give Me Great Ratings . . ." *Newsweek*, 11 November 1991.

2. Ibid.

3. "Bikini Ad Prompts a Lawsuit," *New York Times*, 9 November 1991.

4. "Get Me Repaint," *Newsweek*, 25 November 1991.

5. Anna Quindlen, "Don't Call Me Ishmael," *New York Times*, 23 November 1991.

6. Elinor Lipman, "Are You the Office Sex Pest?" *New York Times*, 23 November 1991.

7. Katie Roiphe, "Date Rape Hysteria," *New York Times*, 20 November 1991.

8. Wolf, *The Beauty Myth*, 25.

9. Alison Jaggar, *Feminist Politics and Human Nature* (Sussex, Eng.: The Harvester Press, 1983), 371, 382–84.

10. Firestone, *The Dialectic of Sex*, 2.

11. Anne Koedt, "The Myth of the Vaginal Orgasm," *The Sixties Papers* (New York: Praeger Publishers, 1984), 471, 473.

12. Ti-Grace Atkinson, "Declaration of War," *Amazon Odyssey* (New York: Link Books, 1974), 47–55.

13. Millett, "Sexual Politics: A Manifesto for Revolution," *Notes from the Second Year*, 111–12.

14. Edward Abbey, *The Fool's Progress* (New York: Avon Books, 1990), 39.

15. Cited in Nancy Gibbs "When Is It Rape?" *Time*, 3 June 1991.

16. Quoted in Wendy Steiner, "Declaring War on Men," *New York Times Book Review*, 15 September 1991.

17. Philip Weiss, "The Sexual Revolution: Sexual Politics on Campus: A Case Study," *Harper's*, April 1991.

18. "When Is It Rape?"

19. Ibid.

20. Neil Gilbert, "The Phantom Epidemic of Sexual Assault," *The Public Interest*, Summer 1991.

21. Ibid.

22. Ibid.

23. Ibid.

24. Ibid.

25. Ibid.

26. Weiss, "The Sexual Revolution."

27. Ibid.

28. Cited in Margarita Levin, "Caring New World: Feminism and Science," *The American Scholar*, Winter 1988.

29. D'Souza, *Illiberal Education*, 197–98.

30. Weiss, "The Sexual Revolution."

31. Leslie Carbone, "Re-Education in the Name of Tolerance," *Campus Report*, October 1990.

32. Gilbert, "The Phantom Epidemic."

33. "Women See Hearing from a Perspective of Their Own Jobs," *New York Times*, 18 October 1991.

34. Charles Sykes and Brad Miner, "Sense and Sensitivity," *National Review*, 8 March 1991.

35. Magda Lewis, "Interrupting Patriarchy: Politics, Resistance, and Transformation in the Feminist Classroom," *Harvard Educational Review* 60, no. 4 (November 1990). Also, all subsequent references to Lewis article.

PRESUMED VICTIMIZED

1. Jim Sleeper, *The Closest of Strangers*, 172.

2. Ibid., 173.

3. Julie Buchanan, "Color by the Numbers," *WI: Wisconsin Interest* 1, no. 1 (Winter/Spring 1992).

4. Sleeper, *The Closest of Strangers*, 164.

5. Herman Belz, *Equality Transformed* (New Brunswick, N.J.: Transaction Publishers, 1991), 3.

6. William R. Beer, "Resolute Ignorance: Social Science and Affirmative Action," *Society* (May/June 1987).

7. Ibid.

8. Ibid.

9. Belz, *Equality Transformed*, 2.

10. Ibid.

11. Ibid., 139.

12. William Raspberry, "PUSHed and Pulled," *Washington Post National Weekly Edition*, 3–9 September 1990.

13. Beer, "Resolute Ignorance."

14. Sleeper, *The Closest of Strangers*, 176.

15. Beer, "Resolute Ignorance."

16. Linda Lichter, *Public Opinion*, August/September 1985.

17. Frederick R. Lynch, "Affirmative Action, the Media, and the Public: A Look at a 'Look-away Issue,' " *American Behavioral Scientist* 28, no. 6 (July/August 1987).

18. Steele, *The Content of Our Character*, 15.

19. Ibid., 24.

20. Ibid., 33.

21. Donald Kinder and David Sears, "Prejudice and Politics: Symbolic Racism Versus Racial Threats to the Good Life, *Journal of Personality and Social Psychology* 40 (1981).

22. Byron M. Roth, "Symbolic Racism: The Making of a Scholarly Myth," *Academic Questions* 2, no. 3 (Summer 1989).

23. National Research Council, *A Common Destiny: Blacks and American Society* (Washington, D.C.: National Academy Press, 1989), 120.

24. *A Common Destiny*, 147.

25. John B. McConahay and Joseph C. Hough, Jr., "Symbolic Racism," *Journal of Social Issues* 32, no. 2 (1976).

26. Donald Kinder and L. M. Sanders, "Righting Benign Neglect: A Proposal to the NES Planning Committee and Board," cited in Donald Kinder, "The Continuing American Dilemma: White Resistance to Racial Change 40 Years After Myrdal," *Journal of Social Issues* 42, no. 2 (1986).

27. James R. Kluegel, "If There Isn't a Problem, You Don't Need a Solution," *American Behavioral Scientist* 28, no. 6 (July/August 1985).

28. Roth, "Symbolic Racism: The Making of a Scholarly Myth."

29. Ibid.

30. McConahay and Hough, "Symbolic Racism."

31. Roth, "Symbolic Racism: The Making of a Scholarly Myth."

32. Paul M. Sniderman and Philip E. Tetlock, "Reflections on American Racism," *Journal of Social Issues* 42, no. 2 (1986).

33. Paul M. Sniderman and Philip E. Tetlock, "Symbolic Racism: Problems of Motive Attribution in Political Analysis," *Journal of Social Issues* 42, no. 2 (1986).

34. Roth, "Symbolic Racism: The Making of a Scholarly Myth."

35. Sniderman and Tetlock, "Symbolic Racism: Problems of Motive."

THE RACIAL NIGHTMARE

1. SUFR (Students United for Respect) is an organization on the Notre Dame campus.

2. Dave Anderson, "Martyrs Without a Cause," *New York Times*, 13 December 1990.

3. "Barry's Free Ride," *The New Republic*, 7 May 1990.

4. Andrew Sullivan, "Call to Harm," *The New Republic*, 23 July 1990.

5. Jim Sleeper, "New York Stories," *The New Republic*, 10 September 1990, 17 September 1990.

6. Robert D. McFadden et al., *Outrage: The Story Behind the Tawana Brawley Hoax* (New York: Bantam Books, 1990), 109.

7. Ibid., 114.

8. Ibid., 150.

9. "Talk Grows of Government Being Out to Get Blacks," *New York Times*, 29 October 1990.

10. Ibid.

11. Ibid.

12. James Traub, "A Counter-Reality Grows in Harlem," *Harper's*, August 1991.

13. Quoted in Sleeper, "New York Stories."

14. Joe Klein, "Spring Fever," *New York*, 7 May 1990.

15. Arthur M. Schlesinger, Jr., *The Disuniting of America* (New York: W. W. Norton, 1992), 56.

16. Ibid., 69–70.

17. George James, *Stolen Legacy* (San Francisco: Julian Richardson Associates, 1976).

18. Quoted in Mary Lefkowitz, "Not out of Africa," *The New Republic*, 10 February 1992.

19. Schlesinger, *The Disuniting of America*, 75.

20. Ibid.

21. Quoted in Schlesinger, *The Disuniting of America*, 77.

22. Lefkowitz, "Not Out of Africa."

23. Quoted in Schlesinger, *The Disuniting of America*, 65.

24. Ibid., 101.

25. Ibid., 78.

26. Ibid., 94.

27. Ibid.

28. Sleeper, "New York Stories."

29. Quoted in Sleeper, "New York Stories."

30. Erika Munk, *Village Voice*, 17 July 1990.

31. "Turning Boycotts of 2 Korean Greengrocers in Brooklyn Into Green Power," *New York Times*, 7 June 1990.

32. Klein, "Spring Fever."

33. Traub, "A Counter-Reality."

34. "Cuomo, Strolling, Discusses Slavery," *New York Times*, 2 June 1990.

35. Cartoon by Babin for *Times Union*, Rochester, New York; reprinted in *Washington Post National Weekly Edition*, 16–22 September 1991.

36. "As a Brooklyn Community Seethes, Bitterness Flows 2 Ways," *New York Times*, 23 August 1991.

37. "As a Brooklyn Community Seethes."

38. David Mills, "The Judge v. 2 Live Crew," *Washington Post National Weekly Edition*, 25 June–1 July 1990.

39. Lewis Lapham, "Acceptable Opinions," *Harper's*, December 1990.

40. Tom Wicker, "Home of the Brave?" *New York Times*, 14 June 1990.

41. Jon Pareles, "Rap: Slick, Violent, Nasty and, Maybe, Hopeful," *New York Times*, 17 June 1990.

42. Henry Louis Gates, Jr., "2 Live Crew, Decoded," *New York Times*, 19 June 1990.

43. Michele M. Moody-Adams, "Don't Confuse 2 Live Crew With Black Culture," *New York Times*, 25 June 1990.

44. Mills, "The Judge vs. 2 Live Crew."

45. Joe Klein, "Race: The Issue," *New York*, 29 May 1989.

46. Schlossberg, *Idols for Destruction*, 69.

47. Klein, "Race: The Issue."

48. David Maraniss, "McGee Steers with His Own Code of Ethics," *Milwaukee Journal*, 22 July 1990.

WRONG QUESTIONS, WRONG ANSWERS

1. Eva Etzione-Halevy, *The Knowledge Elite and the Failure of Prophecy* (London: George Allen & Unwin, 1985), 44.

2. Ibid., 2.

3. Ibid., 67.

4. Ibid., 1.

5. Irwin A. Hyman and John D'Alessandro, "Good, Old-Fashioned Discipline: The Politics of Punitiveness," *Phi Delta Kappan* 66, no. 1 (September 1984).

6. Ibid.

7. Daniel Duke, "Student Behavior, the Depersonalization of Blame and the Society of Victims," in Keith Baker and Robert Rubel, eds., *Violence and Crime in the Schools* (Lexington, Mass.: D. C. Heath, 1980), 31–47.

8. Wilson and Herrnstein, *Crime and Human Nature*, 521.

9. *A Common Destiny*, 275.

10. Ibid., 275–76.

11. Ibid., 525.

12. Mead, "The New Politics of the New Poverty."

A MORATORIUM ON BLAME

1. James Q. Wilson, "The Rediscovery of Character: Private Virtue and Public Policy," *The Public Interest*, no. 81, Fall 1985.

2. Ibid.

3. Ibid.

4. James Q. Wilson and Richard Herrnstein, *op. cit.*, 431

5. Ibid., 432.

6. Ibid., 433.

7. Ibid., 435.

8. Ibid., 528–29.

9. Ibid., 528.

10. Ibid.

11. *The Wall Street Journal.*

12. Louis W. Sullivan, "Where Have All the Fathers Gone?" *The Chicago Tribune*, 28 January 1992.

13. David Whitman "Exodus of the 'Couch People,' " *U.S. News & World Report*, 28 December 1991.

14. Ibid.

15. Daniel Bell, *op. cit.*, 25.

16. People for the American Way, *Democracy's Next Generation*, 1989, 27.

17. Arthur M. Schlesinger, Jr., *op. cit.*, 17.

18. Bell, *op. cit.*, 155.

19. I Corinthians, 13:13.

20. Christina Hoff Summers, "Teaching and Virtues," *Imprimis* 20, no. 11, November 1991.

21. Ibid.

22. Viktor Frankl, *The Unheard Cry for Meaning*, (New York: Washington Square Press, 1978), 61.

23. Ibid., 52.

24. Saul Bellow, *op. cit.*, 313.

INDEX

Printed in the United States
208350BV00004B/11/A

9 780312 098827